DIONYSOS
Exciter to Frenzy

Dionysos: Exciter to Frenzy

DIONYSOS
Exciter to Frenzy

Vikki Bramshaw

Published by Avalonia
www.avaloniabooks.co.uk

Published by Avalonia

BM Avalonia
London
WC1N 3XX
England, UK

www.avaloniabooks.co.uk

Dionysos: Exciter to Frenzy
Copyright © 2013 Vikki Bramshaw
All rights reserved.

First Edition, September 2013
ISBN 978-1-905297-67-2

Design by *Satori*, for Avalonia.
Cover Art *'Dionysian Spirit'* by Samuel Hack © 2012
Interior illustrations by Dimitris Christeas © 2012

British Library Cataloguing in Publication Data. A catalogue record for this
book is available from the British Library.

About the Author

Vikki Bramshaw is an author specialising in pre-Christian religion and esoteric traditions. Some of her passions are religious history, theurgy, initiatory rites, and trance. Her first book, *'Craft of the Wise: A Practical Guide'* was published with John Hunt Publishing in 2009, after which Vikki wrote for several anthologies with Avalonia including *Swaying with the Serpent* (featuring in *Hekate: Her Sacred Fires*, 2010) and *'The Scorpion & the Bridal Bed'* (featuring in *VS: Thou Art That - That Thou Art*, 2011). In this book, *'Dionysos: Exciter to Frenzy'*, Vikki explores the numerous facets of the god Dionysos revealing the hidden faces of the thrice-born god and the extent of his influence in the mysteries of the ancient world, through the cycles of nature and beyond.

Vikki has also completed several courses as part of her ongoing research, including *The Origins of Human Behaviour* with Oxford University. She is also a trained *Holistic Healer* with the SHA, a qualified *Equine Sports Massage Therapist*, and has studied an introductory course in *Counselling and Transactional Analysis* with Peter Symonds College of Winchester.

Find her on the web: www.craftofthewise.co.uk
or write to:

Vikki Bramshaw
c/o BM Avalonia
London
WC1N 3XX
United Kingdom

Contents

Map Key:

1. Naxos (island)
2. Lesbos (island)
3. Mt. Parnassos (mountain and settlement) and Delphi (settlement/temple complex), mainland Greece
4. Knossos (palace/temple complex), Crete
5. Athens (city), mainland Greece
6. Pylos (settlement), mainland Greece
7. Chania (settlement), Crete
8. Thebes (settlement – modern Thiva), mainland Greece
9. Eleutherai (modern Gyphtokastro), Bulgaria
10. Port Thorikos (settlement – modern Porto Rafti), mainland Greece
11. River Erasinos (near Lake Stymphalia), mainland Greece
12. Mt. Ida, Crete
13. Mt. Ida, Turkey
14. Dikteon caves, Crete
15. Eleusis (settlement – modern Eleusina), mainland Greece
16. Euboea (island) Mt. Ochi, at Karyai, (modern Karystos)
17. Dodona/Dodonaean Grove (modern Dodoni, Ioannina), mainland Greece

18. Samothrace (island)
19. Mt. Kithairon, mainland Greece
20. Mt. Didyma (modern Didyma), Turkey
21. Orchomenos (settlement), mainland Greece
22. Lerna (settlement) nr Argos, mainland Greece
23. Thrassos (island, modern Thasos)
24. Miletos (settlement), Turkey
25. Elis (district), Greece
26. Ephesus (settlement/temple complex), Turkey
27. Ikarion (modern Dionysos), mainland Greece
28. Erineos (settlement), mainland Greece
29. Sparta (settlement), mainland Greece
30. Limnae (settlement/temple complex), Thrace (Turkey)
31. Iolcus (settlement), mainland Greece
32. Corinth (settlement), mainland Greece
33. Chios (island)
34. Tenedos (island)

Dionysos: Exciter to Frenzy

Introduction

"O, blessed are you, the fortunate one who knows
the rituals of the gods ...
whose spirit merges
with these Bacchic celebrations
frenzied dancing in the mountains
our purifying rites –
one who reveres these mysteries
from Kybele, our Great Mother
who, waving the Thyrsus,
forehead crowned with ivy
serves Dionysos." [1]

This study was born out of a series of synchronicities, prophecies and other mystical occurrences which happened to our small ritual group in Hampshire.

Hampshire is a seemingly unlikely place for the Dionysian current[2] to manifest. Both trained to our third degrees in Alexandrian Wicca, myself and fellow ritualist Peter Ralls began taking applications for our own ritual group in 2005. We were not a conventional Wiccan group; having received training with teachers from several different occult traditions, we were already working outside the standard Wiccan framework. After a few years we adopted the more general term of Initiatory Witchcraft, which allowed us to explore alternative mystery traditions and magical practices. It was all semantics of course - but it helped us in some way to remain true to our journey. In a way, my first book *'Craft of the Wise: A Practical Guide to Paganism & Witchcraft'* which was published in 2009 marked this moment; an initiatory journey for me in itself – drawing a line beneath my previous work whilst also leaving one or

---

[1] The Bacchae, 100-112 Euripides, c. 400 BCE, trans. Ian Johnston
[2] Spirit or emanation of Dionysian ethos, philosophy and/or worship

two clues at the new direction our ritual group was taking. *Craft of the Wise* did not attempt to cover this new ground.

Within Initiatory Witchcraft many of the ritual themes are received intuitively, and then reconstructed with historical research into that particular mystery tradition or practice. A lot of it is down to synchronicity, messages and intuitive work. There is very little scripted work. It is based on studying and recreating the more mystic aspects of ancient traditions. However, we often use the ritual framework from Wicca as a structure for the practice of the mysteries (either magical or theurgic) because it does seem to work in terms of creating coherence and structure. We also found, through our own experiences, that the ethos of Wicca and Witchcraft (and the very nature of the gods and forces working within them) behave in a very similar way to the ecstatic cult of Dionysos, and gods and goddesses of a similar ilk – and are therefore conducive with the ritual and practice of Wicca. Ultimately, they seem to follow the same *'current'* in the universe.

The Dionysian experience transcends physical boundaries and cultures; it is found all over the world from Asia to Africa and right across Europe. Dionysos was worshipped by so many people – in so many places and in so many ways – that it is difficult (if not impossible) to define exactly how and when he was worshipped. Certainly, it's a difficult task to interpret the information we have on the rites of Dionysos – our modern perspectives and cultural differences will no doubt blur our understanding of their original meaning. For instance, creating a calendar of Dionysian festivals is a near impossible task; even the Athenian festival calendar, which is well known in modern academia, draws upon much older fragmented sources from elsewhere, which had already been altered and changed to fit into the Athenian way of life. By the time these ceremonies were being performed in Athens, many of the original meanings of the rites had already been forgotten (which is why some say the Athenian rites of Dionysos are in fact the Dionysian rites in their most *'impure'* form). Dates of festivals and ceremonies changed too, depending on whereabouts in Greece you were – unlike today, time was measured locally and festivals would often be celebrated at slightly different times of the year depending on where you lived, or even what your trade was. Therefore I have tried to interpret the material that was available as accurately as possible, by making judgments (that make sense to me) in terms of the modern day months in relation to the viticultural cycle and the climate - but please, if you wish to interpret things differently, DO SO! Dionysos is all about freedom and expression.

It was just this lack of structure which initially marked our encounter with the mysteries of Dionysos – and his theurgic ritual counterpart, Hekate. Whilst running our ritual group, our solitary practices outside of the group began to change. Independently of one another, our private rituals became less structured, more intuitive and prophetic. They incorporated trance, and deep and sometimes disturbing personal meditations; ecstatic music, movement and dance, and strangely intoxicating dreams. My personal experiences also involved serpent energy; and I eventually found this force was a guise of Hekate.[3] At the same time as I was unravelling the mysteries of the Serpent in Greek mythology, Peter was having the same sort of ecstatic experiences but with the Bull-Horned God; who eventually revealed himself to be the bull-formed snake-wielding Dionysos. Ironically, on petitioning Dionysos for a bigger and better working space, we came into possession of a flat in the area of St Denys (or as per a map from the 1600s, '*S.Dionies*') in Southampton. With the arrival of Christianity and the canonisation of Pagan gods to Christian saints, Dionysos had become Saint Denys, or Saint Denis.

We began to bring our private practices into the group setting and worked with Dionysos and Hekate together. Initially, we were quite surprised to find that Hekate was so keen to work with Dionysos, and vice versa; an enigma which became clear with just a little more research into Hekate's history as a unifier of opposing principles, her involvement in the Orphic Mysteries and her role of consort to Dionysos-Sabazios as the goddess Bendis[4] (or Brimo). Another similarity shared by Dionysos and Hekate was their role in aiding mortals to achieve a ritual state of consciousness, a role they both offered to the process of theurgy - something we were working with intensively in our ritual group. The Dionysian current was both guiding our rituals and shaping our fate. After working with these deities exclusively for an extensive amount of time, we decided to

[3] Hekate Her Sacred Fires, edited by Sorita d'Este, 2010: P.83
[4] Hekate Her Sacred Fires, edited by Sorita d'Este, 2010: P.40

dedicate our ritual group to Dionysos and Hekate alone. I took a back step from training in order to focus on my own path and develop the material that would in time become this book.

This book is written from a modern Western Mystery Tradition viewpoint – the only viewpoint I can give. I would like to stress that the material in this book is only my own interpretation of what has already been written about the god, together with my own inspiration and ritual experiences. I hope that I have managed to step far enough away from modern practices (whilst still recognising parallels) in order to view the evidence from an objective and impartial point of view - but inevitably my interpretations will be influenced by modern thinking. As the author Robert Brown writes, *'our acquaintance with earlier times is probably insufficient to enable us to judge whether ... a particular assumption is* (correct) *or not'* [5] that is, no matter how well read we are on a subject we will always be influenced by our modern way of thinking and preconceptions; but perhaps we have to accept this on some level as part of the natural evolution of the Dionysian cult.

Certainly, the ethos and rites of Dionysos transcend the boundaries of time and seem just as relevant to the mystery tradition movement today as they ever were. Some readers may be of the opinion that I have tried to *'shoehorn'* an ancient tradition into a modern ethos - and perhaps in many ways I have! But of course the truth is, by his very nature there is no *'right'* or *'wrong'* way of following a Dionysian path; we find Dionysos where people need him the most, regardless of their cultural background. The aim of this book is to present a historical study of Dionysos and a reliable basis upon which the Dionysian current can develop and grow. I believe that the way we work with the ancient gods should always be evolving and transforming in tune with the modern world, just like Dionysos himself - but that it is just as important that we unify well researched ancient practices with our modern interpretations.

I cannot emphasise enough the importance of reading the original epics by such writers as Nonnus, Ovid, Euripides and Homer; whilst they are sometimes difficult to read, and the purpose and accuracy of their work is constantly disputed, they will always

---

[5] The Great Dionysiac Myth Vol.1, Robert Brown, (1877) 2000: P.29

provide the best insight into the ancient way of thinking as well as priming you with the background on Dionysos that would have been known well by our ancestors. I would also encourage reading the limited – but excellent – academic material about Dionysos by writers like Walter Otto, Karl Kerenyi and Robert Brown. I urge you to read these approaches because whilst they do not attempt to bring together the practices in a workable sense, they present the information in its purest form. These authors paved the way to understanding the cult of Dionysos, and without them this book would not have been possible. I would also like to take this opportunity to thank my fellow *'ritualist in crime'* Peter Ralls for his invaluable input in the early stages of this project and his contributions to the research on the political and cultural implications of the Dionysian cult in particular; and Dimitris Christeas for the sketches which can be found throughout this book (also for correcting some of my Pidgin-Greek!) And lastly, I would like to thank Samuel Hack who captured the essence of the Dionysian spirit in the stunning painting used on the front cover of this book.

Certainly, the Dionysian philosophy suggests that it impossible to develop spiritually without also embracing the realities of life – for Dionysos is a god of substance. The ancient Greeks had two different words for our word, *'life'*: the first was *bios* which referred to the literal, mortal existence of an individual, and the other was *zöe* which referred to the *'spirit'* of life. This ethos was reflected at the core of Dionysian religion, which recognised both the reality of existence and also a profound spiritual awareness. Dionysos is sometimes described as *"other-worldly without being world-denying"*[6] the Dionysian cult brought religion and the corporeal into one without negating the importance or viability of either; arguably, perhaps something that is missing in many spiritual and religious paths available today.

Vikki Bramshaw, May 2012

---

[6] Dionysos, Richard Seaford, 2006: P.83

Chapter 1

Who is Dionysos?

"He who leads the throngs becomes Dionysos."[7]

Who is Dionysos? Portrayed as the leader of lustful processions and drunken debauchery, he appears a hedonistic god, at best - but this is a gross generalisation, and negates the true complexity of Dionysos' nature.

Dionysos can certainly be described as a *'complex'* character. He is *Dionysos Dimorphos*, *'dual-formed'*, and *Dionysos Dimetor*, *'born of two mothers'*. His dual nature bestows him with the authority of a liminal god: he who stands on the threshold between the worlds as a god of prophecy and initiation, and he who traverses the processes of birth, life, death and rebirth. As an ascended god Dionysos occupies the heavens, yet he also dwells in the depths of the underworld acting as a guide for souls, spirits and shades. As the bull-formed lord of death and rebirth, he is *Dionysos Dikerotes 'the two-horned one'*. He is the hunter, yet also the hunted - and he is dead, yet also alive; these cycles of opposition were the driving force behind his cult rites. Dionysos offers us the joyous freedom of choice, yet he is also the toxicity that we ourselves administer by our erroneous decisions; he is *Dionysos*

---

[7] The Bacchae, 115, Euripides, c. 400 BCE, trans. Karl Kerényi

Bromios, *'the roarer'* and loud-shouting god of pandemonium; *'yet silence and stillness often fell upon those who were possessed by him'*.[8] Often symbolic of extreme and contrasting states of being, he embodies the primal emotions that drive us and makes us who we are.

Neither was the cult of Dionysos a small one; his following was perhaps one of the most widely spread of the ancient mysteries, and stood as a serious rival to the emerging cult of Christianity. We find record of Dionysos' worship to the west in Italy; to the east in Turkey; to the north in Romania and Bulgaria, and to the south in Libya - and pre-Dionysian ritual and culture relating to later Dionysos worship all over the Mediterranean. We also find striking similarities in terms of practice with shamanic cultures from other parts of the world, such as West Africa, the Caribbean, and even northern Europe. As Katie Gerrard writes, *'the term 'shamanic' has come to represent a whole range of traditions that embrace ecstatic and trance techniques'*[9] - whether Dionysianism as a whole can be described as a *'shamanic'* path is of course debatable, however many of the accounts of the earlier Dionysian cults do show similarities, particularly in terms of techniques, themes and overall atmosphere.

Despite the widespread nature of his following, Dionysos had no central priesthood.[10] Dionysian cults were regional, and often organized internally by their founding members. Worship was freeform, focusing on different qualities of the god and practicing different rites, depending on where you lived and your social status. Even within the confines of Athens alone, the way Dionysos was worshipped greatly varied depending on the individual cult you joined, your role within it, and whether you were initiated or not. Other than the common idea that Dionysos played a part in the processes of life, death and rebirth, we cannot know if they shared any other concrete beliefs; and as Albert Henrichs writes, the so-called religion of Dionysos is more *'a modern abstraction, the sum total of the god's numerous facets, symbols and cults'*.[11] But the Dionysian influence

---

[8] Dionysus Myth & Cult, Walter F Otto (1960) 1995: P.94

[9] Seidr: The Gate is Open, Katie Gerrard, 2011: P. 187

[10] Jewish & Christian Self-Definition, 'Changing Dionysian Identities', Albert Henrichs, 1982: P.151

[11] Jewish & Christian Self-Definition, 'Changing Dionysian Identities', Albert Henrichs, 1982: P.151

on the world was assured. Dionysos left behind a worldwide legacy - as his worship was instrumental (if not almost entirely accountable) for the creation of theatre and drama which originated in ancient Greece and was performed for Dionysos as an offering in his honour. However, it's also important to remember that theatre and comedic street revelry were not the first concern of Dionysos until classical times[12] and that, as will become apparent during this book, the Dionysian cult was for the most part *chthonic* in nature - a cult of possession, trance and prophecy, with themes of death, initiation and transformation.

Ancient Origins

The name *Dionysos* is first recorded in the Linear B script from Pylos - a settlement on mainland Greece - and Chania, on the Greek island of Crete. It is a Greek name, of late Minoan origin. Certainly, a large percentage of worship to Dionysos as we know him today occurred within mainland Greece and its surrounding islands, but in truth there was no local centre for Dionysos that we know of, and his worship was spread all the way across the Mediterranean Basin and beyond. Perhaps one of the best clues signifying his mixed heritage is the supposed location of his legendary homeland, Mount Nysa: many scholars declare that it stood in central Greece, whilst according to the historian Herodotus, Nysa was in Ethiopia. And the writers Antimachus, Diodorus and Nonnus referred to an Arabic Nysa, whilst Apollonius Rhodius mentions a Nysa in Egypt – and the philosopher Xenophon knew of a Nysa in Syria!

Historically speaking, the Dionysos we know today is actually a conflation of many different gods, demi gods and daimons who originated in all different parts of the world: an amalgamation of god and spirit forms. This is where things can get difficult in terms of modern interpretation depending on your personal theology; but for the panentheist like myself, it is easy to consider that the Dionysian *'current'* or ethos was present in several different places at once, and was simply given different names by different cultures. Indeed like the Egyptian goddess Isis, Dionysos was known for his *'many faces'*

---

[12] The God Who Comes, Rosemarie Taylor-Perry, 2003: P.56

and was often described by our ancestors as *'he of a thousand names'*.[13] This is not to say that the gods are not individual in their own right; having worked closely with a number of gods who are considered *'the same'* by academics, I can safely say from experience that they are not! In my opinion, the gods are like the seas; the Pacific, the Atlantic, the Mediterranean, for instance - they are all one body of water, yet they possess varying salt contents, temperatures, depths and geology, and unique marine life. They are by no means *'the same'*. Like water, the gods are ever changing, ever moving, influenced by the people around them and we cannot define them; and they slip through our fingers if we try to contain them. The ancients saw things this way too - the majority of pre-Abrahamic religions were open to recognising their own gods in the gods of other cultures, and quite often two deities were synchronized for cultural or political reasons. These unified deities of the same current brought with them cultural diversity from their homelands.

"The bull-Dionysos of Thrace, when he came to Crete, found a monstrous god, own cousin to himself." [14]

Dionysos finds his origins in the local bull and bee god of Crete; the god of the starry heavens in Egypt, and the hunter resurrection god of Thrace and Phrygia amongst many others - all of whom share commonalities considered part of the Dionysian current. Dionysos is also closely identified with other deities who share a similar nature, such as the Sumerian *Dumuzi*, the Egyptian *Osiris*, the Phrygian *Attis* and the Indian *Shiva*, as well as minor gods and household spirits of ancient folk magic - all of whom may have influenced the way Dionysos was worshipped and portrayed. So although the name of Dionysos is perhaps most commonly known for its connection to mainland Greece, it is clear that for a complete picture we must also look further afield. Whilst it is impossible to study all of the possible origins of Dionysos here, I have tried to identify a few of the most *'likely suspects'* below.

---

[13] The God Who Comes, Rosemarie Taylor-Perry, 2003: P.7

[14] Prolegomena to the Study of Greek Religions, Jane Ellen Harrison 1908: P.481

Crete

First we turn to Crete, and an early god worshipped there named *Zagreus*. As the hunter and capturer of wild animals, Zagreus was often depicted flanked by lions or leopards; themes which would persist on throughout later Dionysian imagery and lore. He was also associated with the snake - a symbol which was also likely inherited from the god *Sabazios* of Thrace and Phrygia, but was mostly lost to the later Dionysos – possibly due to the Dionysian current becoming less associated with wild animals and more associated with agriculture and viticulture as time went by. It is also known that Dionysos became *'urbanised'* as he became integrated into the Athenian pantheon, something that would have distanced him from some of his more primal, animalistic origins.

Zagreus was also embodied in the bull and the oxen (or perhaps more anciently, their ancestor the Auroch) and often described as bull-horned, or bull shaped. The iconography of the bull would find its way into later Dionysian imagery and ritual; worshippers of Dionysos wore horns in imitation of the god, and his icon was sometimes constructed in bull form. The bull Dionysos was considered both a chthonic and solar god and therefore significant in both the upperworld and the netherworld, as the solar sun and the chthonian torch. As a dark and chthonic deity, the Bull Dionysos was summoned from the depths of the underworld with trumpet blasts; yet as a god of fertility and life, the same bull god played an important part as *Basileus* (divine monarch) during royal marriages and *hieros gamos*.

"My suitor was a river god ... who in three shapes was always asking me from my father ... coming now as a bull in visible form, now as a serpent sheeny and coiled, now ox-faced with human trunk, while from his thick-shaded beard fountain water sprayed." [15]

Zagreus is considered by many as the closest we have in terms of an *'original'* Dionysos: a synchronisation of a local Cretan deity with the god Sabazios from Thrace and Phrygia. Crete was known for its

---

[15] Trachiniae, 10-15, Sophocles, c. 450 BCE, trans. Sir RC Jebb - On *Achelous*, the chthonic river god who has many similarities with Dionysos and could be considered as another guise of him.

'*extraordinary mixture of races and consequently religions*'[16] and it is likely that many of the roots of Dionysian ethos reach back to Minoan Crete. However on the Greek mainland, Dionysos Zagreus was considered a '*foreign stranger*' - he was integrated, but occupied a much lower position that he had in Crete (where he had easily matched the Olympian Zeus in importance and status). On the mainland however, many of the roles which Dionysos carried out were already assigned to other deities, and therefore the vast diversity of his character became lost over time. He still held his title as the '*highest of all gods*' - but only at Mount Nysa, which came to be known as his kingdom.

Thrace & Phrygia

"*Sabazios ... is as Dionysos. He acquired this form of address from the rite pertaining to him; for the barbarians call the bakkhic cry 'sabazein.*"[17]

In terms of Dionysos' connection with the natural world, Sabazios of Eastern Thrace and Phrygia is probably our original '*god of the wilds*'. Although Zagreus (and Dionysos after him) is sometimes described as a '*nature*' deity, it is likely that (unlike the modern view of a nature god) this association was more in terms of *control over nature* rather than communing with it.

Sabazios is a very specific god in his own right who became conflated with Zagreus, the local horned deity of Crete. Certainly there appears to have been a presence of a Dionysian current in Minoan Crete *before* the arrival of Sabazios, particularly in terms of tauromorphic (bull-formed) imagery; and in the epic *Dionysiaca* the poet Nonnus describes this Zagreus as the '*former Dionysos*', suggesting that Zagreus represented the Dionysian current before the Mycenaean Greeks took over Minoan Crete. Yet, the Greek historian Diodoros Siculus writes that Sabazios was the '*more ancient Dionysos*'. So whilst the popular opinion is that the Dionysian current was introduced to Hellas (Greece) from Thrace and Phrygia, it is just as likely that the Thracian and Phrygian cults were influenced by those of Crete.

---

[16] Robert Brown: The Great Dionysiac Myth Vol.1, Robert Brown, (1877) 2000: P.128

[17] Suidas s.v. Sabazios (trans. Suda On-Line) (Byzantine Greek lexicon C10th CE)

Sabazios displayed many cult symbols which would later be ascribed to Dionysos. In particular his association with wild animals, specifically those which cannot truly be tamed such as reptiles and big cats – and of course bulls, which despite being common agricultural animals can possess a dangerously unpredictable nature. Sabazios was also said to have first domesticated and yoked pairs of oxen, to draw ploughs. A relief from Plovdiv in Bulgaria dated C3[rd] BCE depicts Sabazios in the company of a bull – but also a mounted horseman. Whilst the later Dionysos was not directly associated with horses, many deities considered analogous to him were, and several characters from Dionysian mythology (and history) are noted for their connection with horses – especially those of a particularly free spirit which were harder to tame, such as Alexander the Great's black stallion, *Bucephalus*. Horseback riding would have been considered a position of honour and kingship, as well as a significant aid for hunting – all functions of Dionysos.

It is perhaps fitting then that Sabazios was also a god of fire; an element that was equally unpredictable as some of the cult animals of Dionysos, and just as important as part of his worship. Fire was often equated with ferocious wild beasts; and the fire of the funeral pyre was described as a predatory creature, tearing apart' the body with 'a *furious jaw*'.[18] As both a bringer of untamable heat and an underworld guide for the deceased, it is likely that Dionysos (in particular the Dionysian face of Bakcheus, the ecstatic fire-born god) would have been equated with this fiery and consuming guise of Sabazios. Indeed, wine pots were sometimes used as urns for human ashes, perhaps indicative of how wine and the journey to the afterlife were considered akin to one another. Strabo accounts that the followers of Sabazios would dance across hot coals and lead nocturnal processions carrying blazing torches. They also carried a sacred bronze hand, a cult image decorated with symbolism relevant to the god such as snakes, and pinecones. We may also suppose that this fire symbolised the *fire inside* that is, the primal forces of man and nature. A reminder of these rites to Sabazios and the Great Mother still exist today on the Strandzha mountains in Bulgaria, where on the Catholic feast of St Athanasius the local people similarly dance across hot coals at night,

---

[18] Homo Necans: Greek Sacrificial Ritual & Myth, Walter Burkert, 1986: P.52

whilst honouring a sacred metal hand[19] reminiscent of the bronze hand of Sabazios. Another similar rite occurs in several villages in northern Greece, where a similar night-time fire walking festival is held every year.

"The smoky glare of torches sees you above the cliffs of the twin peaks, where the Corycian nymphs move inspired … by the cries of your divine words."[20]

Their nocturnal rites were in honour of Sabazios together with the meter theon *Hipta*, a similar mother goddess to Kybele who was incorporated into the rites of the Orphic Mysteries. In other cases, Sabazios was coupled with *Bendis*, and was accounted to have been either her son or lover. Bendis was a Thracian huntress-goddess who was depicted wearing a peaked trapper hat, long cloak and knee-high fox-skin hunting boots. She was possibly a predecessor to Artemis, herself considered akin to Kybele and allied with Dionysos. Plato writes that Bendis introduced the first horseback relay in Athens which involved the participants passing a blazing torch to each other as they galloped around the track; perhaps in honour of her consort Sabazios, who was skilled in horsemanship.

As well as sharing similar cult symbols, the rites of Dionysos would also reflect the earlier practices of the followers of Sabazios. The orator Demosthenes described the rites of Sabazios, *'In the day-time you marshaled your gallant throng of bacchanals through the public streets, their heads garlanded with fennel and white poplar, and as you went, you squeezed the fat cheeked snakes, or brandished them above your head, now shouting Euoi Saboi!'* [21] customs which are strikingly similar to the rites of Dionysos and Orphic practice. A similar chant was documented by Strabo, who wrote that many of the processional chants to Sabazios included the ritual cry *'evoe saboe!'*[22] . It is possible that the name of Sabazios continued to be used in later Dionysos rites, with the chant *'sabazeu'* sometimes being used to call Dionysos in his bestial form.

---

[19] The Greek Colonisation of the Black Sea, GR Tsetskhladze, 1998: P.79

[20] Antigone, 1126-1135, Sophocles, c. 440 BCE, trans. Sir RC Jebb

[21] On the Crown, 260, Demosthenes, c. 300 BCE trans. CA Vince & JH Vince

[22] Geography, 10.3.18, Strabo, c.7 BCE

The word *saboi* was also used to describe the worshippers of Sabazios, who celebrated his rites of birth, sacred marriage and sacrifice away from the general public in relative secrecy. Certainly, the ways of Sabazios (and later, Zagreus and Dionysos) would have appeared unfamiliar and alien to the Greeks; there was an air of mystery around the cult, which remained in the Dionysian current even when the festivals of Dionysos had reached Athens. True Dionysian cult members remained at the fringe of society - either as eccentric minorities or, in comparison, well structured and self-funded organizations which were recorded as being of genuine concern to the overall control of the state. Like Dionysos, Sabazios was also a favourite of women of all ages, who featured prominently in his rites.

It is possible that Dionysos finds a further connection to Sabazios through fermented beverages. '*Sabaia*' was a beer made from barley and water in ancient Illyricum[23] described as an '*ordinary person's drink*' which was intimately connected to the hunter-gatherer culture as well as grains, cereals and beans - goods which would later be sacred to Dionysos. Whilst Dionysos is a god of many diverse forms, it is likely that a significant part of his character as we know it today was built around (and transmitted with) the knowledge of fermented beverages. Many of Dionysos' myths symbolically embodied the discovery of different types of alcohol, and individual stories are likely to have been conceived in order to record each settlement's first encounter with the production of it. So in order to discover the possible origin of this particular element of Dionysos, we can start by looking towards Libya and Egypt where it is believed that winemaking first originated and then quickly spread across to Phrygia, Thrace and Attica. It is also possible that the Libyan anthromorphic hunting culture was transmitted to the neighbouring Minoan Crete.

Sabazios would later become an alternate name for Bacchus, the Roman equivalent of Dionysos; although in many ways the two deities were very different.

---

[23] *Prolegomena to the Study of Greek Religions*, Jane Ellen Harrison 1908: P.419

Egypt

The ancients were captivated by the movements of the cosmos: both the Egyptians and the ancient Greeks followed the cycle of Sirius (the brightest star in the night sky). The rising of Sirius in summer was considered as their New Year. Similarities have been drawn between the cult of Dionysos and the Egyptian demi-god *Iachen* who was seen as the embodiment of the Sirius star and the *'tamer'* of heat - and from whom it is likely that Dionysos partially derives. It is perhaps also here that we partially find the origins of *Dionysos Meilichios, 'the mild'* - the dark, nocturnal god of winter coolness who was petitioned at the height of summer to return to the land of men and put out the flames of the summer's heat.

As torchbearers of the underworld, both Iachen and Meilichios were associated with the *'nocturnal sun'* – particularly in the mild underworld realm of Elysium, which Virgil describes as having its own sun.[24] Our ancestors were fascinated with the sun's disappearance during the night and due to the apparent descent of the sun into the underworld, it was believed that the sun alternately took the form of two opposing states: a solar daytime sun and a nocturnal *'underworld'* sun. Incidentally, it is here we find the possible meanings of the word *Nyktelios*, an epithet of Dionysos meaning *'night sun'*, or *'night light'*. The underworld sun was sometimes equated with the moon, and other times described as a primordial chaos which emitted rays of light through the underworld, but did not give off any heat. Dionysos Meilichios illuminates the underworld that would otherwise be in complete darkness, and Zagreus is also described as such. He is the shining light which writers described as emanating from the darkness of ancient honey-caves, and the spark of potential which was buried and concealed in the underworld and guided those who dared to enter.

Worship of Dionysos himself was known in the later dynasties of Egypt, particularly in the Egyptian city of Thebes, the so-called *'mystic city of the seven gates'.*[25] Like Mount Nysa, the location of Thebes often differed between accounts and it is likely that the mythological

---

[24] Aeneid, 6.637ff, Virgil, c. 29 - 19 BCE, trans. J Dryden
[25] The Great Dionysiac Myth Vol.1, Robert Brown, (1877) 2000: P.22

Thebes is in fact a combination of the Thebes in Egypt and the Thebes in Greece (Dionysos finds his origins in both places). According to legend, the city of Thebes was founded by Kadmos (the father of Semele, the mother of Dionysos). The stories of Kadmos usually refer to him as having founded the Thebes in Greece, but Kadmos himself was said to have been of Phoenician origin - and he is sometimes called Kadmeion, meaning *'son of the east'* pointing towards the Thebes of Egypt. The legendry Thebes is also mentioned by Pentheus in the epic *The Bacchae* together with a curious statement about *'two suns'* - usually explained as being a result of the King's vision being blurred, but possibly a hint at something of deeper meaning; Pentheus sees *'two suns, two images of seven-gated Thebes.'* [26] to which Dionysos responds, *'...now you're seeing just what you ought to see.'*[27]

"Iakchos, O Iakchos, the light bringing star of our nocturnal rite. Now the meadow brightly burns, old men's knees start to sway, they shake away their pains and the long cycles of the years, through your holy rites."[28]

From Iachen, we also find the word *Iakchos* used as a descriptive name (or *'epithet'*) of Dionysos at Knossos (a palace/temple complex on Crete) from the Minoan name for the star Sirius. Described as *'the light bringer star'* Iakchos was later considered a god in his own right, as torchbearer in the nocturnal rites of the Eleusinian mysteries and ascribed to be the son of Demeter and Zeus. Despite his importance in such mysteries, the word Iakchos is often considered a simple epithet of Dionysos; however it is likely that Iakchos (as Iachen) actually defined several important aspects of Dionysos' worship, in particular that of Crete – and also in relation to Ariadne, the Minotaur, and the starry skies.

---

[26] The Bacchae, 1128-1129 Euripides, c. 400 BCE, trans. Ian Johnston

[27] The Bacchae, 1128-1136 Euripides, c. 400 BCE, trans. Ian Johnston

[28] Frogs, 340, Aristophanes, c. 400 BCE, trans. M. Dillon

Chapter 2

Fermented Beverages

'Wine is art. It's culture. It's the essence of civilization and the art of living.'[29]

Dionysos is well known for his association with wine; yet this association is a complex one. Certainly wine was used in his cults; but exactly to what excess, and for what purpose? In order to understand its relevance in his worship we need to look at the origins of Dionysos more closely; a search which does not start with wine or grapes - but mead, and honey.

Honey & Mead

"To Zeus and Dionysus, a gift of honey."[30]

Prior to the cultivation of sugar our ancestors would have used honey to sweeten their foods, as well as to aid the fermentation process of Mead, or *'honey-water'* - the first drink of Dionysos which predated the production of wine (and even agriculture) by thousands of years. Honey itself was a symbol of nourishment, and the title of *Bee* was given to the priestesses and seers of Delphi, Ephesus and Eleusis. Originally, honey would have been collected from wild bees, which usually involved breaking open rock or wood to access the colony; and traditionally, mead was made at the time of the rising of Sirius which marked the height of summer and the month of the greatest heat - as well as the first month of the year for both the Hellenes and the Egyptians. The Roman philosopher Pliny the Elder

---

[29] Harvests of Joy, Robert Mondavi, 1999: P.4
[30] Mycenaean Linear B Tablet, 1250 BCE

recorded the traditional instructions for making mead.[31] The water would be kept for 5 years and then mixed with honey; it would then be reduced down, and more honey added. The mixture would then be poured into fermentation skins (usually goat) and left to stand for 40 days to aid the fermentation process.

In some versions of his myth, Dionysos was considered akin to the mead itself, and sources recall that Dionysian mystery cults held awakening rites for Dionysos in the caves to mark the 40 days of the mead's production and the final opening of the fermentation skins, which was seen as synonymous with his birth. I would also suggest that Dionysos' birth within the cave recalls the earlier prehistoric foraging for wild honey, as it would not have been uncommon to find wild bee colonies inside caves; dark places that reached deep into the earth, and which already had the chthonic connection that would be an important part of Dionysos' diverse character (particularly the first incarnation of Dionysos, the Cretan Dionysos-Zagreus, who was born from a goddess of the *under-earth*). Indeed, caves have been discovered in which rock art depicts people collecting honey and making mead in this way.[32]

We also find evidence of another honey based drink called *melikratos* being used in Dionysian cults, which combines two very ancient and primal foods – honey, and cow's milk. *Melikratos* was used for libation, consecrating sacred items, and as an offering to the dead. Indeed, wherever we find the veneration of bees we find the reverence of cattle, and this was especially so with the Dionysos of Crete who was intimately connected to both the bull and with bees. In one account by the poet Virgil[33] sacred cattle were sacrificed and their bodies lain out for 9 days after which bees were seen to swarm from the body as the resurrected life force of the god; a process known as *bougonia* (meaning *'oxen-born bees'*). Whilst in Homeric myth, a young bull was sacrificed during the season of Opora (summer heat) its leather hide transforming into a skin of mead. [34] Other stories tell

---

[31] Natural History XIV, 31.36 Pliny the Elder, 77-79 CE (Perseus Project)

[32] The God Who Comes, Rosemarie Taylor-Perry, 2003: P.19

[33] Georgics, 4.538-58/425-28, Virgil c. 29 BCE

[34] The God Who Comes, Rosemarie Taylor-Perry, 2003: P.20

of how Dionysos turned into a bull to escape the Titans, before being torn to pieces by them, and being reborn as a bee.

Eventually man semi-domesticated the bee, and honey began to be harvested from man-made hives. It is believed that the domestication of bees first occurred in Egypt and Mesopotamia, but one of the cultures which came to excel at the production of honey was Crete, which retained Dionysos' ancient association with honey for much longer and with more vigour than mainland Hellas. Some legends account that it was Dionysos himself who discovered mead after he was born, as well as teaching man how to domesticate bees. The continued use of both mead and *melikratos* in the more chthonic and zoomorphic Dionysian cults (such as those on Crete and also Phrygia) is a likely reminder of a more bestial or animalistic culture, which predated agriculture and the cultivation of soil.

Grapes & Wine

"Wine ... brings the primeval world to life again. It is doubly significant then, when in the transformed world not only milk and honey but streams of wine (flow) forth from the earth before the eyes of the dancers, who are bewitched by the presence of Dionysos, and sport with the elements.'[35]

Dionysos is well known for his connection with wine: one possible meaning of his name is *'lord of wine' (Deo-oenos-os)* but to what extent was its involvement, and how was wine used in Dionysian rites?

It is certainly likely that several aspects of Dionysos' character, festivals and worship were formed to reflect the production of wine right through to its export to other countries (just as they had with mead, but this time on a greater scale) and with it, a new and exciting culture of Dionysos began to develop and spread across the Mediterranean. This process probably began with Dionysos Zagreus in Crete, as a continuation of the Minoan wine and mead culture. Although it is believed that the production of wine probably originated in Libya, the knowledge of viticulture spread rapidly to

---

[35] Dionysus Myth & Cult, Walter F Otto (1960) 1995: P.101

neighbouring countries with mainland Hellas and the island of Crete quick to incorporate it into their economies and culture.

Greece soon became an important centre for winemaking, and began exporting wine from such places as Port Thorikos[36] southwards towards the island of Naxos and northwards to Thrace, taking the myths of how Dionysos created wine with them. A small temple to Dionysos stood in Thorikos, linked by a path which led through vineyards up to the town of Ikarion (present day town *'St Dionysos'*). Ikarion was the location of an important Dionysian sanctuary, and a place recalled by many writers as the first town to have welcomed Dionysos and his gift of wine. It is also at Ikarion that we meet our pseudo-historical character, a local leader named Ikarios, who according to some accounts received knowledge of how to produce wine directly from Dionysos. We find several other characters associated with Dionysos and who were said to be accountable for the discovery of wine[37] and in many cases these pseudo-historical characters probably represent aspects of Dionysos himself. One such character is the King Amphiktyon from Athens, who was said to have received the skill of viticulture by taking part in a Dionysian procession.

But more importantly, it is within these legends that we also find details about the practice of mixing wine with water, to create ritual drinks. Despite the common image of Dionysian drunken revelry, it is evident that much of the wine used within early Dionysian rites was actually *watered down*, and would not have been strong enough to actually intoxicate anyone drinking it. Many accounts show that when pure, unmixed wine was used, just the tiniest sip of wine was taken - an act that was purely symbolic at best – and the remainder of the wine poured upon the floor or the altar, rather than finished off by the celebrants. One such example of restrained consumption is known to have occurred during the festival of Anthesteria, when the first wine of the year would be mixed with water in a jug and shared out among the celebrants. The celebrants would drink their small cup of wine, and then whatever was left over was poured upon the floor

---

[36] Present day Porto Rafti

[37] In many of these cases these pseudo-historical characters probably represent Dionysos himself

in an act of libation[38] to honour Dionysos. This wine-tasting rite was called the *Neoinia* or *'new wine'*.[39] This offering was seen as a fitting sacrifice, and the wine was considered akin to life-blood of Dionysos and the power of regeneration. This connection between blood and wine remains today in Christian communion, where wine is seen as the blood of Christ. (The bread of communion, however, was not originally believed to be the flesh of a male deity but the body of the goddess – chiefly the goddess Demeter of the Eleusinian Mysteries during which grain, seeds and fruit were used in a similar way). Several accounts in Hellenic literature state that just three shallow cups of diluted wine is all that is recommended in any situation to remain under control, and Dionysos himself issues a rather amusing yet cautionary word on exceeding the three cups in the poem *Semele or Dionysos*, written by Eubulus: *'three bowls do I mix ... one to health, which they empty first, the second to love and pleasure, the third to sleep. When this bowl is drunk up, wise guests go home. The fourth bowl is ours no longer, but belongs to violence; the fifth to uproar, the sixth to drunken revel, the seventh to black eyes, the eight is the policeman's, the ninth belong to biliousness, and the tenth to madness and hurling the furniture.'*[40]

With one foot in each world, *Dionysos Acratopotes 'pure wine'*, stood in a balance between two paradoxical states - the clarity and freedom of spirit that was given by taking a sip of the afterlife, and also the wide spectrum of emotions and states of being which finally led to blind drunkenness: first happiness, then affection, perhaps violence and then, most certainly, illusion and insanity. This insanity was described as *'the wrong kind of madness'*. The cautionary legend of Ikarios, the leader of the town of Ikarion, also reflects this ethos of *'responsible drinking'*. After Dionysos had introduced wine to him, Ikarios allowed the members of his court to drink too much. Believing that Ikarios had poisoned them, they murdered him. The term *'everything in moderation'* comes to mind – and indeed, wine was described as *'both a joy and a burden'* upon mankind. As a god of wine, Dionysos was known as *Psychodaiktes 'Destroyer of the Soul'* and *Hypnophobes 'Terrifier During Sleep'* – but also *Luaios 'Deliverer from Care'*, *Theoinos*, *'Exhilarator'*, and even *Iatros*, *'The Healer'*. The ancients were

---

[38] Dionysus Myth & Cult, Walter F Otto (1960) 1995: P.100

[39] Antiquities of Greece Vol.1, John Potter, 1740: P.416

[40] Semele or Dionysos, fr. 93, Eubulus c. 300 BCE

well aware of both the benefits *and* dangers of alcohol - and given this sort of evidence, I believe it's unlikely that drunkenness would have been regularly encouraged in Dionysian ceremonies in his honour, at least in earlier Dionysian rites.

"Good wine is a good familiar creature if it be well used."[41]

However just like the domestic yet unpredictable bull, or the changeable states of being experienced through intoxication, Dionysos has a complex and dual-formed nature - and we should be careful not to sanitize the Dionysian practices for the sake of our modern ideas of morality. Although we have evidence that wine was often used in moderation, there *certainly are* also accounts of drunken revelry during his rites - a fact which cannot (and should not) be denied. For example, wine was sometimes used during the initiatory rites of inner mystery cults as a way to experience pure chaos: an impulse of ecstasy[42] and a part of Dionysos' nature which also warrants recognition. Nevertheless, this was just one side of Dionysos and in terms of what was actually practiced, evidence suggests that a combination of several different trance inducing methods were used to induce ecstatic Dionysian orgiastic rites - the consumption of wine was just one part of the overall technique and experience. Certainly, Homer did not consider wine a very important aspect of Dionysos' worship - he failed to mention a connection with it at all.[43]

We should also keep in mind that as time went by, the true meanings behind the myths and rites of Dionysos may have been partly lost. The earlier rites of Dionysos were performed by very few and from the fringes of society; and it is quite likely that over time the meanings behind some of the Dionysian symbols (such as the partaking of wine) became lost. Certainly, as the Dionysian practice became embraced by the Romans in Italy (who worshipped Dionysos as his equivalent, the Roman god *Bacchus*, in the rites of the *Bacchanalia*) the elements of self gratification that the Dionysian cult had permitted seemed to become the primary focus of the cult, and this eventually led to *the Senatus Consultum de Bacchanalibus ('Senatorial*

---

[41] Othello, Scene II, William Shakespeare, 1603
[42] The God Who Comes, Rosemarie Taylor-Perry, 2003: P.18
[43] The Great Dionysiac Myth Vol.1, Robert Brown, (1877) 2000: P.21

Decree concerning the Bacchanalia') a complete ban of the Bacchanalia in Italy in 186 BCE. However, it is not known if the ban was truly a result of true, corrupted hedonistic rites or more to do with the political consequences of abolishing a very influential political organisation - which by this time had its own economic resources, was highly organised, and was largely out of the control of the general authorities.

The poet Nonnus wrote that Dionysos was the first to create wine. However wine, and the grapevine from which it came, were also thought of as the *embodiment* of Dionysos. The harvesting of grapes from the branches of the vine plant was seen to be reflected in the myths of Dionysos' dismemberment, and pests such as goats (which stripped the delicate vines) were considered as enemies of Dionysos and he was sometimes called upon as *Aigobolos*, *'goat smiter'*. In a similar way, Dionysos became associated with foxes and honoured as *Dionysos Bassarios* (*'Fox'*) because foxes were believed to eat the grapes. One is reminded of the fable:

"Driven by hunger, a fox tried to reach some grapes hanging high on the vine but was unable, although he leaped with all his strength. As he went away, the fox remarked, 'Oh, you aren't even ripe yet! I don't need any sour grapes.' People who speak disparagingly of things that they cannot attain would do well to apply this story to themselves.' [44]

The connection between Dionysos and wine was a favourite subject for artists, and imagery of Dionysos and his followers drinking wine featured on many pieces of pottery and frescos. It also became significant in the shape of Hellenic tableware; the favourite cup of Dionysos was the *kantharos* [45] or *cylix*, a two-handled symmetrical cup which came in both a jug-like shape and a shallower dish-like shape. The symmetrical design and two handles reflected the dual nature of Dionysos (and perhaps equipped the owner with a slightly more steady hand, after they had consumed the wine!) With the arrival of Christianity and the canonisation of Pagan Gods to Christian Saints, the kantharos later became known as the two-

---

[44] The Concise Dictionary of European Proverbs, 1998: P.989 (proverb 986: Phaedrus)
[45] Ashmolean Catalogue: Heracles to Alexander the Great, 2011: P.170

handled cup of Saint Denys / Saint Denis, and it was presented in the 19th century to the Abbey of St Denys in France where it was used to hold the communion wine. (Incidentally, the inhabitants of the town of Saint Deny's are called *'Dionysiens'*!![46])

So, an association with wine was certainly a very recognisable trait of Dionysos – however it will become clear throughout this book that wine was just *one* of the many important roles which were assigned to him. As a foreign latecomer to the Greek world, it is likely that many of Dionysos' roles were overshadowed by native deities who already held those functions, which brought his association with wine more to the forefront. This is demonstrated on Greek coins from the period which show the image of Dionysos alongside other more well-known deities, together with less familiar Dionysian symbols such as the *kista mystica*, the ivy plant, the *thyrsus*, the serpent, the leopard, the bull and even the shining rays of the sun – all discussed later in this study.

The Agathos Daimon

O' holy Agathos Daemon, bring to fulfillment all favours and your divine oracles. [47]

The Agathos Daimon was a primitive, pre-Olympian fortune spirit of ancient Greek folk religion and magic. Its origin is uncertain; however it remained popular throughout ancient Greece and into the Roman period as a household spirit of wine, grain and prosperity. The daimon was also often synchronised or identified with other deities including Hermes, Zeus and of course, Dionysos.

Its form was that of a genderless snake, and it was often depicted with symbols of good fortune and abundance such as the *cornucopia* (horn of plenty) corn baskets and ears of grain; as well as chthonic symbols such as poppies and the caduceus, the symbol of Hermes the psychopomp. Later in antiquity the Agathos Daimon came to be considered as a masculine spirit, and was complemented with a

---

[46] The Great Dionysiac Myth Vol.1, Robert Brown, (1877) 2000: P.326
[47] PGM IV 3165 – 3170

female spirit named *Agathae Tyche* [48] who is identified with the Phrygian mountain mother of Dionysos, Kybele.

It was traditional to offer a libation of unmixed *'pure'* wine to the Agathos Daimon on the second day of the month; this could be done by pouring the wine upon the ground, but in a domestic setting it usually involved evoking the daimon as part of the tasting of neat wine after a banquet. Oil and grain is also known to have been offered; indeed Wine (*Oino*) was not the only daughter of Dionysos: there was also Seed (*Spermo*) and Oil (*Elais*). In the Athenian calendar, this offering would occur the day after the New Moon, when the tips of the crescent (or *'horns'*) of the moon were beginning to show. The libation was poured as an offering of thanks for the food received during the previous month, and as a supplication to ask for good fortune during the next. This household ritual was particularly popular during the Anthesteria, which marked the opening of the new wine, the return of the ecstatic Dionysos and the day of *Pithoigia* – the second day of the Anthesteria when the wine fermentation jars were opened and connected this spirit with good fortune.

The Agathos Daimon is perhaps most famously known for its worship in Alexandria in Egypt where according to legend, Alexander the Great destroyed a great earth serpent whilst building the city and so erected a temple in its honour. Some readers might notice that this tale of slaying the serpent also seems reminiscent of another legend: that of *Python*, the *'earth dragon'* of Delphi, who some consider is Dionysos in serpent form. The slaying of the serpent may have been symbolic of the usurping of the oracular site of Dionysos (and the Great Mother) by the Olympian Apollo, who was thereafter revered as the oracular god of Delphi.

Whilst established in Egypt, the Agathos Daimon became associated with the solar cycles and was sometimes evoked as a descriptive title for the sun god, Re; and in the *Greek Magical Papyri*, the Agathos Daimon is mentioned in a spell to the Greek sun god Helios.[49] However - the whole spell seems more suited to Dionysos than it does Helios. It is often supposed that Dionysos was not

---

[48] The Religions of the Roman Empire, John Ferguson, 1985: P.82
[49] PGM 1596-1715

concerned with magic and the occult, largely because his name is not often mentioned in significant magical texts such as the *Greek Magical Papyri* (PGM). However, when we observe the overall material available as a whole, we start to see that this is not the case; and it is quite possible that the lack of his name in important texts such as the PGM may well be attributed to his synchronisation/identification with other deities such as Osiris, Helios and Abraxas – all of whom are mentioned in the PGM numerous times.

In fact, both Dionysos and his followers were known for their occult abilities and we see these techniques being carried out in both legend and history including shapeshifting, divination, necromancy, curses, miracles (such as turning water into wine) conjuration, communicating with animals, raising energy and even the magical use of herbs and resins. Certainly as a liminal deity, Dionysos is a prime candidate for occult abilities which require an ability to traverse the worlds: he shares this realm with other deities who stand on the threshold betwixt and between and are known for their skills with magic and the occult, such as Hekate. The followers of Dionysos are also known for their occult abilities, such as the Orphic priests – and the Dionysian Maenads, who often lived on the fringes of society and travelled into the untamed wilderness by night to work their rites. A large proportion of necromancers in ancient Greece were also Dionysian women. The Dionysian cult is also known to have made use of a number of ritual fetishes or charms, such as the *phallos* ('little mouths') the *eiresione* boughs, protective *palladia* charms, tools of oscillation, and *defixiones* (curse tablets). And during the Mysteries of Eleusis we find an object known as the *kesatot*, the *'magic arm-bands of the Bacchae'* which according to some sources were used to capture souls. It is possible that these arm bands were a mark of initiation, demonstrating that the initiate had navigated the underworld during his mortal life and prepared for the journey of his soul, which was handed over to Dionysos after death. Some writers also associate these practices with necromancy and raising the dead.

'Wherefore thus saith the Lord God; Behold I am against your pillows (kesatot) wherewith ye there hunt the souls to make them fly, and I will tear them

from your arms and will let the souls go, even the souls that ye hunt to make them fly.'[50]

Throughout ancient Greece the Agathos Daimon was associated with oracles, divination and initiation. The spirit was involved in particular with the oracle of *Trophonios*, another chthonic god who shares many Dionysian attributes. Here, the querant had to undergo various initiatory stages of bathing and anointment before descending down into the earth, where they *'lay in state'* in a tight underground chasm; here they would receive the oracles. Afterwards, they were instructed to visit the altar of Agathos Daimon and offer their prayers, sacrifices and sacred grain and seed (honey-cakes in particular) in exchange for the insight they had received. The Agathos Daimon was also considered as an intermediatary spirit between gods and mortals, referring the requests of mortals onto the gods concerned.

---

[50] Ezekiel 13:20

Chapter 3

Mythology & Cult Narrative

With a deity as old as Dionysos, and with so many different possible origins and cult centres all across the globe, it is not surprising that we have a wide variety of different versions of his myth. Evidence suggests that his worship easily reaches back to the Bronze Age, at least 1500 BCE; and his origins in the Bull God of Crete began as early as 7000 BCE. His hunter instincts, together with a link to wild animals such as the leopard and the auroch, might even tentatively suggest a connection to the earliest hunter gatherers of Africa.

Despite his ancient origins, many of the sources we have available to us in terms of Dionysiac myth are relatively new in origin. For instance *Metamorphoses* was written by Ovid no later than 8CE, and even *The Bacchae* by Euripides (one of the few accounts that has reached us in its entirety) was written no earlier than 410 BCE. The Homeric epic *The Iliad*, which was written around 800 BCE, is thought to be one of the most important texts available and considered *'intimately acquainted with his cult and his myths'* [51] - yet was still written relatively recently when we consider that by this time, the god had been worshipped in that particular form for at least seven hundred years. The epic *Dionysiaca*, 48 books of poetry relating the life and times of Dionysos, was written by Nonnus in 550 CE and is consistently challenged in regard to its accuracy – largely due to the fact that it is of a comparatively late date. It is generally accepted that *'by 400 BCE the character of the god was fixed and determined, and that anything written after this date cannot be trusted'.*[52] However I would argue that this epic is simply another retelling of the ancient myths. Nonnus collected together as many legends as possible, both the well known

---

[51] Dionysus Myth & Cult, Walter F Otto (1960) 1995: P.53
[52] The Great Dionysiac Myth Vol.1, Robert Brown, (1877) 2000: P.10

and the obscure, and wove them together into one entire narrative. As such, his epic may well have served to preserve fragments of Dionysian legend which would otherwise have been lost.

Certainly, it is likely that much of the material we have today originated in older legends, which would have been transmitted orally via cult and ritual theatre, well before they were formally written down in the epics. It is difficult to say which parts of the Dionysos myth are the oldest, or the most genuine – if of course there really can be such a thing as a *'genuine'* myth. Certainly, before the myths of Dionysos became well-known poetic epics, his cult narratives would have been constantly changing and transforming. Myths would also have been altered to suit the particular requirements of different cults and organisations, and may have been added to or altered in order to reflect events happening in society. Several myths include Dionysos playfully wooing various goddesses, for example; perhaps indicative of the cult of Dionysos and mead/wine making being introduced to new civilizations, and his worship being incorporated into other local cults.

"... there was born of Zeus and Persephone 'a Dionysos' ... whose birth and sacrifices and honours are celebrated at night and in secret ... The younger one (Bromios) *also inherited the deeds of the older* (Zagreus) *and so the men of later times, being unaware of the truth and being <u>deceived because of the identity of their names</u>, thought there had been but one Dionysos."* [53]

A short note on Dionysos & the Orphic Mysteries

It would not be possible to write about Dionysos without mentioning the Orphic Mysteries – if only for the purpose of explaining certain variations and contradictions that you might come across when researching Dionysian mythology. The Orphics were selective counter-cultural religious groups - possibly also influenced by eastern philosophy, in particular the legends of Kadmos (the father of Semele, the mother of Dionysos) who considered themselves transcendental initiates of Dionysos. First appearing circa 500 BCE, these groups were a distinct offshoot from the Dionysian mysteries -

---

[53] Library of History, 4.4.5, Diodorus Siculus, c. 60 – 30 BCE

in particular the milder cults of Dionysos, such as those of *Dionysos Athenaios*. Whilst it is generally believed that many aspects of the Orphic myth and cult became integrated into the Athenian worship of Dionysos, we must also consider that the Orphics were just as equally influenced by earlier Dionysian mysticism, myth and practice.

The cult itself was based around a central figure named Orpheus, a pseudo-historical poet who was believed to be the hunter son of Apollo.[54] According to the Orphics, Orpheus had invented the mysteries of Dionysos – but only after Dionysos had demanded that Orpheus do so – an interesting concept which seems to convey that Orpheus *himself* was reluctant to carry the Dionysian message. Although he is often identified with Kadmos, in many ways Orpheus can more easily be identified with Pentheus – the grandson of Kadmos and King of Thebes who refused to follow Dionysos. He was eventually torn apart by Dionysian Maenads, a tale which was echoed in Orphic legend when Orpheus was murdered by Maenads after refusing their advances. Although the tale of Orpheus *'inventing'* the Dionysian Mysteries was taken literally by Orphic initiates, it is extremely unlikely that Orpheus even existed, let alone invented Dionysian practice. Evidence for the Dionysian cult reaches *much* further back, and tales similar to those given in the Orphic mysteries were being told at least a century before the *Orphic Hymns* were first written.

Despite his identification with Pentheus, it is likely that *'Orpheus'* was also a Thracian name for Dionysos (or a god who was akin to him) especially as Orphism itself is usually described as being of Thracian/Phrygian origin. If this is true, then many elements of Orphic mythology and mysticism probably originated in the earliest forms of the Dionysian current – perhaps those we name Sabazios and Zagreus. These found their way into the later Dionysos, and were finally put to use by the Orphic Mysteries. There are also possible links with the Egyptian god Osiris, who was identified with Dionysos and the stories of Kadmos. Certainly, many elements of the later stories of Dionysos can be attributed to the earlier Zagreus; for instance we can identify certain elements within the legends of

---

[54] Apollo himself was often considered a more ethical and orderly inversion of Dionysos.

Dionysos Bromios detailed by Nonnus (such as those involving the discovery of mead) which can be attributed to the earlier tales of Zagreus. So, whilst Zagreus and Bromios are often considered to be *'separate'* deities, they are in truth one of the same; guises or incarnations of Dionysos. This is not a case of conflation (two identities becoming confused) but a distinct mythological link. In fact without it, the foundations of Dionysos' whole nature start to become undermined. As well as being accredited with the *'invention'* of the Dionysian mysteries, Orpheus was also said to have written the so-called Orphic myths themselves, which featured Zagreus and Persephone as two of the central characters. But in fact, as Pausanias tells us, they were scribed by a writer named Onomakritos who *'in the orgies he composed for Dionysos made the Titans the authors of the god's sufferings'* [55] – that is, he introduced the Titans to an already existing (and much older) story. *'As a papyrus fragment from the holy books tells us, it belongs to the Dionysiac belief, and it was from this that the Orphics took it over.* [56]

On a side note, it is also obvious that Onomakritos gave the Titans a much more malignant character than they had possessed before as the elder gods of Gaia. In any case, these stories would later be embraced by Nonnus in his epic, the *Dionysiaca* in which *Dionysos Zagreus* is identified as the first incarnation of Dionysos, the child of Persephone who according to the Orphics was elevated to the throne of Zeus – but who was then torn to pieces by the Titans who cooked and devoured his body. Furious, Zeus punished the Titans by striking them with his lightning bolts which turned the Titans to ash – and from these ashes, the human race was designed. The act of dismembering Dionysos is often suggested as having brought about *'original sin'* (much like Eve taking the apple in the Garden of Eden) for humans were made from the bodies of the sinful Titans. However this has been challenged, proposing that this idea was actually only conceived in the 1800's from a Christian point of view.[57] Indeed, looking at the story from a more *'pagan'* angle, it seems more logical that our bodies are Dionysiac; if we did indeed come from the ashes of the Titans who ate the flesh of Dionysos, we are part of him - as

---

[55] Description of Greece 8.37.5, Pausanias, c. 200 CE

[56] Dionysus Myth & Cult, Walter F Otto (1960) 1995: P.191

[57] See Tearing Apart the Zagreus Myth, Radcliffe Edmonds, 1999

well as those older gods who were the children of Gaia herself. To quote from Aleister Crowley's Gnostic Mass, *'there is no part of us that is not of the gods!*[58]

According to Orphic mythology, the heart of Zagreus is then salvaged by Zeus who offers it to Semele to drink as a potion; he is then reborn as *Dionysos Bromios* to his second mother, Semele. In many ways the Titans can be seen as the initiators: transforming Zagreus into the second incarnation of Dionysos – Bromios - and giving life to mankind. Despite these tales of Zagreus being attributed to the later Orphic mysteries, many of them can in fact be considered pre-Orphic, as several of the concepts were already being used in the Dionysian elements of older cult rites and belief systems. For instance, it is believed that the many older rites and legends of *Bakcheus* of Naxos were put to use by the later Dionysian mysteries and then the Orphic Mysteries. Also, the mystery cult at Delphi already maintained a set of myths and rites surrounding the dismemberment of Dionysos as part of their agricultural season: the *'tearing'* of the god at the winter festival, and the burial (or *'planting'*) of his dismembered parts at the spring festival.[59] Festivals were also held at this time to Persephone and *Zeus Meilichios* (the sacred snake-god or chthonic daimon of the ancient Hellenes, who housed the spirits of departed ancestors[60]) and the two were considered a pair at the ritual *'planting'* of Dionysos; the joining of Zeus and Persephone is of course the basis for the Orphic tale of Zagreus. It is also likely that the *'enthronement'* of Dionysos, which was at the heart of Orphic mythology and was probably used in their initiations, finds its origins in the ecstatic dances of Samothrace, whose women danced in circles around an idol upon a raised platform. [61]

Despite the common origins of their rites and mythology, the philosophy of Orphism was in many ways a direct contrast to the Dionysian cult. Unlike the female-led Dionysian mysteries, Orphism was largely male dominated. They also frowned upon the older, more corporeal Dionysian practices – such as sacrifice and orgiastic rites –

---

[58] Liber XV The Gnostic Mass, Aleister Crowley, 1913: Part VIII

[59] Greek Mysteries, Michael Cosmopoulos, 2003: P.231

[60] The God Who Comes, Rosemarie Taylor-Perry, 2003: P.4

[61] See Tearing Apart the Zagreus Myth, Radcliffe Edmonds, 1999

as corrupt: *'Orpheus ... reclaimed them from bloodshed and barbarous rites'.*[62]
And unlike the Dionysian world view, the Orphics rejected the
positive role of the physical world in religion and mysticism, and
adhered to the idea of transcendence as a way to escape physical
matter (rather than embracing the physical as a tool to facilitate the
spiritual journey). Whilst the Dionysian mysteries had embraced a
physical expression of the mysteries as key to the release of the spirit
(i.e. in the form of rituals, song and dance, trance and ecstasy, and
festival processions) Orphism largely abandoned them. Their practice
became more of a philosophical doctrine which embraced theoretical
mysticism such as astrology and science. According to the Greek
philosopher Proclus, Pythagoras himself was an initiate of the Orphic
mysteries[63] and many of their concepts found their way into
Pythagoreanism. But the elitism and secrecy of the Orphic mysteries
would eventually become its undoing. Unlike the Dionysian
mysteries, which despite its initiatory elements had on the whole
remained a cult for *'the average person'*, Orphism had become suitable
only for the privileged and influential, and gradually found its
numbers dwindling. From its ashes, several new cults of a Gnostic
nature began to form in its place such as Neoplatonism - and even
Christianity, all of which had one thing in common: *'salvation'* from
the material world that Dionysos and the other old gods had so
treasured.

Whilst the Orphic mysteries often contradicted the Dionysian
world view, it did serve to introduce elements of *'learned'* rather than
'experienced' mysticism (such as philosophy and astrology) into
remaining Dionysian cults - and of course, into our culture as a
whole. It also provided us with the *Orphic Hymns*, poems based on the
cult of Orphism and believed to have been written around 300 BCE.
Certainly, without the Orphics we would not have anywhere near as
much information about the original Dionysian cult as we do today.
The Orphics simply *'reworked'* ancient mysticism, serving to preserve
many lingering and perhaps forgotten fragments of the declining
Dionysian tradition within its framework for us to discover.

---

[62] Frogs, 1030, Aristophanes, c. 400 BCE, trans. Frere
[63] The Works, Ralph Cudworth, 1829: P.80

The Dual-formed God

"Dionysos I call loud-sounding and divine, inspiring God, a two-fold shape is thine; thy various names and attributes I sing, O' firstborn, thrice begotten, Bacchaen King. Rural, ineffable, two-formed, obscure, two-horned, ivy-crowned, and Euion pure. Bull faced and martial, bearer of the vine, endued with counsel prudent and divine: Eubouleus, whom the leaves of vines adorn ... hear my voice O' lord ! Come blessed Dionysos, begot from thunder, Bacchus famed. Bassaros God, of universal might, whom swords and blood and sacred rage delight ... come with much rejoicing mind.'[64]

Dionysos is often considered a dual deity; a quality that was arguably one of his most important characteristics. As a demi god (born of a mortal mother and a divine father) Dionysos already had one foot in both worlds; he was the embodiment of duality which lay at the heart of almost every Dionysian myth and cult festival. He was *Dionysos Dimorphos, 'the dual-formed one'*, and the force that brings opposites together - two halves of a whole. The late 19th century philosopher Nietzsche spoke of Dionysos as a metaphor to describe the transition between creation and destruction – both *'destructively creative'* and *'creatively destructive'*. Whilst Nietzsche was speaking about modern culture, his use of Dionysos as a metaphor was quite appropriate: the simple idea that one extreme state of being cannot exist without its direct opposite. Love and hate, hot and cold, peace and war, mildness and frenzy, childhood and maturity, soberness and drunkenness, presence and absence, and birth and death – and specifically, the concept that something must be destroyed in order for something else to begin. The author Robert Brown writes that Dionysos was *'both the nurturer and destroyer of things ... he was, at the same time, the mildest and most terrible of divinities.'*[65]

If we accept that several key elements within the Orphic tales of Zagreus and Persephone (also reflected in the *Dionysiaca* by Nonnus) are in fact reminders of lingering or forgotten fragments of more ancient Dionysian mysticism and mythology, then it is possible to consider the first two incarnations of Dionysos mentioned in Dionysiaca - *Zagreus* and *Bromios* - as dual counterparts, two necessary

---

[64] Orphic Hymn 53 to Amphietus
[65] The Great Dionysiac Myth Vol.1, Robert Brown, (1877) 2000: P.132

halves of a whole. In the *Dionysiaca*, Dionysos makes a transition between his incarnation as *Zagreus* (the mild and nocturnal god) and his new incarnation as *Bromios* (the roaring and frenzied fire-born god). This transition between two states was sometimes interpreted as a premature or *'early'* birth, and actual or *'later'* birth - a concept that was common in Hellenic religion and mythology. When Zagreus dies (or transforms) his soul 'lives on' as Bromios. *Zagreus, who was dead, becomes alive again*[66] in the body of Bromios. This second guise of Dionysos was more commonly known as Bakcheus (or, to add confusion, simply Dionysos!) but when Nonnus wrote the *Dionysiaca* he referred to him as one of his epithets, *Bromios* – possibly to avoid this confusion in the story, and individualise this otherwise wide-reaching guise of the god.

Theories on the Dionysian Cycle of Duality

DIONYSOS DIMORPHOS	
DIONYSOS ZAGREUS (MEILICHIOS)	**DIONYSOS BROMIOS (BAKCHEUS)**
'The Mild' and 'The Kindly'	'The Ecstatic' and 'The Raving'
Dark and Cool – Shade Face	Bright and Hot – Bright Face
Figwood Dionysos	Vinewood Dionysos
Death, Resting, Nocturnal & Mild	Growth, Alive, Manifest & Chaotic
Child of the Underworld	Manifest in the Upperworld
Coolness - "Tamer of Heat"	Fire Born God - "Encourager of Heat"
Descent, Resting, Preparing	Return/Coming, Raving, Celebrating

---

[66] The Great Dionysiac Myth Vol.1, Robert Brown, (1877) 2000: P.75

Fermentation of Mead and Wine – Waiting	Enjoyment of Mead and Wine & Making More
Death in the Underworld and Rebirth into the Manifest World (upperworld of men)	Cycle of Presence and Absence in the Manifest World (upperworld of men)

No matter what we choose to name these two phases of the god, the theme between them remains the same: a transition between *mild and nocturnal*, and *frenzied and fire-born*. These solar and chthonian themes are represented by absence and presence: sun up, sun down - inside, outside; metaphorically, the solar aspect of the god is stood on top of the mound, whilst the chthonian god is hidden inside it. His two forms can even be seen reflected in viticulture: the growth of the grapes is solar, whilst their fermentation inside pots and skins is chthonian and hidden.

The Dionysian rites and festivals reflected this exchange between the two forms of the god, and the underlying themes of death and rebirth. In Athens, both forms of Dionysos were celebrated annually and in tune with the solar year, with the Mild Dionysos ruling over *Dadophorios* (the three winter months) and the Ecstatic Dionysos ruling over the remaining hotter and lighter nine months of the year.[67] It was believed that Dionysos would simultaneously be sacrificed and reborn, his soul simply transferring from one form into another. Specially chosen bull-calves (named *axios tauros*, '*worthy bull*') were believed to be the embodiment of Dionysos and '*worthy*' of carrying his spirit or soul; these calves were sacrificed throughout the year to emulate the theme of death, dismemberment and resurrection. It is interesting to note that during sacrifices to the chthonic gods, the head of the animal being sacrificed would be turned down[68] (towards the underworld) rather than the usual position of animals being sacrificed to Olympian gods whose heads would be turned upwards (towards the heavens). In a similar way, the Olympian gods had

---

[67] Later, Apollo would usurp the lighter part of the year, leaving Dionysos with only the three winter months.

[68] The God Who Comes, Rosemarie Taylor-Perry, 2003: P.78

elevated altars, whereas the more chthonic deities such as Dionysos and Hekate more often had low altars or sacrificial pits.

The timing and frequency of when each guise of the god was believed to be present during a Dionysian festival cycle was entirely dependent on where the festival was being performed. For instance, the Athenian festivals embraced both sides of the God within a single twelve month calendar year similar to our own, whilst the trieteric festival cycles of other Dionysian revelers (generally outside of Athens) celebrated each guise of the god *biannually* (the festival cycle spanned over two years, and an entire year was given to each form of the god - with a third year concluding the cycle and marking the beginning of another). Much of the material in this book is built around the Athenian festival cycle; although many of their festivals incorporated the themes and rites of earlier Dionysian mystery cults, and were inspired by their older customs.

The duality of Dionysos – a god of life and death and presence and absence – was often seen to be embodied in the grape vine which appeared dry and dead during the winter yet burst forth with green leaves and juicy fruit during the spring and summer. It produced intoxicating liquor which allowed the Bakkhoi of Dionysos to alter their consciousness, to prophesise and *thyein*, 'rave' – releasing the spirit and leaving behind the boundaries and cares of the earthly world. It is symbolic of the liminal capabilities of Dionysos; he who traverses between two worlds. Kerényi identified that the ivy, another plant sacred to Dionysos, was also symbolic of his duality: first sending out creeping *'shade-seeking'* stems of juvenile leaves (the embodiment of *Dionysos Meilichios*, the Dark Lord) then later adult leaves on fertile stems, which produce berries and seek full sunlight (the embodiment of *Dionysos Bakcheus*, *'the manifest one'*).

With evidence of descent and return and embodiment in the growth cycle of plants, it is perhaps tempting to assume that Dionysos is a vegetation god. The concept of *'the vegetation god'* was made popular by the work of JG Frazer in *The Golden Bough*, and quickly became integrated into neo-pagan philosophy. However whilst Dionysos was embodied in certain agricultural and natural flora, these plants were often chosen more because of their significance in terms of duality and cycles of opposition and their role in the natural world, rather than the world of agriculture. Reflecting his dual nature, the Dionysian rites contained within them the message of balance and opposition - dismemberment and rejuvenation, descent and return, imprisonment and liberation, love and loss; mysteries celebrated by his followers which *within the moment of ritual trance, unmasked themselves to reveal their names to be life and death.*[69] And like Dionysos, his followers learnt to traverse the worlds.

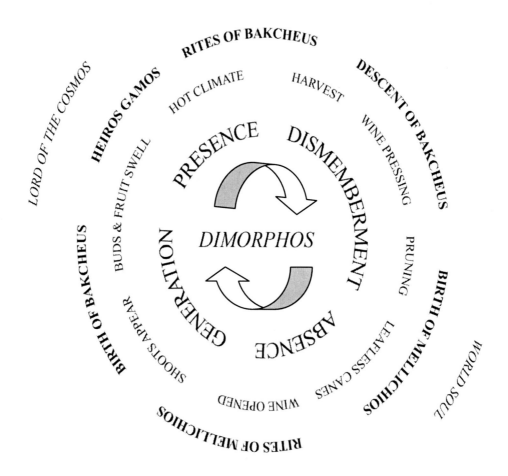

---

[69] Dionysus Myth & Cult, Walter F Otto (1960) 1995: P.121

Dionysian Masks & Duality

"The mask ... an image out of which the perplexing riddle of his two-fold nature stares – and with it, madness. This is the mask."[70]

The mask was one of the most significant symbols of Dionysos and was used in both his public festival processions and within the more secretive mysteries celebrated by his cult. Originally, the face of the reveler may have been disguised with white pigment, soot or mud or stiffened linen, or large leaves of different plants wrapped around the face to create a vacant expression or alter ego. Later, these methods were replaced by man-made masks which were carved out of wood and bone or fashioned out of leather; it remained popular however to disguise the face with clay or ash, and sometimes vermillion, or green and red plant juices.[71] Masks were sometimes worn upon the face in Dionysian rites; usually, it was animal masks of satyrs and centaurs that were worn in this way, but facial masks of Dionysos himself were also sometimes worn, both man shaped and bull horned; perhaps in order that the wearer might become the embodiment of the god. More often however, the mask itself was considered the embodiment of Dionysos in its own right – sometimes carried in, or covering, the sacred *liknon* (winnowing basket) and other times elevated up high on a column or post whilst his followers honoured him beneath.

The mask itself is an enigma; it takes the form of a living face, yet it is not alive. It can be made to appear as any shape – animal, human or god – and conceals the real identity of its wearer. Inside the mask, the wearer is free of his or her usual limitations; he or she is nameless, timeless, and powerful. The wearer is hidden, yet in plain sight; and they can become any character they imagine themselves to be, whilst beneath their costume their physical body remains unchanged. The mask also allows the wearer to withdraw from the material world: behind the mask, the wearer could focus more freely on the purpose of their rites. Their sight is clouded, allowing prophetic visions to occur. Their breathing is stifled - taking them into a deeper, altered state of consciousness. Their hearing is changed – and trumpets,

---

[70] Dionysus Myth & Cult, Walter F Otto (1960) 1995: P.86

[71] Dictionary of Greek & Roman Antiquities, William George Smith, 1870: P. 363

drums and words rumble in their ears. In modern terms, the wearer of the mask was in effect shapeshifting: altering his consciousness for a period of time to experience the thoughts and feelings of another being – an ability which Karl Kerenyi[72] described as the *'second sight'* and reflected the changeling-skill of Dionysos.

The power of liminality that the mask was believed to hold meant that it was also considered an important tool when communicating with ghosts and shades of the underworld and certainly, bestial masks which aided the wearer to connect with their primordial roots would have aided communication with the ancestors: voluntary atavistic trance and prophecy which was channeled into masked ritual and theatre. The spring festival of Anthesteria, which celebrated Bakcheus' return from the underworld and the opening of the first barrels of wine, was also a time for honouring spirits who had followed Dionysos up into the upperworld of men. Wine was probably used in conjunction with masks during these sorts of rites. A bronze mask of Dionysos (dated between 200 BCE - 100 CE) now part of a collection at the British Museum, was originally a pair of supports for the handle of a ritual drinking vessel which was a cross between the traditional wine-mixing bowl and the ritual *situla* (bucket). It depicts Dionysos with a beard of grapes and ivy berries, and two small horns rising from his temples.[73]

Dionysos was not usually represented by an actual statue in the pre-classical (archaic) era; his image was perhaps considered too changeable to be embodied by such a consistent form. Instead his form usually took the shape of a mask, which was hung on a wooden column or pillar and elevated up high for all to see. Creating masked post-gods is an ancient practice; the first image of a mask on a column is dated 6000 BCE.[74] The Dionysian post-god is often depicted on vase paintings with ivy or vines creeping up the wooden column and around the mask. Often, a cross-post was attached to the main column, creating a scarecrow-like figure which would be dressed in black robes or animal skins and could be carried about in festival processions; a man in black. Sometimes the post-god was carried into

[72] Dionysos: Archetypal Image of Indestructible Life, Karl Kerényi, 1996: P.80

[73] http://www.britishmuseum.org

[74] Greek Religion, Walter Burkert (1931) 1985: P.13

the mountains and thrust into the earth, creating an impromptu ritual space; the mask and the robes or skins would be thrown over it and the physical presence of Dionysos could be achieved in any place, at any time. In other cases the mask and skins were hung upon a living tree - a permanent fixture within a sacred grove which for a period of time became the incarnation of Dionysos. The masked pillar was often used in conjunction with other cult items (such as leopard skins, cowbells, and the ithyphallic thyrsus – a staff topped with a pine-cone) and was not considered to represent Dionysos in his entirety. Indeed after the rites or festival season was over, the masked column figure would often be taken apart again and packed away; a process that may have been symbolic of Dionysos present and Dionysos absent.

The Carved Masks of Figwood & Vinewood

The carved wooden masks of Figwood and Vinewood were worshipped as the two opposing forms of *Dionysos Dimorphos*: the *'resting, nocturnal and mild'* god, and the *'alive, manifest and chaotic god'*, respectively. These two opposing faces of the god can also to some degree be considered as analogous with the first born nocturnal child of the underworld (Zagreus) and the second born *'loud shouter'* (Bromios/ Bakcheus) in their dual aspects - but are perhaps more representative of the cycle of *'presence and absence'* which Dionysos himself traverses; symbolic of the agricultural and viticultural cycles which the festivals largely revolved around. The Figwood and Vinewood masks are best known for their use by the cult of Dionysos on the island of Naxos (just off mainland Greece) however there is also mention of similar masks and epithets being used in Athens, perhaps suggesting that their use may have been more widespread than first thought. Naxos is, however, well known for its connection with Dionysos and his myths; it is otherwise known as *'the sea girt Dia'*, or *'Dionysias'*.[75]

The Vinewood mask was symbolic of the present, ecstatic god *Dionysos Bakcheus*. Whilst he could be considered as sharing characteristics with *Dionysos Lysios* (the Light One, or Liberator) we

[75] The Great Dionysiac Myth Vol.1, Robert Brown, (1877) 2000: P.25

must not confuse *'light'* with *'gentle'*. The light and dark guises of Dionysos are simply representational of his *'absence'* or *'presence'*, or his position in either the upperworld or the underworld. The concept of light as *'good'* and dark as *'evil'* is a notion which would not have existed for the followers of Dionysos who saw life and death as synonymous; for instance, whilst modern neo-paganism tends to associate ghosts and spirits with the darker, wintery side of the year, early Dionysians invited ghosts and spirits to their springtime celebrations. This is not limited to ancient Greek religion: many other cultures from all over the world honoured the dead throughout the year. And readers from cooler climates such as the British Isles must also be careful not to interpret the Dionysian summer months with pleasure and plenty. For those in the Mediterranean, the heat of the summer sun would have made for hard work, water shortages, failing crops, and possibly even famine. Whilst he brought new life, celebration, and a spectacle of miracles, Bakcheus was also the devourer of raw flesh, and the loud-shouting god of pandemonium. He was the inventor of wine, he who offered his Bacchic initiates/followers the clarity and freedom of the spirit - but at the cost of illusion and insanity. He was also the one who punished those who refused to follow him, by cursing their crops. Whilst associated with the underworld, and death of a different nature, it was the dark Dionysos of the Figwood, the resting *'Mild One'*, who brought peace; rather like the relief of a cool evening after a relentlessly hot summer's day. This same Dionysos was sometimes seen as the bearer of the underworld flame, or the cool nocturnal sun. Incidentally, one Greek vase from the Hellenic period depicts the head of Dionysos with vine branches running down between his eyes, splitting his face into two halves. One eye is believed to represent the day-time sun, and the other the nocturnal sun.[76]

The Figwood mask, *Dionysos Meilichios* (possibly from the term for the fig *Meilicha*, meaning *'mild fruit'* and from the chthonic being named *Meilichios*) can be considered as representing the abundance and rest which follows a good harvest, and also an element of katabasis: descent into the underworld - in agricultural terms, the waning of the year into the cooler months. It is unlikely that the cults of Naxos followed the same ethos as those of the Eleusinian but it is

---

[76] The Great Dionysiac Myth Vol.1, Robert Brown, (1877) 2000: P.343

possible that the Eleusinian mysteries were influenced by the themes which were observed by the Naxians, and their masks. This is perhaps why the Figwood Dionysos was considered 'mild' yet also 'chthonic' – of the dark under-earth 'the absent one'.

The Orphics also spoke of a figwood mask, which was given to the goddess Hipta (or Rhea) the nurse of Dionysos. She placed it in a winnowing basket for safety, around which a snake entwined. The fig was also associated with the Eleusinian tales of Kore, who was snatched by Hades and taken down into the subterranean depths to become his queen, as Persephone. Her abduction was said to have happened at Erineos, a village which came to be named after the wild fig trees (*erineos*) which grew in abundance nearby. Dionysos was sometimes equated with Hades and it is possible that this was the mystery that was revealed to initiates in Dionysian rites which were integrated into the Eleusinian mysteries in Hellas. Hellenic vase paintings of Dionysos with the Underworld Queen Kore/Persephone further his connection with Hades and the Eleusinian cults. The fig tree was a widely grown food crop across the Mediterranean, and as a fundamental part of the daily diet it was considered sacred to *Dionysos Sukites*, '*of the fig tree'* who discovered the fig. A similar fruit - the date - was also a staple food in the Mediterranean and sacred to the Sumerian god *Dumuzi*, the '*wild bull*' who was considered the embodiment of the harvested fruit –and like Dionysos was also associated with the underworld and the dance of life, death and resurrection. It was also associated with fertility and the Sumerian sacred marriage rites were described as being carried out upon a '*bed*' of dates. Dumuzi's name also means '*strong one*', and as the Chaldean Tamzi he is the '*Sun of Life'* who was associated with the fierce heat of the midsummer months - both were functions of Dionysos.

Images on Attic *lekythos* (oil flasks) depict that during *Khoes Day* (part of the festival of Anthesteria) a double mask was worshipped - possibly by placing two masks (one figwood, and one vinewood) back-to-back, so that one face looked out from each side. Maenads would mix wine with water in front of the masks, and drink and dance before it - celebrating the dual nature of Dionysos, his return to the upperworld of men, the conception of his next incarnation and the opening of the first wine.[77] A similar figwood mask was used in the town of Ikarion and was considered so important that it was eventually copied into marble around 530 BCE, and continued to be used in the same fashion - although changing the material to marble may have meant that the symbolic meaning of the mask's original material may have been lost after a time.

The sense of duality that these two masks give – either used separately to focus on one individual quality, or together as a unification of his twofold character – is perfectly symbolic of *Dionysos Diphyes* and *Dimorphos*, *'two formed'*. Not only are the two masks iconic of the two guises of the god, but the mask itself is symbolic of the altered state of being that is experienced by the wearer. The mask itself expresses the balance between life and death: its form is that of a living face, but its eyes are hollow and dead. Yet for that moment when the mask is worn, the eyes become alive, and it is as if the mask itself is breathing. A similar account of a carved mask of Dionysos was one made of olive wood which was pulled out of the sea by a fisherman near the island of Lesbos.[78] The fisherman consulted the Pythia, who told them that the mask should be revered as *Dionysos Phallen*, *'of the head'*. The mask was placed inside a wooden chest and worshipped. This is similar to the Spartan account of Dionysos' birth, which recalls that Dionysos was washed up on the shores of Sparta in a wooden chest. In true Dionysian form, the mask of Dionysos Phallen was described by the geographer Pausanias as *'outlandish, and unlike the normal features of Greek gods.'*[79]

Dionysos - who stands astride the worlds and the paradoxes of life and death, dark and light and resting and raving – represents the unification of these forces: two halves of the mask, together – balance and opposition as one. This is what his Bakkhoi aimed to achieve with the masks; they stood with one foot in *bios*, the material world of the mortal, and the other in the realms of the gods; confronting their mortality and celebrating *zöe*, the ecstasy of the spirit of life.

---

[77] It is said that the name of this festival day comes from the wine pitchers used during the ceremonies.

[78] Dionysus Myth & Cult, Walter F Otto (1960) 1995: P.88

[79] Description of Greece, Book 8, Pausanias (c. 200 CE) 1979: P.473 trans. WHS Jones

The Masked Thespian

"The desire of escaping from self into something new and strange, of living in an imaginary world, breaks forth in a thousand instances in these festivals of Dionysos."[80]

Represented by the universal symbol of theatre – the two contrasting masks of comedy and tragedy, the ecstatic and mournful masks of Dionysos – the cult of Dionysos was also instrumental in the beginnings of dramatic performances. Theatre as we recognise it today originated in the formalised ritual plays of the Rural and City Dionysia, although theatrical performances and mythical reenactments were given in offering to Dionysos throughout the year by his followers. Thespis, a Hellenic poet who lived during the C6[th] BCE, is believed to have been the first person to stand on stage and play a fictitious character during the intervals between the dithyrambs to Dionysos. He was the first actor, and is credited with the invention of tragedy as well as bringing the use of masks into *'fictional'* theatre. Thespis was born in Ikarion (present day town St Dionysos) the location of an important Dionysos sanctuary and also a place recalled by many writers as the first town to have welcomed Dionysos and his gifts of wine and theatre. A Figwood mask was also used there in the local rites, symbolic of *Dionysos Meilichios.*

According to the philosopher Aristotle[81] early ritual drama was improvised and acted out by the Bacchic followers of Dionysos as part of *dithyrambs* - chorus songs which lamented both the absence of the god and celebrated his return, fitting for a god of duality - and were first performed on the circular grain threshing floors and market places of ancient Hellas. Dithyramb choruses were originally performed by initiates of the mysteries, and sometimes depicted in song a description of the initiate's experience of the passage to the underworld. It is important to remember that for a very long time, dance and drama were seen as synonymous with ritual; they reflected profound mystic experience and as such, certain ritual practices of consecration and purification were carried out before and after the performances. The circular motion is also of interest; like us, the

---

[80] Dictionary of Greek & Roman Antiquities, William George Smith, 1870: P.363
[81] Aristotle: Poetics, Richard Janko, 1987: P.194

ancient Greeks believed the world was round – albeit flat. By working rituals and magic in circles, they attempted to create a microcosm of the macrocosm (similar to one of the aims in ritual circles today). The ancient city of Thebes, the 'mystic city of the seven gates' was also created in a circular shape and each of its seven gates was given a planetary association to represent the surrounding cosmos. Therefore to move in a circular motion was to quite literally move with the dance of the cosmos. A similar circle dance, described in Euripides *The Bacchae* was performed by the followers of Dionysos, and the whole mountain and its beasts joined in with the dance.

> *"Hero Dionysos come*
> *to thy temple home ....*
> *rushing with thy bull-foot, come!*
> *noble bull, noble bull...*'[82]

Aristotle also accounts that the comedic aspects of theatre originated in part from the ithyphallic rites of Dionysos which featured satyrs (masked followers of Dionysos) wearing oversized figwood phalli to the festival rites. Incidentally, the Satyrs themselves were never representative of the god himself, who was described as *'bull-footed'* (a slang term for the phallus or a *'riggy'* animal). Accounts are given of revellers moving through the town procession shouting obscenities and insults at the crowd - creating a sense of absurdity to the rites of *Dionysos Bakcheus*. The Eleusinian processions (which involved the guise of Dionysos known as Iakchos) are believed to have also included this sort of entertainment during their festivals; masked figures were said to appear to the initiates of the procession half way through their journey, as light relief, to amuse - but also to create a bizarre, *'raving'* atmosphere which added to the experience of the festival. Other accounts suggest that the satyrs were originally part of the tragic stage, and that the *'ad lib'* nature of their theatre was a place where social structure could be questioned without fear of retribution from the authorities: as a god of liberation and revelry, Dionysos' stage was certainly the place for questioning the *'status quo'*, and experimenting with social boundaries.

---

[82] 'Dithyramb of Ellis' Themis - A Study of the Social Origins of Greek Religion, Jane Ellen Harrison, 2010: P.210

Theatre removed both the actors and the audience from everyday consciousness, and allowed them to be absorbed by theatrical narrative. This is much like the drama of today, such as theatrical productions and cinematic film which offers escapism to some and inspiration to others. The same can be achieved on an even deeper level through effective ritual; so consuming are these narratives, and so thought provoking, that they can change the way we think and view the world. Comedies, which originated in the Bacchic phallic dances, songs and enthusiastic processions, can bring cheer to many a sad soul and it is to Dionysos that we must give our thanks for this gift. Incredibly, theatre reached even beyond the boundaries of conflict – with bands of actors safely travelling into otherwise hostile territories, and able to perform peacefully. As such, theatre became internationally popular and this would mark the beginning of entertainment which would become such an important element of the modern word. Without Dionysos, we would have neither drama nor comedy - at least in the forms we have come to know them.

Zagreus (Meilichios)

"Mistress Earth and Zagreus who art above all other gods!"[83]

The Dionysian form known as *Zagreus* was recognised by many other epithets for the Nocturnal Dionysos – and when discussing him outside the perspective of Orphic mysticism or the tales of Nonnus, I have chosen to refer to him as the Naxian *Meilichios, 'the Mild One'*. You will find I refer to Zagreus and Meilichios interchangeably throughout this book, depending on the context.

Meilichios is sometimes considered the unmanifest Dionysos; metaphorically, he is the *'seed'* beneath the earth, waiting to sprout into the upper world. His name is possibly derived from the Greek word for *'honey'* or *'fig'*. The word is also sometimes used as an epithet for Zeus, but in fact comes from an earlier chthonic *daimon* (spirit being) of the same name; who one could argue had more in common

---

[83] Alkmeonis fr.3, Author Unknown, See Epicorum Graecorum Fragmenta, G. Kinkel, 1878

with the chthonic cult of Dionysos than it did the Olympian cult of Zeus. In support of this, it is interesting to note that shrines to Zeus Meilichios were often built on rocky, mountainside terrains, fitting for the mountain-born Dionysos. The chthonic spirit Meilichios was the more benign side of a daimon god known as *Maimaktes*[84]. Maimaktes could be benevolent or malevolent[85] depending on the sacrifices that were offered to him – but like Dionysos, he was a god of the common people, bestowing welfare to the vulnerable or the lower classes. But he had a bloodthirsty nature, too; and in truth, Meilichios possessed this nature also! Whilst Meilichios was the silent god of winter dormancy, he was also feared as Lord of the Dead; Hunter of Souls. Associated with underground caves, Meilichios holds the epithet, *Ailianos, 'gaping one' - 'he who makes the ground burst'*: he stands at the gateway between the worlds, as lord of the absent and dead.

Yet, Meilichios had his own moments when he reached upward to touch the upperworld. He was drawn out from the depths of the sea by his initiates/followers (commonly referred to as *Bakkhoi* or *Bacchants* [masculine] *Bakkhai* or *Bacchantes* [feminine] although the former masculine terms are used to describe his followers in general)[86] who made offerings at the seashore and sung songs at the edges of lakes to the sound of trumpets.[87] According to the Athenian festival cycle, this invitation into the upperworld marked the beginning of the three winter months of the Mild and Dark God's rule.

Meilichios is just one guise of this far-reaching chthonic god. As the horned god of the underworld he is the predator, yet also the prey: the hunter becomes the hunted and similarly, myths recall how Zagreus was murdered by the Titans and withdrew to the dark womb of Semele, in preparation to be reborn.

---

[84] Prolegomena to the Study of Greek Religions, Jane Ellen Harrison 1908: P.8

[85] Horos Dios: An Athenian Shrine & Cult of Zeus, Gerald Lalonde, 2006: P.45

[86] Parallel Lives 'Demosthenes' 18.260, Plutarch c. 75 CE

[87] Account by Socrates. See Dionysos: Archetypal Image of Indestructible Life, Karl Kerényi, 1996: P.180

The Myths of Zagreus

The First Incarnation of Dionysos

"Zagreus ... son born to Zeus in dragonbed by Persephone, the consort of the black robed king of the underworld..."[88]

The first incarnation of Dionysos was *Dionysos-Zagreus* the son of Persephone, the goddess of the underworld. An exact account of his birth is absent, but the themes are fitting for a child born of the underworld. He is usually depicted as an infant – although when identified with Meilichios as the Lord of Souls or the 'Pillar God' he often appears as an older, bearded figure.

Perhaps the oldest legend recounting his birth is that of the awakening from a *'leather sack'* (mead fermentation skins) inside a dark mountain cave. Rites were carried out to acknowledge his birth, such as those held by the followers of Dionysos in the *Korykion antron* (*'cave of the leather sack'*) on the slopes of Mount Parnassos, mainland Hellas.[89] Dionysos was associated with the mead itself; which, fermenting inside the skins, was likened to the unborn baby Dionysos in the womb. The bees are described as Dionysos' nursemaids, being essential in the production of the honey which was a symbol of the young Dionysos himself. Other legends tell of how the baby Dionysos was nourished by milk and honey, which was offered to him by his nursemaids when they received the boy from Zeus.

The legend of the leather sack was also recalled by the playwright Euripides, who wrote about a Dionysian mystery cult who carried out these sacred rites in the Idaean Caves of Crete. These caves were said to have burst forth with blood at the birth of *Dionysos Melissaios*, *'bee man'* – a sacred blood, which has been linked by some modern writers to honey. In later versions of his myth the young Dionysos is credited with the actual discovery of mead himself, *'he would cut a fennel stalk and smite the hard rocks, and from their wounds they poured for the god sweet liquor.'*[90] This passage is usually assumed to be referring to wine but it

---

[88] Dionysiaca, 5.562ff, Nonnus c. 500 CE trans. Rouse

[89] Or by other accounts, Phrygia

[90] Cynegetica, 4.230 ff, Oppian c. 300 CE trans. Mair

could just as likely be referring to honey, or mead; elsewhere in the text, the same author writes that Dionysos *'brought the gentle bees from the oak and shut them up in hives'.*[91] Later in history the symbology of the leather sack (fermentation skin) was surpassed by the *liknon* an agricultural tool which was an important part in the Eleusinian Mysteries - in some tales Dionysos was said to have been born from the liknon as the *liknites, 'spirit in the winnow'.* This deity, who was associated with abundance via wild honey, was now associated with the abundance of the domestic seed. It may also have been followed by the *pithoi,* the clay fermentation pot which was used in the production of wine and was later celebrated during *Pithoigia* on the 11th day of the month of Anthesterion when the first of the newly fermented wine was opened.

"Zagreus appears little in literature ... he is essentially a ritual figure, the centre of a cult so primitive, so savage, that a civilized literature instinctively passes him by."[92]

The father of Zagreus is held to be Zeus; however it is important to note that the Zeus of Cretan mythology is considered by many to be a conflation of Dionysos-Zagreus himself. When the Mycenaen Greeks took over Minoan Crete, they noticed similarities between the god they found there (Dionysos Zagreus) and their own leading deity, Zeus. Many myths with a Cretan influence began to ascribe Zeus with many of Dionysos' attributes and associations, giving us good reason to speculate that the Cretan Zeus is in fact Dionysos. Incidentally, the first part of Dionysos' name, *'Dio',* is from the same root word as Zeus (via the Proto-Indo-European *'Dyeus'*). This is related to the Latin *Deus* (simply meaning *'god'*). With this in mind, we can probably treat the Cretan Dionysos and the Cretan Zeus as one god; a father and son duo in a cyclical sense. As Cretan mythology no doubt had an effect on the later mythology of mainland Greece, we must consider the possibility that Dionysos continued to be an integral part of the mainland Zeus, albeit a hidden one.

---

[91] Cynegetica, 4.230 ff, Oppian c. 300 CE trans. Mair
[92] Prolegomena to the Study of Greek Religions, Jane Ellen Harrison 1908: P.481

<u>Conception & Birth</u>

'Fates made him perfect ... the god with ox's horns, crowned with wreaths of snakes – that's why the Maenads twist in their hair wild snakes they capture.'[93]

According to legend the goddess Demeter hid her daughter Persephone in a cave in Crete, to protect the maidenhood of the beautiful young woman. The mouth of the cave she guarded with serpents, to assure that no man – mortal or god – could enter. But Zeus,[94] struck by the beauty of Demeter's daughter, took the form of a snake and in this disguise crept part the guards. Entering the cave he wooed Persephone in his serpent form; and by this *'dragon bed'*[95] union, *Dionysos Zagreus*: the horned baby of the underworld, the shapeshifter, was conceived. The appearance of the snake is a likely reminder of the snake daimon *Meilichios*; or a reminder of the Phrygian *Sabazios*, to whom it was said all snakes belonged. When the boy was born, Zeus took him up into the heavens and set him upon his throne in Olympus, the home of the gods, and armed the young Dionysos with two lightning bolts for protection which he instructed the boy to keep hold of at all times.

Dismemberment & Death

But the wife of Zeus, the goddess Hera, grew angry that her husband Zeus had betrayed her by sharing Persephone's bed, and to spite them both she sent the Titans (elder gods who opposed the Olympian gods) to murder the child. This would be the first of many attempts Hera made to destroy Dionysos. The Titans drew near as the child Zagreus sat upon his throne, watching his court dancers weave and spin before him and unaware of the danger that closed in. Yet still, Dionysos was protected by the lightning bolts which Zeus had given him; and somehow the Titans had to separate the boy from his weapons. And so they enticed the child with toys; spinning tops, dolls and balls. Excited by the new playthings placed before him, Zagreus left his throne and put down his lightning bolts. As he played with his new toys, the Titans offered the boy another toy – a hand

---

[93] The Bacchae, 129-135, Euripides, c. 400 BCE, trans. Ian Johnston

[94] We can also consider Hades, who is often termed 'the underworld Zeus' as Dionysos' father.

[95] Dionysiaca, 5.562, Nonnus c. 500 CE trans. Rouse

mirror. Zagreus had never seen his reflection before, and whilst he was distracted admiring his face in the mirror, the Titans attacked. First they struck him with knifes. The young boy fought well for his life, using his shapeshifting abilities to assume many forms such as that of a snarling lion, a wild horse, a goat-kid, a deformed baby, a serpent, a tiger and lastly, a horned bull. But the frustrated Hera, who had been watching from afar, let out a staggering roar and the bull dropped to the ground, stunned. It was now that the Titans set upon him, striking him with their infernal knifes and then tore him apart. Once he was dismembered they first boiled the parts of his body in a cauldron upon a tripod, then placed the flesh on spits and cooked him over the fire, and then ate him up.

Zeus punished the Titans by blasting them with his lightning bolts and turning them to ash. According to legend, this ash would be used to make up the bodies of the human race. Zeus also punished Gaia, the mother of the Titans, by raining down hellfire upon the earth; in all directions the earth was aflame and the lands burned in the fires of Zeus - even the sea boiled with his heat. But then, seeing Gaia's scorched body, Zeus began to feel pity for her and put out the fires by flooding the earth.

The end of the little boy's existence was the beginning of a new life for Dionysos. Zeus had managed to salvage the heart of his dead son which he then ate, taking the spirit of Dionysos back into himself. He then impregnated Semele, who would become the mother of Bromios – Dionysos the second-born. Zeus then gave the remaining parts of his son that had not been eaten to Apollo, to scatter upon the earth. Some say that his phallus was recovered by the gods of Samothrace, who placed it in a cave on the island and instructed the islanders to begin the Samothracian rites in its honour.

Bromios (Bakcheus)

The following spring, *Dionysos Bakcheus 'the Ecstatic One'* was born into the world of men. The Dionysian form known as *Bromios* was recognised by many other epithets for the Ecstatic Dionysos – and when discussing him outside the perspective of Orphic mysticism or the tales of Nonnus, I have chosen to refer to him as the Naxian *Bakcheus 'the Ecstatic One'*. You will find I refer to Bromios and Bakcheus interchangeably throughout this book, depending on the context. It was this aspect of the god whom Nonnus named in his epic the Dionysiaca as *Bromios, 'the roarer'*.

"Dionysos as Bakcheus awoke the holy madness which he himself again, after it had reached its highest point of intensity, stilled and tranquilized as Meilichios."[96]

Bursting forth into the material world, he brought with him new life – he was *Dionysos Euboulês 'most manifest'* and *Dionysos Auxites, 'bringer of growth'*. Indeed wherever Bakcheus/Bromios travelled, life and fertility followed. His presence was said to result in the miraculous growth of grapes: *'one-day vines'* which instantly flowered to produce ripe fruit whenever the god appeared. He had the same miraculous effect on wine: streams flowed with wine in his presence, and jugs of water turned to wine. Yet, in the height of summer, Bakcheus also brought the unbearable heat of the midday sun, and even drought. The guise of Bakcheus is connected with the Solar/Sun guise of Dionysos, which is discussed in more detail later on in this book. Whilst it was he who had brought the springtime buds, it was also he who threatened their very existence. It is because of this paradox that the people petitioned for the return of the nocturnal god – Zagreus (or Meilichios) the *'Tamer of Heat'* or *'Kindly One'* - the torch-bearing underworld god who ruled over the cooler months.

The Myths of Bromios

The Second Incarnation of Dionysos

"Semele was kept for a more brilliant union, for already Zeus ruling on high intended to make a new Dionysos grow up, a bullshaped copy of the older Dionysos..."[97]

Conception & Birth

By eating the heart of Zagreus, Zeus had taken the soul of Dionysos into himself; he then made love to a pregnant mortal named Semele whose unborn child was to become the next incarnation of Zagreus - *Dionysos Bromios*. By doing so, Zeus believed

---

[96] Psyche (Vol 6) Erwin Rohde (1925) 2006: P.287
[97] Dionysiaca, 5.562-6.168 Nonnus c. 500 CE trans. Rouse

that he had safeguarded the soul of Dionysos. The spirit of the vibrant god was apparent even before he was born, and Semele found herself compelled to dance whenever she heard the sound of a flute, and Dionysos danced in her womb. But Hera heard about Zeus and Semele, and learnt that a child had been conceived of their union. Angry that Zeus had been unfaithful yet again, Hera devised a plan. Disguised as an old woman, she appeared to Semele and persuaded her to ask Zeus to appear to her in his true form; for this, she said, was his most magnificent appearance. And so Semele convinced Zeus to show her his true self - but his form was accompanied by storms, and thunder, and lightning which was so mighty and deafening that Semele (being a mere mortal) was almost terrified to death. She was then accidentally struck by Zeus' lightning, which finally killed her.

"I see my mothers' tomb — for she was wiped out by that thunderbolt. It's there, by the palace, with that rubble, the remnants of her house still smouldering from Zeus' living fire ... but I praise Cadmus. He's made his daughter's shrine a sacred place ... with leafy shoots of grape-bearing vines."[98]

The *Homeric Hymn to Dionysos* also accounts that shrines were built thereafter for Semele, and Hecatombs offered to Dionysos at the place of his birth at the trieteric festivals (festivals held over two years with a concluding third year). As luck would have it the unborn child in Semele's womb survived the lightning - for cooling ivy vines wrapped around him and protected him from the heat that had killed his mother. Zeus then quickly transferred the unborn child into his thigh; a temporary womb which would bring the baby to term. Zeus later gave birth to Dionysos - the bull-horned and serpent-crowned child - at Phoinie, on Mount Nÿsa[99]. And so the Second Incarnation of Dionysos – Dionysos Bromios, or the Olympian Dionysos – was born; incidentally, another possible meaning of the word *'Dionysos'* might be *Dio-nÿsa* or *Theo-nÿsa*, *'the Zeus of Nÿsa'*.

Bromios (or Bakcheus) is depicted in many different forms: as a child, a desirable youth, or an older bearded man - depending on

---

[98] The Bacchae, 7-15, Euripides, c. 400 BCE, trans. Ian Johnston

[99] Possibly present day Mt Kithairion, although more likely a place of fantasy - a combination of several different sites where the cult of Dionysos practiced.

when, why and how he is evoked. Legend also knows him as the most vengeful incarnation of Dionysos.

Childhood

Some legends say that Dionysos was brought up on the mountain where he was born, by *Nysos* the god of the mountain and his daughters the *Nysiades*. Other tales recall that Dionysos was taken by Hermes to the mountains of Phrygia, were he was brought up by Rhea (or Kybele) and her *Nymphai* the river spirits, reminiscent of the origins of Sabazios and the tales of the Korykion Antron leather sack.

Rhea was also said to have taught him mystic rites, and spoke an oracular prophecy to Dionysos instructing him in the art of making wine. As an infant, Dionysos quickly forgot this prophecy; however when he grew older and he was out wandering the hillsides, Dionysos spied a snake wrapped around a vine plant (the snake in this tale is also reminiscent of the earlier Sabazios, to whom all snakes belonged). On seeing the snake - its jaws running with grape juice from the vine plant – Dionysos thought of the prophecy that Rhea had once bestowed upon him about how to create wine - the grape juice running between the snake's teeth reminded him of the wine press that Rhea had described during her oracle. Acting on the instruction of her prophecy, Dionysos created a hollow in the earth which would become the first wine press. He then instructed his Satyrs (or '*Sileni*') to begin treading the grapes, '*crushing the fruit with many a skip of the foot, crying euoi!*'[100] Illustrations of this scene might also be depicting actual masked wine-traders from the period, and the Dionysian dance of *Epilinios* '*the grape-treading dance*', was performed in remembrance of this event.

"*He trod the grapes with dancing steps … the Satyrs also, shaking their hair madly in the wind, learnt from Dionysos how to do the like. They pulled tight the dappled skins of fawns over their shoulder, and they shouted the song of Bacchos.*"[101]

Incidentally, the word *euoi* appears again, this time as an obscure character from Hellenic mythology called Euoi who is identified with

---

[100] Dionysiaca, 12.330ff, Nonnus c. 500 CE trans. Rouse
[101] Dionysiaca, 14.143ff, Nonnus c. 500 CE trans. Rouse

the Dionysos who saw the snake. Euoi is also accounted to have invented wine, and then crafted the first hollow bull horn to drink it with. It is interesting that even though the earlier bull god Dionysos-Zagreus began to be overlaid by the Dionysos of viticulture (wine making) his ancient bestial hunter origins are still evident in this story in the form of the hollow bull horn. Another example of this is one of his titles *Dionysos Asterius,* which links him with Sirius the hunting dog, his Minoan and Egyptian origins in Iakchos/Iachen, and also Orion the hunter. Orion was also sometimes considered as the force which led Rhea to prophesise and Dionysos to discover wine.

A different account from Laconia (Sparta) about the arrival of Dionysos describes how Semele's father cast the baby Dionysos and the body of his dead mother into the sea in a wooden crate, which eventually washed up on the coast of Laconia where he was brought up by Ino, sister of Semele and the wife of King Athamas of Orchomenos. Legend says that Semele's sister Hera became jealous that Dionysos still lived and sent madness upon Athamas, who ended up killing one of his own sons.

So Hera continued to pursue the boy, who she believed should not be allowed to live. Some legends say that Zeus changed Dionysos into a ram to save the boy from Hera, whilst others recall that Dionysos mimicked a baby goat in play, bleating and pretending to walk on hooves in order to mislead her. He also tried dressing up as a woman in coloured garments and perfume, but Hera was not so easily deceived and grew angry with those still giving shelter to Dionysos. Eventually Hera drove the Nymphai insane, and turned their sons into Satyrs: "*the form of a creature with long ears, and a horse's tail sticking out straight from the loins and flogging the flanks of its shaggy-crested owner; from the temples cow's horns sprouted out, their eyes widened under the horned forehead, the hair ran across their heads in tuft, long white teeth grew out of their jaws, a strange kind of mane grew of itself, covering their necks with rough hair, and ran down from the loins to feet underneath*".[102] Hermes came and took the boy away to safety, and the Satyrs would become some of Dionysos' most trusted followers.

---

[102] Dionysiaca, 12.330ff, Nonnus c. 500 CE trans. Rouse

Hermes carried Dionysos in a sacred box of pine to the top of a mountain at Karyai (present day Mt. Ochi on the island of Euboea) to stay with a minor god named *Aristaios*. Aristaios was wise in animal husbandry and making olive oil and cheese, and was also said to be the first to bring beekeeping to the people. According to some versions of the myth, it was here that Dionysos first struck rocks with his thyrsus (a wooden staff tipped with a pine cone) and they burst forth with honey-mead, 'sweet liquor'.[103] Coincidentally, the shape of the modern honey dipper seems to parallel the shape of the ancient thyrsus.

Whilst staying with Aristaios, Dionysos also learnt how to skin an animal and prepare its meat – and it is within this tale that we also find a hint at Dionysos' link with destruction and resurrection. First separating the limbs of the animals from their carcasses, he proceeded to cast them on the ground, only to put their limbs back together and for the animal to return to life. The vengeful Hera makes an appearance in this version of the story too; trying to send Aristaios mad. In *Cynegetica* the Greek author Oppian accounts that the Nymphai, fearing that Hera might hear the baby Dionysos put him back in his pine box and covered it with deer skins and vines, dancing round it and drumming with the local women to veil the noise of the crying child. It was here that the Nymphai and the accompanying women of Euboea are said to have first experienced the mysteries of Dionysos.

At a young age, Dionysos had already managed to acquire many important skills and arts. Despite a challenging start to his life, he had been cared for by some notable foster carers (first Rhea[104] and then Aristaios) and he had already been instructed in the mystic rites, beekeeping, mead making, animal husbandry, oils and cheeses, how to skin and prepare meat - and even the art of resurrection. He had also established several of his cult rituals and celebrations including the trieteric festivals – and Mt. Nÿsa, the mountain upon which by some accounts he had been born, became his kingdom.

---

[103] Cynegetica, 4.230 ff, Oppian c. 300 CE trans. Mair

[104] Or Ino and Athamas

Yet Hera pursued him still; after a time Dionysos began to feel the effects of the madness inflicted upon him. Suffering from insanity, he began to wander away from his kingdom. First he entered Asia, where he introduced the art of viticulture and the cult of Dionysos to the people of Syria and Egypt. Wherever Dionysos travelled, the gift of wine followed with streams of wine flowing forth and grape vines miraculously flowering and ripening. Having conquered their shores, he then travelled on; according to the Latin writer Hyginus in his *Astronomica*, he headed north towards the sacred oracular sanctuary at Dodona where he believed he might be able to seek a cure for his insanity from Zeus. On his way to Dodona, Dionysos came across a wide and deep swamp which stood between him and the sanctuary. It appeared impossible to cross by foot and all seemed lost – but then, some donkeys approached. Sitting upon one of them, Dionysos was able to ride across the swamp without having to touch the water and on reaching the other side Dionysos regained his sanity, and was cured. As a gesture of gratitude he placed the donkeys among the stars: *Asellus, Australis* and *Asellus Borealis,* in the constellation of Cancer.

Further Adventures:

Conquest of India

Cured of madness, Dionysos continued his wanderings with a mind to conquer further territories. This time he looked towards India and after an instruction from Zeus to assemble a great army, Dionysos began to gather together a whole host of gods, daimons, sea spirits, centaurs, cyclops and satyrs to invade their shores. In a golden chariot driven by snarling lions, Dionysos led his foreboding army, who advanced *'to the sound of flutes, drums, pipes and crashing cymbals'.*[105] It must have been a truly terrifying sight to the armies of men: '...*seated in thy golden chariot, thy lions with long trappings covered, all the vast coast of the orient saw thee...'* [106]

---

[105] Dionysus Myth & Cult, Walter F Otto (1960) 1995: P.93
[106] Oedipus, Lucias Seneca, 413 ff c. 100 CE

Having led the successful conquest of India, Dionysos then triumphantly returned to Mt. Nÿsa and his surrounding kingdom upon the back of an elephant; a foreboding creature which terrified those who had not seen such a beast before. But when he attempted to reclaim his kingdom from the mountain god Nysos whom he'd left in charge during his absence, the god Nysos refused to give it back. Not wanting to cause a disagreement with Nysos (whom had cared so well for him in his early years) Dionysos stepped back and asked Nysos to kindly step down; but Nysos refused to submit. Dionysos waited three years before deciding to reclaim his kingdom; he eventually did so by dressing up his warriors in women's clothing, and convincing Nysos they wanted to join in with the state festivals. As soon as his disguised army was inside the walls, they stormed the city and took back Dionysos' kingdom. By some accounts he instituted the trieteric festivals thereafter, which he named the *Trieterikos* - festivals held over two years with a concluding third year.

The Rebellion of Kings

Certainly, Dionysos was quite a force to be reckoned with and was notorious for punishing those who refused to acknowledge him. On one such occasion Dionysos was passing through southern Thrace, teaching people about viticulture, when his cult was met with a hostile reception by King Lykourgos of Edonia. Lykourgos drove Dionysos out of the Kingdom, forcing him to seek refuge with the sea goddess, Thetis. But the Satyrs and Maenads who had accompanied Dionysos were not so lucky; Lykourgos hunted them down and imprisoned them, beating them unmercifully. As a punishment, Dionysos turned his land barren, scourged him with rods, and then made him go insane; and in his madness Lykourgos murdered his son, cutting him down as if he was a vine. And as the crops began to fail, an Apollonian oracle was issued declaring that Lykourgos should be offered to the gods in order for fertility to return to the land – and so he was sacrificed by his own people. Other accounts say that Lykourgos was sent to the Land of Sinners, where he was set to perform the eternal task of drawing water with a broken pitcher.

A similar myth was featured in Euripides' *The Bacchae*. This time Dionysos arrived in Thebes, where according to some accounts Dionysos was conceived. Zeus recalls in the *Iliad* [107] '*I loved Semele in Thebai* (Thebes) *... and she bore Dionysos, a source of joy to mortals*'. Here, his cult was quickly embraced by the local women who took to the mountains to worship in abandoned frenzy and orgiastic rites. Indeed one of the revelers was *Agaue*, the mother of Pentheus and the King of Thebes. Agaue was also the sister of Dionysos' mother, Semele. Pentheus was infuriated when he discovered that his mother and the other women of the city were indulging in such distasteful rites, and immediately outlawed the worship of Dionysos throughout the land. He persecuted all those who remained faithful to Dionysos, imprisoning the Maenads and any other Dionysian worshipper and sent his guards out to arrest Dionysos himself. The guards soon found a stranger by the name of Dionysos, and much to their surprise he went willingly into their custody; he later introduced himself as the human leader of the Dionysian revelry. Whoever this stranger was, he certainly wielded the power of a god. Once within the city walls he enchanted the King who mistook a young bull for the stranger, and bound the bull instead of the man. Dionysos then effortlessly slipped past Pentheus and escaped, taking the imprisoned Maenads with him; their shackles miraculously dropped from their wrists and ankles and their prison doors swung open. Suddenly realising he had been tricked, Pentheus rushed outside only to be confronted by what would turn out to be a mirage of the stranger; another phantom conjured by the god, who Pentheus rushed at with his sword until he realised that he had been deceived yet again. Frustrated, Pentheus then saw the stranger stood inside his house! The stranger repeated a warning:

"Pentheus, though you hear my words, you obey not at all. Though I suffer ill at your hands, still I say that it is not right for you to raise arms against a god, but to remain calm. Bromios will not allow you to remove the Bakkhai from the joyful mountains." [108]

The stranger named Dionysos asks Pentheus, did he wish to journey up to the mountains, to see his mother and the other women,

---

[107] Iliad XIV 317-27, Homer c. 800 BCE

[108] The Bacchae, 790-791, Euripides, c. 400 BCE, trans. TA Buckley

and observe their rites for himself? For if he did, he would lead him there; as long as Pentheus disguised himself as a woman, dressed like a Maenad to avoid detection. So Pentheus dressed up as a woman in a dress and wig; yet another trick to mock him, for the streets of Thebes shook with laughter as Pentheus walked out of the city.

'Women, the man is caught in our net. He will go to the Bakkhae, where he will pay the penalty with his death. Dionysos, now it is your job; for you are not far off … First drive him out of his wits … since if he is of sound mind he will not consent to wear women's clothing, but driven out of his senses he will put it on. I want him to be a source of laughter to the Thebans … now I will go to fit on Pentheus the dress he will wear to the house of Hades, slaughtered by his mother's hands.'[109]

As Pentheus followed the stranger up into the mountains, he started to notice that the stranger had began to change appearance; *'horns seem to grow on your head. But were you ever before a beast? For you have certainly now become a bull.'* All along, the stranger had been the god Dionysos in disguise, although Pentheus still did not know it. On reaching the mountainside where the Maenads gathered, Pentheus asked his guide to take him higher, where he could view the *'shameful acts of the Maenads'* for himself. At that moment, Dionysos seized hold of the top branches of a pine tree and pulled it down; *'…it was bent just like a bow … in this way the stranger drew the mountain bough with his hands and bent it to the earth, doing no mortal's deed.'* He then placed Pentheus on the top most branch, and let the pine go upright again. Atop the uppermost branch, he was seen by every Maenad there. Dionysos then cried out in a booming voice, *'women, I bring the one who has made you and me and my rites a laughing stock. Now punish him!'* The women descended on the pine tree, but could not climb it. They clawed at the bark and roots, but the tree did not give. Finally they tore at the branches and dragged the tree up from the ground. They set upon Pentheus; his mother was the first to scratch at his flesh as he was torn apart piece by piece. Just like the story of the Egyptian Osiris, the parts of Pentheus' body were scattered far and wide; only his head (or phallus) was retained, which his mother fixed on the end of her staff.

---

[109] The Bacchae, 850-860, Euripides, c. 400 BCE, trans. TA Buckley

There are several similar stories of how notable women, usually the daughters, sisters or mothers of Kings, refuse the cult of Dionysos and are driven mad. One such story is that of the daughters of King Minyas of Orchomenos, who refused to join the celebrations of Dionysos and were turned into bats.

"… they keep themselves aloft on parchment wings; and when they try to speak they send a tiny sound that suits their size, and pour their plains in thin high squeaking cries. Houses they haunt, not woods; they loathe the light; from dusk they take their name, and flit by night."[110]

Pirates at sea

On his way to the island of Naxos, Dionysos met a crew of Tyrrhenian pirates. By some accounts, he hired the pirates to sail him home to Naxos; by other accounts, they came upon him by chance and picked him up from the shore, or from his own boat. But whichever way he found himself upon their ship, they mistook him for a mere mortal —of royal kinship perhaps – and planned to use him as a hostage or sell him as a slave. Seizing Dionysos, they bound his wrists and ankles – but soon found that the ropes and chains would not hold him. He truly was a mighty god. The ship suddenly came to an unnatural halt in the sea; the deck began to flow with wine, and vines grew throughout the ship and up the mast; bunches of grapes ripening before the pirate's eyes. Then wild beasts appeared: first a lion, and then a roaring bear. The lion pounced upon the ship's captain, whilst the rest of the crew jumped into the sea, terrified. As they did, they were turned into dolphins. All the while, Dionysos *'sat with a smile in his dark eyes'.* [111] Just one of the crew was saved this fate – the navigator, who had tried to persuade the other pirates to release Dionysos. To him Dionysos said, *'Take courage … you have found favour with my heart. I am loud-crying Dionysus whom Kadmos' daughter bore of union with Zeus.* [112]

---

[110] Metamorphoses 4. 1 & 272 & 389 ff, Ovid, c. 100 BCE – c. 100 CE trans. Melville
[111] Homeric Hymn 7 to Dionysos, c. 700 – 400 BCE, trans. Evelyn-White
[112] Homeric Hymn 7 to Dionysos, c. 700 - 400 BCE, trans. Evelyn-White

His One True Love: Ariadne

"… his love is ecstatic and binds him forever … There is good reason for our calling Ariadne the chosen one, for it is quite remarkable how little the myth speaks of any other true love affair."[113]

Dionysos met *Ariadne*, the daughter of King Minos of Crete, on the island of Naxos. By some accounts, she had been abandoned on a beach at Naxos by Theseus, the hero whom she had fallen in love with[114] and whom she had helped slay the Minotaur. Betrayed by Theseus, Ariadne was inconsolable; yet on meeting Dionysos she grew to love him far beyond that which she had ever felt for Theseus. And the feeling was mutual; Ariadne is recalled as being one of the very few *'true loves'* of Dionysos.

Dionysos and Ariadne were married and he bestowed upon her the *Crown of Amphitrite,* a treasure which he had retrieved from the depths of the sea during his journey to Naxos. It was a beautiful celebration and according to some accounts, the Dionysian miracle of rivers flowing forth with wine took place for the very first time that day. Following their marriage, Ariadne and Dionysos went on to bear many children including *Oenopion* (*'wine'*) *Staphylus* (*'grapes'*) *Euanthes* (*'flowering'*) and *Tauropolus* (*'bull-herder'*).Together with her sea women Ariadne joined the retinue of Dionysos, following him on his travels to Argos.

War against the Argives & the Death of Ariadne

Dionysos, Ariadne and their band of sea women and satyrs then travelled towards the city of Argos on mainland Hellas, where they intended to introduce the cult of Dionysos. But on their arrival they were met with a hostile reception from the city's people, who were led by the hero Perseus. The city refused to acknowledge the cult of the god and his ruling, and so Dionysos declared war against the city and Perseus. Those who refused to acknowledge Dionysos were driven mad and the women of the city were said to have been seen in the surrounding hillsides, devouring the flesh of their own children.

---

[113] Dionysus Myth & Cult, Walter F Otto (1960) 1995: P.177

[114] Other accounts tell that Dionysos and Ariadne were already a couple before she ran away with Theseus.

During the battle, Ariadne – the one true love of Dionysos – met her death. Some sources recall that she was slain by the spear of Perseus, whilst others recall that she was turned to stone after glancing at the head of Medusa, which Perseus bore. Many other Dionysian women were also slain by Perseus, and buried in a common grave in front of the temple of Hera in Argos. By some accounts Ariadne was also buried there, but in her own separate grave. The Greek traveler and author Pausanias writes that after the war had ended, the city began to honour Dionysos, and adopted his cult and ruling. Part of the city's temple to Hera was set aside for Dionysos, which Dionysos named Cresius (the Cretan).

"Come now (Dionysos) lay down your thyrsus, let the winds blow battle away, and fix the self-made image of mortal Ariadne where the image of heavenly Hera stands."[115]

Descent into the Underworld & Ascent to Olympus

Dionysos consulted his father, Zeus, who gave him permission to descend into the realms of the dead and retrieve his wife Ariadne, who had been slain by the Argives. According to some versions of the legend, Dionysos began to search for an entrance to the underworld without success, until he came across a man named Hypolinus, or Polymnus, who stated that he would show Dionysos where to find the gateway to the Hades – but only if Dionysos offered *'a reward that could be given without loss'*,[116] i.e., a sexual repayment – and Dionysos agreed. And so Hypolinus showed him the way and Dionysos descended into the Alkyonian Lake, the gateway to the chthonic underworldly realms, where he found Ariadne. The exact location of the lake is not known; it may have been in Lerna or perhaps in Argos; both sites have a history of nocturnal rites used to call Dionysos up from the deep and celebrate his return. Other accounts recall that Dionysos brought Ariadne/Semele back up through a gateway he found amidst the chthonic altars which stood in the temple of Artemis at Argos.

---

[115] (Hermes speaks to Dionysos) Dionysiaca, 47.665, Nonnus c. 500 CE trans. Rouse
[116] Astronomica, Part 2 II.5, Hyginus, c. 100 CE, trans. M Grant

When Dionysos had returned from the underworld with Ariadne, his crown then rested in the stars; having journeyed between the worlds, his earthly existence was complete. Dionysos had now received full god status, and could dwell with the other gods in Olympus. Dionysos renamed Ariadne to *Thyone*, goddess of frenzy and trance, and sharing his immortality with her *they both* ascended up to the heavens to take their place beside the immortals. By some accounts, the price he paid for sharing his immortality with her was an effeminate demeanor; perhaps symbolic of the unity between them. Dionysos then set Ariadne's crown into the heavens, as the semi-circular star constellation *Corona Borealis*. But finally; what of his promise to Hypolinus? When Dionysos finally returned to the upperworld of men, he found that Hypolinus had in the meantime died – but he intended to honour his promise. According to some writers, such as the Christian writer Clement of Alexandria, Dionysos carved a phallus out of figwood beside the grave of Hypolinus, and sat upon it.

Triplicity:
The Third Incarnation of Dionysos

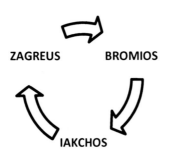

ZAGREUS   BROMIOS

IAKCHOS

'They honoured (Iakchos) as a god next after the son of Persephone (Zagreus) and after Semele's son (Bromios) they established sacrifices for Dionysos late born and Dionysos first born, and third they chanted a new hymn, for Iakchos ... the Athenians beat the step in honour of Zagreus and Bromios and Iakchos all together.' [117]

The first two incarnations of Dionysos - *Zagreus* and *Bromios/Bakcheus* - are perhaps the most striking faces of Dionysos. The first incarnation of Dionysos is his conception and birth as a child of the underworld: the quiet and mild guise of Dionysos. The

---

[117] Dionysiaca, Nonnus 48.962ff, c. 500 CE trans. Rouse

second is his manifest form on earth, or 'most present' form: the chaotic guise of Dionysos. Like two sides of a coin, these two incarnations stand in paradoxical duality.

However according to Nonnus in his epic *Dionysiaca* there is a third incarnation of Dionysos: named *Iakchos*. Whilst remaining an incarnation or legacy of Dionysos – as the third *'face'* or *'mask'* – Iakchos is the ascended Dionysos who undergoes the process of apotheosis (ascension into the heavens) before being reborn again to the underworld realms. Iakchos is the passage between the Olympian realm of Zeus and the underworld realm of Hades; the spark of spirit which enlivens the seed that dwells within the leather sack, from which Zagreus will be born once again. He stands between the worlds, a guide to souls in search of the afterlife. This cycle would also come to be reflected in the structure of the trieteric festivals.

DIONYSOS ZAGREUS	DIONYSOS BROMIOS	DIONYSOS IAKCHOS
Son of Persephone	Son/Consort of Semele/Ariadne	Son of Aura/Demeter
CONCEPTION > BIRTH	MANIFEST FORM ON EARTH	APOTHEOSIS & REBIRTH
Child of the Underworld	Most manifest in the Upperworld	Ascension / Afterlife

Iakchos the Third-Born

"Come to dance in mystic revel ... Lord of the frolic and dance, Iakchos, beside me advance!"[118]

Best known for his torchbearing-role in the nocturnal rites of Eleusis, Iakchos was the chthonic guide and *dadouchos* (hierophant) to the initiates of the mysteries: the *'light-bringing star'* who led souls down into the underworld by the light of his shining torches. During the Eleusinian initiations, a blazing statue of Iakchos led initiates into the

---

[118] *Frogs*, 316ff, Aristophanes, c. 400 BCE trans. O'Neill

temple or Hall of Mysteries at which time all lights would be extinguished and the initiate plunged into darkness[119] simulating the journey beyond death and entry into the subterranean realms. Iakchos may be connected to Dionysos Meilichios, the mild and *'nocturnal sun'*; indeed the torchbearing role was not limited to Iakchos and was shared with many other forms of Dionysos. For instance, we find *Nyktelios Lampter*, an epithet of Dionysos meaning *'nocturnal torchlight'* or *'night light'*, who was revered as *'chorus leader of the fire-breathing stars'*.

"(He who) kindles the flaming torches, brandishing one in each hand, Iakchos, O Iakchos! The light bringing star of the nocturnal mysteries ..."[120]

The name Iakchos is often considered as simply another epithet of Dionysos – which, by its use in the mystery traditions, just so happened to develop into a more significant deity over time. In the case of *Dionysos Iakchos*, it has been supposed that the epithet developed out of the ecstatic axiom, *Iakche!* or *Iakchos!* which was called out during Dionysian processions[121] and was believed to be the chant of dead initiates who resided in the underworld. The earliest written evidence of Iakchos being equated with Dionysos is in *Antigone*, by Sophocles, which we might tentatively suggest also hints at the spirits of the dead: *'chorus leader ... master of the voices of the night ... appear O' king with your attendant Thyiads, who in madness dance through the night for you, the steward Iakchos.'* Indeed, the Greek historian Herodotus recalls how, during the battle of Salamis fought between the Athenians and the Persians in 480 BCE, a *'divine host'* of underworld spirits advanced on the Persian army. Chanting Iakchos and kicking up dust of a thousand dead men, their advance sent fear through the Persian troops who were later defeated by the Athenians.

Certainly by classical times, Iakchos was considered an individual deity in his own right. Dressed in the hunting boots of Dionysos and carrying torches reminiscent of the Sabazian processions of fire, this underworld guide is certainly a part of the Dionysian current – but in truth, it is likely that his origins reach much further back than just a simple epithet. It is possible that the name Iakchos is in fact a

---

[119] Homo Necans: Greek Sacrificial Ritual & Myth, Walter Burkert, 1986: P.280
[120] Frogs, 340-342, Aristophanes, c. 400 BCE trans. O'Neill
[121] Greek Religion, Walter Burkert (1931) 1985: P.74

reminder of much older origins – the Egyptian torchbearing demi-god *Iachen*, who may even have partially defined the early Dionysian current. Described as the *'tamer'* of the heat of Sirius (the *'dog star'* - in Minoan, *Iaker*, meaning messenger or fire bringer) Iachen offered magical protection against the destructive heat of fire – a quality which was petitioned by torchlight processions. It is likely that Iachen defined several fundamental features of Dionysian worship - such as his fire-bearing role, and certain elements of his hunter instincts - that of the capturer (or *'tamer'*) of wild or destructive beasts - which would be absorbed into the surrounding cultures, in particular that of Crete.

"Let not Athens sing hymns to a new Dionysos, let him not have equal honour with Eleusinian Dionysos, let him not take over the rites of Iakkhos who was there before him, let not his vintage dishonour Demeter's basket!" [122]

Iakchos also came to be associated with harvest grain, and within the rites of Eleusis he grew to be considered the son of Demeter – the goddess of grain and initiation – who together with her daughter Kore/Persephone presided over the Eleusinian mysteries. Iakchos was considered as Persephone's guide as she journeyed through the earth, between the upperworld of men and the underworld realms of Hades. He also played an important part in the nocturnal rites as *Eubouleus*, another epithet for Dionysos which meant *'counselor'* or *'chthonic guide'* and as such he was sometimes described in the Orphic Hymns as the *Bakkheios Hermes*. A mask of Dionysos would be used to cover the Eleusinian *liknon* (grain winnowing basket) which held the sacred objects to be revealed at initiation. By other accounts, the mask was placed inside the liknon, as one of the sacred objects itself. These sacred objects were used together with ears of grain to communicate the mysteries of Eleusis. Again, it is likely that this is a reminder of a much older association – this time with a fortune spirit of Hellenic folk magic, called the *Agathos Daimon*. . By participating in the mysteries of the grain, the initiate was guaranteed passage into the afterlife and consequently, Iakchos was also responsible for refusing access to those who were not initiated.

Aside from his role as Iakchos, Dionysos was important in the Eleusinian mysteries in his own right and wine vessels from the

---

[122] (Hera to Persephone) Dionysiaca, 31.28ff, Nonnus c. 500 CE trans. Rouse

period often depict his important role as *'lord of the sanctuary'* watching over the birth of Iakchos in the Hall of Mysteries. In fact Demeter, Kore/Persephone and Dionysos were often considered a divine triad within Eleusis and Athens, and the accounts of Dionysos being present at the birth of Iakchos (an embodiment of himself) further defines Iakchos as an individual incarnation in his own right:

> *"Bakkhos (Dionysos) took into his care the boy (Iakchos) and presented him ... babbling 'Euoi' ... the goddess gave him in trust to the Bakkhante's of Eleusis... wearing ivy tript around the boy Iakkhos, and lifted the Attic torch in the nightly dances of the deity lately born."*[123]

In comparison to many of the other Hellenic gods, Dionysos was a particularly corporeal, earthly, and almost *'human'* god; yet he too had his moments of ascension. According to some accounts, when Dionysos retrieved his mother Semele from the underworld he ascended with her to the heavenly realms of the Olympian gods; and within his role as initiator of trance he aided his initiates to reach higher levels of consciousness. In the Eleusinian Iakchos, we see this element of Dionysian ascension reflected; because whilst Iakchos is a chthonic guide of the netherworldly depths, his role as initiator and the afterlife is also involved in ascension - he epitomises the transcendental elements of initiation, trance, and indeed death. He is the glowing ember in the dark; the guiding light which led his initiates towards a more spiritual, rather than corporeal, ecstasy.

The Mothers of Dionysos Iakchos

Whilst the Dionysos Iakchos of the Eleusinian Mysteries is most often considered as the son of Demeter, several sources give a somewhat different account, all of which are worth investigation. The poet Nonnus gives an extensive account of the Titaness *Aura* being the biological mother of Iakchos. He later relates that Dionysos *'hands over'* Iakchos (after Aura tried to murder him) to Demeter, to take part in her mysteries. Thereafter, Iakchos is referred to as the son of Demeter.

---

[123] Dionysiaca, 48.848, Nonnus c. 500 CE trans. Rouse

Sometimes the Eleusinian Mysteries referred to Iakchos as the son of Persephone, Demeter's daughter - who is also attributed as the mother of Zagreus, the first incarnation of Dionysos. This could be simply because the two goddesses were often equated with one another, or it might suggest that one of the secrets of the Eleusinian Mysteries was that Iakchos and Zagreus - similar in purpose and origin - were equated with one another.

We find accounts by the playwright Aristophanes of the mortal Semele as the mother of Iakchos: *'Semeleian Iakchos, giver of wealth'* [124] and *'Iakchos, son of Semele, they called him.'* [125] Euripides also hints at Iakchos' Semelian origins; throughout the play he lists Dionysos as being born of Semele and refers to Iakchos once within the play as the *'Bromian god'* clearly describing Iakchos as Dionysos under another name. In this sense he is conflating Iakchos with Dionysos in general, and it is logical that Euripides is referring to Iakchos as born of Semele. Incidentally the name of Semele still exists in modern Bulgarian Thrace in the Slavonic name *'Zemlya'*, meaning *'earth'* [126] so it wouldn't be too much of a stretch of the imagination to conflate these two earthy goddesses.

Although *'Demeter'* was one of the names found in Minoan Crete (and therefore would have pre-dated the Thracian/Semelean influence by quite some time) we do not know that Dionysos was ever considered the son of Demeter on Crete. It was only when his character was recognised that he started to be connected with her and became a consort in her mysteries at Eleusis.[127] However it is possible that Semele and Demeter were identified, or conflated: Demeter of course is from *Dea Mater*, which would have been used for any Mother goddess, including the Thracian/Anatolian *Kybele* (described as the *'bronze-rattling Demeter'*[128] of the Phrygian mountains) and not just for the Demeter of the Hellenic myths. The people who worshipped Kybele created an enormous door with two lions either

[124] Scholium on Aristophanes, Ranae, 479 (Source: Eleusis, Karl Kerényi (1960) 1991: P. 156)

[125] Eleusis: Archetypal Image of Mother & Daughter, Karl Kerényi (1960) 1991: P.94

[126] Myths of Greece & Rome, Jane Harrison, 1927: P.72

[127] The Great Dionysiac Myth Vol.1, Robert Brown, (1877) 2000: P.82

[128] Isthmian Odes 7.3, Pindar, c. 458 BCE

side, carved out of the mountainside; Kybele was believed to use this door to travel to and from the mortal world. If iconography is anything to go by, it appears that the Minoan bull god in his youthful guise is usually shown beside a mountain mother, which likely would resemble Kybele. And Kybele, according to Euripides *The Bacchae*, set the Dionysian mysteries in motion - and even joined in with them. It is likely therefore that both Semele and Demeter are simply variations of the Great Mother, who have been equated in this particular myth.

But what of Aura? Her nature also suggests a link to the mountain and earth mother goddesses *Dea Mater* and *Kybele*; she is the mountain maiden who came to be considered as the personification of mountainside and hillside breezes, and as the huntress companion of Artemis, Nonnus describes Aura as the *'boar-slayer daughter of Kybele'*. This suggests that, like Semele, Aura is simply another name for *Dea Mater* or *Kybele*; the Great Mother.

"Not alone has Bacchus himself or the mother of Bacchus (Semele) *attained the skies ... the heavens wear the crown of the Cretan maid* (Ariadne)." [129]

Dionysos Iakchos was embraced in the Eleusinian mysteries as the torchbearer of nocturnal rites, and the legends spoke of his descent to the underworld to retrieve his dead mother. Yet here again we see a confusion between two versions of the same myth from two different sources – this time, between Semele (as the mother of Dionysos) and the lover of Dionysos, Ariadne. It is very likely that Ariadne and Semele were equated in ancient times: both shared a mortal status; both took the new name *Thyone* after they ascend to Olympus; and both shared a love for Dionysos. It was very common in ancient pagan religion to consider the mother of a god also his lover, and vice versa. I chose to focus on Ariadne within my own version of this particular descent myth, because in my own opinion, she is likely to be a truer expression of the consort to the older, bull-formed Dionysos who finds connections to the Minoan bull god of Crete (from where this particular story, as well as many of the original festival themes, are likely to have originated). The cult of Ariadne shared many similarities with the cult of Dionysos, especially the arts

---

[129] Hercules Furens 16, Seneca, c. 100 CE, trans. Miller

of trance and dance. Additionally, Ariadne was considered the *'Queen'* of Dionysian women; in particular, a band of Maenads from the Aegean Islands known as the *'sea women'* who she led in trance and choral dance. She was also closely associated with Aphrodite, the goddess of love and of the ocean, and in Amathus on Cyprus she was worshipped as *Ariadne-Aphrodite.* [130] In short whilst Dionysos stands as perhaps one of the oldest guises of the Bull-Horned Hunter God of the wilds, his consort – whether we choose to name her Demeter, Persephone, Semele, Aura, Artemis-Taurike, Ariadne or even Kybele – is the Great Goddess, the Mountain Mother, the Mistress and Huntress of horned and wild beasts, and keeper of both the earth below and the skies above.

The Myths of Iakchos

The Third Incarnation of Dionysos

"O Iakkhos! O Iakkhos! Come to tread this verdant level, come to dance in mystic revel, come whilst round thy forehead hurtles many a wreath of fruitful myrtles . . . Come, arise, from sleep awaking, come the fiery torches shaking, O Iakkhos! O Iakkhos!" [131]

Conception & Birth

According to the epic *Dionysiaca*, Iakchos was the son of the Titan goddess Aura (daughter of Kybele) and the third incarnation of Dionysos. *Eros*, the god of love, had enchanted Dionysos and made him captivated by Aura, but she did not return his affections; and so Dionysos wooed her *'with a cunning potion'* [132] probably wine, until she was too intoxicated to object to his advances. From this union, Aura conceived twins: Iakchos and his brother.

Childhood

When the twins were born the vengeful Aura - furious with Dionysos for his trickery - meant to murder the boys and left them in a den of ferocious panthers and lions. But much to Aura's surprise,

---

[130] Dionysus Myth & Cult, Walter F Otto (1960) 1995: P.182

[131] Frogs, 316ff, Aristophanes, c. 400 BCE, trans. Frere

[132] Dionysiaca, 48.567ff, Nonnus c. 500 CE trans. Rouse

the panthers nursed the twins, and the venomous snakes which also inhabited the cave only served to protect them. Hearing their cries, the goddess Artemis rushed to help the boys but was too late to save the brother of Iakchos: frustrated, Aura had grabbed the brother of Iakchos and thrown him up in the air. As he hit the ground he was killed; Aura then swallowed him whole. Artemis seized the remaining boy, Iakchos, and took him to safety. She handed him back to Dionysos, who then gave him to the nymph Nikaia to care for.

"(Artemis) stilled her anger. She went about the forest seeking for traces of (Dionysos) in his beloved mountains, while she held (Iakkhos) ... until shamefast she delivered the boy to Dionysos her brother. They honoured him as a god next after the son of Persephone (Zagreus) and after Semele's son (Dionysos)."[133]

Further Adventures

Nonnus accounts that when the boy was grown, the former Dionysos introduced Iakchos to the mysteries of Eleusis, and he became the attendant to the goddess Demeter. Such was his importance to the mysteries - and to Demeter herself - that Iakchos grew to be considered as her son. Many of the Attic festivals of Dionysos would come to be involved with the Eleusinian Mysteries, and vice versa. From then on, Iakchos took the role of torchbearer and a leader of the mysteries and he also acted as the sacred guide to Persephone and Semele as they traversed the worlds. Iakchos would offer his guiding light to the souls of the dead, too. According to some sources, Hermes would take the dead to the place of judgment, and then Iakchos would guide the souls as they journeyed towards the afterlife.

---

[133] Dionysiaca, 48.240ff, Nonnus c. 500 CE trans. Rouse

Chapter 4

Dionysos Polymorphos: A God of Many Forms

"May he appear in all his diversity of shapes ..."[134]

Invoked as *Dionysos Polymorphos 'of many forms'* Dionysos has been known by many different names and by many different appearances. In his human form he could appear as a tyrant or a saviour – or a child, a lover or a father. And as an anthromorphic deity, Dionysos could also appear in animal or plant form, – as a predator or its prey – reinforcing the bond between humanity and the natural world. Many of these forms were vastly different, contrasting and often diametric.

Certainly, Dionysos was not one to be limited by the boundaries and order of physical form; yet he was a very tactile god of earthly concerns and favoured taking a physical shape. Ovid wrote that there was *'no god more present'*[135] than Dionysos: that is, out of all the ancient

---

[134] Dionysiaca, Nonnus 1.11, c. 500 CE, trans. Rouse

[135] Metamorphoses, 3.638-691, Ovid, C1st BCE - C1st CE trans. AS Kline

gods Dionysos was one of the few who people felt that they could reach out and touch and as such he was also known as *Dionysos Euboulês 'most manifest'*. The fact that the practice of god-possession (invocation) was almost entirely unique to Dionysianism in the ancient Greek world is perhaps a testament to this. He was considered as closer to the common people than many of the other gods of the time, and was believed to interact and manifest amongst them on a very real level; no doubt this aspect of his character was related to his status as a demi god, born of a mortal mother. Dionysos could change his appearance from one form to another whenever he so pleased: indeed the ability to shapeshift was one of the powers the infant Dionysos Zagreus first showed he had when he assumed different forms to confuse the Titans. This ability to transform from one shape to another is a common motif in Dionysian myth, and Nonnus writes that the King Deriades of the Indians spoke of how impossible it was to conquer Dionysos because he kept changing into a myriad of forms: *'a lion, a bull, a boar, a bear, a panther, a snake, and now a tree, fire, water.'*[136]

Indeed, Euripides wrote that Dionysos excelled at epiphanies – that is, appearing in physical form. He would usually perform miracles when he materialised; and when Dionysos made an appearance (especially if he was displeased) he made sure that everyone knew about it! One myth tells of how, when the daughters of King Minyas of Orchomenos refused the cult of Dionysos, he made snakes appear amongst their wool, grapevines grow all around their furniture and milk and wine pour from the ceiling. They were eventually driven mad by the god's wrath, bloodily disemboweled one of their sons, and transformed into bats. Dionysos performed similar miracles to demonstrate his power when he was kidnapped by Tyrrhenian pirates, and could not resist tricking the rebellious King Pentheus with his many different forms. Yet in contrast, his epiphanies also marked fortuitous events and the arrival of his physical form was celebrated annually in Athens.

Dionysos was associated with the highest mountains and the deepest oceans; the heavens above and the chthonic world beneath. As a liminal deity, his realm was both above and below – or at least

---

[136] Dionysus Myth & Cult, Walter F Otto (1960) 1995: P.110

somewhere in between: he bridged the threshold between the mortal world and the realms of the gods, and was able to move between the two worlds at will. This chapter explains just some of the different ways Dionysos is known to have been portrayed in our universe and the natural world.

Life, the Universe, & Everything

"The Chaldeans call the God (Dionysos) IAO in the Phoenician tongue ... and he is often called Sabaoth, signifying that he is above the seven poles that is the demiurgus."[137]

To many of his Bakkhoi, Dionysos was a cosmogenic god: that is, they believed that he was instrumental in the creation of the universe and that he was a prime mover in the very fabric of its existence and divided up into it. Neoplatonism would come to name this force the *World Soul*: the animating power which permeates and connects all living things. The World Soul was also seen as an intermediary force between the *Monad* (the primary source) and the material world. Therefore, the gods who worked within the realm of the World Soul were those who inhabited the betwixt and between; they stood on the threshold between the great primordial source and the individual souls of mortals.

"The demiurge divided the whole mixture into souls equal in number to the stars, and assigned each soul to a star ... and when he had sown them, he committed the younger gods the fashioning of their bodies."[138]

With one foot in the world of potential and the other in the world of the physical, these gods traversed the states of spirit and matter. Neither earth bound nor heaven bound, they lay somewhere in between; the perfect position for deities such as Hekate – and of course, Dionysos. It is here where we find Dionysos as *'the spirit of the universe, who agitates the cyclic starry groups ... around the mighty altar of the world.'*[139]

---

[137] Classical Journal XVI-XVII: Collection of the Chaldean Oracles, Thomas Taylor, 1817-1818

[138] Timaios, 41-2, Plato, c. 360 BCE

[139] The Great Dionysiac Myth Vol.1, Robert Brown, (1877) 2000: P.140

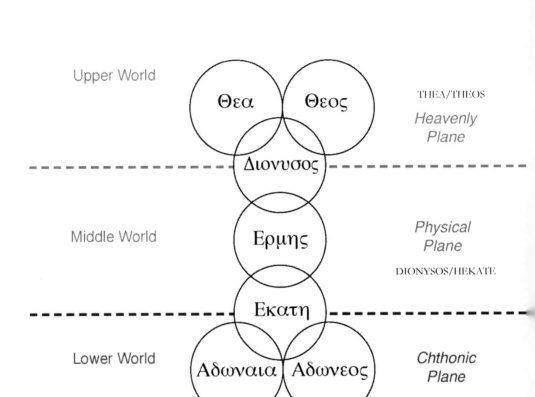

Monad 'The One' →	The World Soul →	The Material World
Primary Source	*Animating Force*	*Matter & Form*
All Soul	World Soul	Individual Souls

Whilst Dionysos was believed to inhabit the liminal realm of the World Soul, his connection to nature and the physical earth itself was significant. The worship of Dionysos, or at least the Dionysian current, was very ancient and had within it the remnants of distinctly animistic practices: primal religious ideas which were derived from materialistic or 'common-sense' ways of looking at things.[140] Whilst

---

[140] Dionysus Myth & Cult, Walter F Otto (1960) 1995: P.7

the individuality of Dionysos was recognised, objects, animals, plants and seasons were also said to *'embody'* the god, and animistic practices such as trance, shapeshifting, frenzied music and movement were common in the cult – all of which are considered today as *'low magic'* practices (that is, rites of the earth). He was also one of the very few deities who was known to physically manifest himself in the physical realm of reality. The world of Dionysos was one universe – a united *bios* of upper, middle and lower worlds all of which he molded to shape and into which he breathed *zöe*, the spirit of life. As such, he was known as *Dionysos Phanes, 'Spirit of the Apparent'* who gave shape and form to physical matter. The Neo-Platonist Olympiodorus wrote that *'Dionysos, when he put his image into the mirror, followed it, and was divided up into the universe'.*[141]

The costume that Dionysos wore also reflected his cosmogenic role, and depicted the composition of the universe. He is described as being attired in a crimson robe like the flowing rays of the sun; and his spotted fawn skin, which was thrown about the shoulder, represented the stars of the sky. About his waist he wore a girdle or belt, which whirled about him in a circular motion and sparkled like sunlight upon the surface of the ocean. Sometimes, he held a blazing torch or wooden staff (thyrsus) which he struck upon the ground, in reference to his underworld mysteries.

The Bakkhoi of Dionysos also wore this sort of outfit in order to bring themselves closer to his mysteries, and by dressing in this way the worshipper became both the earth and Dionysos himself. Plutarch also wrote that a symbolic *'egg'* was honoured during the Dionysian rites which represented generation and in his bull form Dionysos was depicted as an Auroch (the ancestor of the modern bull) charging a cosmic egg and breaking it with his horns. Eggs were popular offerings to underworld deities because of their *'womb-tomb'* like associations; a similar sort of symbology can be found in the mythological wooden chest of Sparta in which the baby Dionysos was concealed, and also the sacred objects which were placed within the *liknon* (winnowing basket) at Eleusis and revealed to initiates during the mysteries. Such a scene can be found within a set of preserved wall frescoes at Villa dei Misteri – *'the Villa of the Mysteries'* located just

---

[141] Dionysos, Richard Seaford, 2006: P.116

outside of Pompeii, where we see a female initiate travelling from the underworld back up into the world of the living. As she emerges from the underworld, she lifts up a cloth which covered the *liknon* to reveal a sacred object – perhaps a phallus or other sculpture. It could also be symbolic of the *liknites*, *'being in the winnow'* perhaps the soul of Dionysos. The concealment and then the revealing of sacred objects was common in both the Dionysian and the Eleusinian mysteries, and may have had much to do with the mystery of *'presence and absence'*, in the Dionysian myths and worldview. Sacred objects such as these were also brought out once a year for the fully initiated to view, usually as part of a nocturnal torchlight procession.

In keeping with his connection to the natural world, Dionysos preferred his worship to be held outdoors rather than inside buildings – something which is almost unique to Dionysos in the Hellenic pantheon. As Richard Seaford writes, Dionysos *'seems more inclined to destroy buildings than construct them'*[142] In this way, a Bakkhoi might embrace their wild side and experience the natural world, away from the limitations of organised society. It seems that Dionysos was not keen on being contained within four walls; and even when artificial structures *were* built for Dionysos, their architecture often reflected the image of nature. Like many neo-pagans today, the followers of Dionysos often held their rites in the open air and in direct contact with the elements. Indeed, many elements of the world can be found concealed in his character, myths and rituals – fire in light and heat, water in lustration and descent, earth in growth and sustenance, and air in motion and sound. During daylight hours, outdoor processions were made across the countryside between sacred sites and even dramatic performances were carried out in open air theatres; and by night, Dionysian revelries were held in deserted rural locations such as rocky mountainsides or by misty lakes and marshes; some accounts report of Maenads returning from their revelries afflicted with hypothermia from exposure to the cold. This is obviously not something that the modern Bakkhoi should seek to achieve! But it is perhaps a testament to the commitment of the Dionysian Maenads to their rites; it has been suggested that they were not even aware of the cold due to the intensity of their trance.

---

[142] Dionysos, Richard Seaford, 2006: P.43

Another preferred meeting place for Dionysian rites was inside caves – which incidentally, for those interested in modern magic, was a favourite working place of the 20th century occultist Robert Cochrane.[143] Indeed, an inscription found on the island of Thrassos dedicates to Dionysos, *'a temple under the open sky ... an evergreen cavern'.*[144] Caves featured heavily in Dionysian ritual and mythology. As Dionysos Zagreus, he was conceived in a cave where his father Zeus wooed his mother Persephone. The birth of Zagreus was embodied in the discovery of honey which was found inside ancient caverns; and later he would come to be embodied in the honey mead which fermented inside leather sacks at the Korykion caves. Maenads made a pilgrimage to these caves every winter as part of their awakening rites to mark this particular myth. The second incarnation of Dionysos was also associated with caves: Dionysos the second born was cared for by Rhea's nymphai inside a mountainside cavern. The mouths of caves were seen as liminal portals, or entrances to the underworld – places of reincarnation and rebirth. Initiations were often held inside caves for this reason; and Dionysian officials, the *antrophulakes* or *'cave guardians'*, were in charge of protecting the caves and the rites held within. Legend speaks of how snakes guarded the caves whilst Dionysos and his mother dwelt within, and perhaps the antrophulakes symbolised Dionysos himself in serpent form.

The association between Dionysos and the earth is almost certainly linked to his deep connection with the goddess – a relationship with the feminine, which was lost or corrupted over time to many other male deities but seems to have become almost a legacy of Dionysos. In Delphi, Dionysos was the Great Earth Serpent, the Protector of the Goddess who had originally presided over the oracular sanctuary before she was usurped by Apollo. And in Eleusis, Dionysos was known as the *'companion and attendant'* to the goddess Demeter. The freedom that he afforded to women (and men who embraced effeminate roles, and were otherwise limited by the patriarchal system) is quite possibly linked to this ancient bond with Mother Earth: *Gaia*, the mother of the Titans, and other goddesses identified with her.

---

[143] See The Roebuck in the Thicket, Evan John Jones, 2001

[144] Inscription 1st Century CE, translation Jaccottet 2003: 31

As a final word, it should be noted that despite their respect and awe for nature, our ancestors' connection with the natural world was not as idealistic as many neo-pagans would perhaps like to believe. For our forefathers, forging a connection with nature meant also to rule and control it. It is here where we meet Dionysos as *Anax Agreus*, *'the hunter'*.

Fire, Sun & Heat

Anyone studying Dionysos for any length of time will soon become aware of his links with fire. In the nocturnal realms of *Meilichios* and *Zagreus*, this fire was the subterranean flames of the underworld which was carried by liminal deities, and the light of the nocturnal underworld sun which illuminated the underworld – particularly the realm of *Elysium* which was said to have its own sun.[145] In this form, Dionysos was *Nyktelios Lampter*, *'night light'*. The followers of Dionysos imitated these infernal flames by constructing sacrificial fire pits, and carrying blazing torches during their rites.

Fire was also considered a purificatory element, and evidence shows that ceremonial tools were purified by fire in the Dionysian-style rites of Macedonia.[146] The body was also believed to be cleansed or vitalized by fire; Strabo accounts of Dionysian processions which led the celebrants of Sabazios across hot coals in Eastern Thrace in a state of purification and devotion. The author George Cox wrote[147] that the Latin words for *spiritus* (spirit) *animus* (mind) and *thymos* (soul/desire) all come from Sanskrit words meaning to *rush* and *shake*, suggesting that magical/oracular abilities and spiritual progression can develop from the movement of the body (in particular furious movement which heats and speeds the blood) creating *'a fire inside'*. This particular state is well known within shamanic traditions across the world, and usually leads to a state of frenzied ecstatic possession: perhaps most obviously within the Northern European practice of *seething* and fire breathing. Incidentally, Plato writes that Socrates described the soul as being drawn by *raging and seething*[148] in

---

[145] Aeneid, 6.637ff, Virgil, c. 29-19 BCE, trans. J Dryden
[146] Ashmolean Catalogue: Heracles to Alexander the Great, 2011: P.141
[147] The Mythology of the Aryan Nations Vol.1, George Cox, 1870: P.31
[148] Kratylos Vol 12, 419c-420b, Plato, c. 500 BCE trans. HN Fowler

connection with our innermost urges and responses; which perhaps suggests a state of purification and connection to primal forces, obtainable by losing the inhibitions and sweating and raging into a state of rapture – as Dionysos does. Generally, these practices were carried out at night and were closely linked with rites of the under-earth; the chthonic realms.

The theme of netherworldly fire is further associated with Dionysos through the Delphic Python, who by some accounts was imprisoned by Zeus underneath Mount Aetna in Sicily – accounting for the occasional seismic and volcanic activity.[149] But as much as Dionysos' links with fire were chthonic, they were also heavenly. As already mentioned Dionysos was often described as being dressed in a crimson robe like the colour of solar flares, with a belt about his waist which sparkled like sunlight. He was also sometimes depicted wearing a solar crown upon his head and with a face of flame, as he flung *'from each plumed arc, glittering and fiery flakes.'* [150] He is *Dionysos Antauges*, *'the Sparkler'* and *Chrysokomes 'the golden haired'* and our familiar *Bakcheus*, the bringer of growth – quite simply he is fire itself, and even the raging Sun. Dionysos was often depicted with a solar sun disc upon his forehead and as such he was known as *Dionysos Karneios, 'the horned sun'.*

Another deity known to be associated with Dionysos and fire is the Titan Prometheus, who like Dionysos, dared challenged the new regime of the Olympian gods. According to Aeschylus' satirical play *Prometheus the Fire Bringer*, Prometheus played a prank on Zeus. He gave two trick offerings to the Olympian god: a delicious piece of beef which was hidden inside a foul-looking ox's stomach, and dry bull bones disguised as a tasty ball of fat. Zeus was disgusted by the ox stomach and chose the tasty fat, but as he took it he realised that within the fat lay only dry bones. Prometheus had deceived him, and Zeus became angry. Knowing how fond Prometheus was of mankind, as a punishment he hid fire from them; but Prometheus eventually stole fire back from Zeus by concealing it inside a Thyrsus, and handing it to mankind.

---

[149] The Divine Thunderbolt, JT Sibley, 2009: P.90
[150] A Vision of Poets, Elizabeth Barrett Browning, 1844

Certainly, several Dionysian themes run through this myth: the struggle between the Titans and the Olympians; the bovine offerings (especially the bull bones) and of course the Thyrsus, the staff of Dionysos. And when Prometheus hands fire to mankind, he offers them a symbol of civilisation; an element of culture which Dionysos was celebrated for bringing to the world. But that is not where the similarities end; like Dionysos, Prometheus was known for his fondness of mankind and was said to have formed our bodies out of clay. It is interesting that this myth is so similar to the Orphic tale of the Titans, whose ashes were used to mould the first humans. A later Roman tale accounts that Prometheus was responsible for the creation of hermaphrodites when Bacchus (Dionysos) got him drunk when he was working on the clay bodies; as a result of his intoxication, he muddled up the genitalia. Indeed, Dionysos himself was often considered as being an effeminate or bisexual male and he was a protector of those who were at the fringes of society and who may have been otherwise marginalised - such as hermaphrodites, who were held as sacred to him. Prometheus is also sometimes identified with *Lucifer* ('*light bringer*') and it is both easy and plausible to see parallels between him and Dionysos, especially as *the liberator*. Incidentally, Lucifer is also connected with Hekate, the consort of Sabazios as *Hekate-Bendis* [151] or *Brimo*.

Dionysos may also be identified with *Iao*, the supreme Phoenician god-name for the Sun. Later, the practices of Mithraic Gnosticism (which partly formed out of Orphism) named their Sun god *Abraxas* – a possible synchronisation of *Iao-Osiris-Dionysos*. This 7-lettered name was also said to represent the seven classical planets and was linked with the World Soul, leading us back to Dionysos as a cosmological prime mover in the creation and movements of the universe. Some scholars believe that Iakchos may also find part of his origins in Iao (IAkchOs). The role of Iao was later usurped by Yahweh/Jehovah. *Abraxas* and *Iao* were both popular names in the *Greek Magical Papyri*, where Dionysian associations can be found in conjunction with other solar deities.

---

[151] Hekate Her Sacred Fires, edited by Sorita d'Este, 2010: P.40

Thunder & Lightning

It is generally believed that thunder and lightning was a divine tool of the heavenly realms; a plaything of the cloud dwelling gods of Olympia. However, there are several accounts which suggest that electric storms were equally equated with the gods of the underworld; and in particular, acted as a divine connection *between* these two realms. In *The Bacchae*, King Pentheus perches is trapped in the branches of a pine tree as Maenads circle the tree below him, waiting to rip him to shreds. Euripides writes how, by the wrath of Dionysos, *'a light of holy fire appeared between heaven and earth'*.[152] To our ancestors, a bolt of lightning quite literally lit up the cosmic connection between above and below; a force which ripped through the material world which sat in between these two realms. Of course, lightning would also have caused some of the first flames that our ancestors would have ever witnessed – linking it with ancestral wisdom and fire.

The legends of Dionysos are rich in tales of thunder and lightning; and certainly they show that lightning was considered as both a gift *and* a curse. According to Orphic legend, which served to preserve many fragments of Dionysian mythology, the infant Dionysos Zagreus held two lightning bolts in his hands - a gift which Zeus had given him for protection. And when the Titans managed to trick Dionysos Zagreus into putting down these weapons (then brutally murdering and devouring him) Zeus punished them with lightning. As the lightning struck them they burst into flames and turned into soot; and from this soot, mankind was formed. The second incarnation of Dionysos would also come to be associated with lightning: whilst he was in the womb of Semele, the goddess Hera (the jealous wife of Zeus) tricked Semele into asking Zeus to reveal his *'true self'* to her. In doing so, she was exposed to his lightning and was killed instantly. Zeus then gathered the infant from Semele's womb and nurtured Dionysos himself within his thigh, until Dionysos was ready to be born. As such, Dionysos came to be known as *Dionysos Ignigena*, *'fire born'*.

The sound of thunder was also associated with Dionysos, and considered akin with the chthonic movements of the earth. The

---

[152] The Bacchae, 1080, Euripides, c. 400 BCE, trans. TA Buckley

sound of the Dionysian revelries was said to equal that of earthquakes by its chaotic nature, and the beating drums of the Dionysian revellers is known to have sounded *'like subterranean thunder'*.[153] Indeed, the sound of an earthquake was described as the *'thunders'* of the nocturnal Zagreus; according to legend Dionysos *'roared like thunder'* as he shook the ground with his earthquakes.

Dionysos was also associated with an object named the *Keraunos* – a word which simply means *'thunderbolt'*, but also contains *Kera* meaning *'horn'*. Probably originating from the symbology of the bull cults of Minoan Crete, the Keraunos was a double-headed axe or spear (similar to a *labrys* or *pelekys*) which was believed to have been shot down to earth by the gods. As legend would have it, these sacred objects were the *'core'* of lightning bolts, which were left behind after lightning had struck the earth. If you were lucky enough to find one (perhaps unearthing an old axe-head whilst ploughing) it could be sold on as a *palladia* – a protective charm against lightning and other misfortunes. [154] These axes were also used by initiates to summon storms, and as such Dionysos was called upon as *Dionysos Pelekys*.[155]

The Keraunos became an important part of Greek culture, décor and legend. Over time, the symbol would also come to take many different forms – from simple axe motifs to elaborate floral embellishments. Illustrated on pottery, statues, furniture and coinage, the lightning-axe stood as a symbol of authority and divinity, and was a particular favourite during the reign of King Philip II and his son Alexander the Great of Macedonia. Ancient Greek coins would also couple the Keraunos with one of the symbols of Alexander's rulership: the golden eagle, a bird which was itself considered to be the *'armor-bearer'* of Zeus.[156] According to Aeschylus, Zeus strikes his enemies *'by means of eagles bearing fire'*[157] destroying their houses with lightning; and the Latin poet Horace describes the eagle as the *'wing'd agent of the levin bolt'*.[158] The janiform shape of the Keraunos (double

---

[153] Aeschylus: Frag 27 (from Strabo, Geography 10.3.16)

[154] The Divine Thunderbolt, JT Sibley, 2009: P.89

[155] The Great Dionysiac Myth Vol.1, Robert Brown, (1877) 2000: P.336

[156] Where the Eagles are Gathered, Steven Bridge, 2003: P.59

[157] Aeschylus: Fragment 81 (from Aristophanes, Birds 1247, trans. W Smith)

[158] Odes, 4.4.1, Horace, 13BCE (from Thespis, TH Gaster, 1975: P. 168)

ended and usually symmetrical) reflected the divine connection that our ancestors recognised between the above and below, and the divinities which resided in those realms. On the island of Tenedos where Apollo was honoured (a deity who came to assume many roles and sacred sites of Dionysos) coins displayed a two-faced Zeus-Dionysos on one side of the coin with a Keraunos on the reverse – together with additional Dionysian iconography such as grapes and a honeybees. [159]

The axe or spear-shaped Keraunos would come to be known as a type of *thunderstone* – a common term generally used to describe any stone item believed to have been thrown down to earth by the gods, usually in conjunction with a storm. Like the Keraunos, these stones were seen to belong to more than just one world: they fell from the starry skies but were found on (or under) the earth. Such stones were found near the ancient Greek city of Orchomenos in Boeotia and were held as sacred at the temple to Dionysos there, and in Delphi a similar stone was found which was placed in the temple of Apollo where it was anointed daily with aromatic oils.[160] Sometimes, thunderstones were meteorites which had quite literally fallen from the heavens, but in most cases they were simply unusual rocks and minerals such as Pyrite. In other cases, they were the fossils of sea urchins[161] whose five ambulacra resembled the 5-pointed star which was sacred in the ancient world. This star was also reminiscent of the Macedonian sunburst which was consecrated to *Dionysos Karneios 'the horned sun'*.

A Keraunos was used during an ancient purification rite carried out by the Idaean Daktyls in the sacred caves on Crete, where they held chthonic rituals to Dionysos and Kybele. The initiate was first required to descend into the caves for nine days, during which he or she underwent purificatory rites which included the eating of raw meat followed by a vow of permanent vegetarianism, or at least a period of abstention from eating meat. They were then expected to give honour to a throne upon which a Keraunos had been placed, together with other accompanying imagery related to Dionysos

[159] Silver Tetradrachm (Phoenician standard) Tenedos c. 400 – 336 BCE
[160] The Divine Thunderbolt, JT Sibley, 2009: P.82
[161] The Star Crossed Stone, Kenneth J McNamara, 2010: P.142

Zagreus. At some point during these nine days, the initiate would also be instructed to engrave an inscription to the Cretan Zeus (Dionysos). The initiate would then be surrounded by Bakkhoi who would clash their cymbals, spin the *rhombos* (bull-roarer) and generally create a cacophony of noise to recreate the sound of a thunderstorm:

"... and bull voices roar from somewhere out of the unseen ... fearful semblances ... as it were of thunder underground is borne on the air ..."[162]

As well as recreating the sound of thunder and aiding the initiate to enter a trance state, this may also have recreated the scene as described by the Greek author Oppian in which the Nymphai who nursed baby Dionysos concealed him inside a box of pine and danced around it – drumming and shouting with the local women, to veil the noise of the crying child from his enemy the goddess Hera. It was during this occasion that the Nymphai and the accompanying women of Euboea are said to have first experienced the mysteries of Dionysos; they may have tried to achieve the same result at the Diktaean caves. Images of this particular legend often show a *keraunos* laying on the ground nearby. Porphyry recalls the words of Pythagoras at his initiation into the cult of the Diktaean Zeus:

"... I have become a mystic of the Diktaean Zeus (Dionysos) and having fulfilled the life of the night-wandering Zagreus, and the raw flesh eating feasts, and holding up the torches of the Mountain Mother (Kybele) and having been purified, Bakchos I invoked..."[163]

The word Keraunos is also used in a direct Dionysian reference in *The Bacchae* when Dionysos punishes Pentheus with *synkeraunosai 'a shattering by a thunderbolt'*. Similarly, Dionysos' mother Semele is given the title of *keraunobolos 'thunder smitten one'*.

Vegetation

Modern paganism has widely accepted the theme of duality and opposition within their festival cycles as characteristic of a dying and

---

[162] Aeschylus (Source: Themis - A Study of the Social Origins of Greek Religion, Jane Ellen Harrison (1912) 2010: P.60-61)

[163] Kretes, Frag.ii. Porphyry (Source: The Great Dionysiac Myth Vol.1, Robert Brown (1877) 2000: P.159)

rising vegetation deity of agriculture: a god or goddess whose rites emulate and celebrate the phases of the solar year and the ebb and flow of the farming cycle. Neo-paganism has come to follow a dying and rising vegetation cycle which is primarily concerned with food production, crops and harvest and the agricultural year (a matter which in most cases is no longer a concern for modern westerners, and therefore is often substituted with growth in other areas - such as prosperity and health). Indeed Dionysos and several of his equivalents from other parts of the world are often considered as sacrificial harvest gods: such as the *'year daimons'* of ancient Hellas who were associated with the growth of crops and the cycles of the sun which fuelled those growth processes. But how accurate can this interpretation really be for a god like Dionysos?

The theory that the religious rites and magic of our ancestors were primarily concerned with obtaining food is perhaps the result of the 19th century anthropological view that our forefathers were rather backward and primitive. But this was not so, for even at the start of the Bronze Age (approx 3000 BCE) whilst the inhabitants of northern and western Europe had only just started making long barrows and had no written language, many civilizations in southern and eastern Europe and Asia had already developed sophisticated societies which embraced medicine and surgery, writing and record keeping, science and literature, art and music and even civil governments, politics and law. The Dionysian theme of duality and opposition meant much more to the ancient Hellenes than a simple farming cycle. Firstly, the Dionysian theme of duality and *'presence and absence'* was also recognised in politics, social and civil equality, trance, shapeshifting, prophecy, travel, trade and invasion and more; in particular, the journey of the soul after death.

So although growing crops was one matter of interest, their ritual and culture revolved around a whole manner of other concerns which included leisure activities and entertainment and an appreciation of *'the finer things in life'* – not dissimilar to our own society today. Did this start with a more ancient association between Dionysos and the growth and decline of crops, like the phenomenon of modern neo-paganism adapting the concerns of northern/western European farming magic? Perhaps; although there is very little connection between agriculture and the older gods from whom Dionysos originates, other than perhaps *Agathos Daimon* - and according to mythology, the prosperity of agricultural crops in general was of relatively little interest to Dionysos.[164] In fact Dionysos quite often released his wrath upon other crops in order to punish those who refused to acknowledge his cult or leadership.

Secondly, his festivals and cult rites were not always celebrated within a yearly (agricultural) sun cycle. In fact some of the earliest Dionysian festivals were only celebrated once every three years (as part of the *'trieteric'* festival cycle) and sometimes even less often than that. This is not consistent with a rite which is specifically designed to aid the growth of annual crops, as is generally believed. However it could be associated with fermentation, and the aging or *'laying down'* of wine to produce different tastes and qualities.

Thirdly, the idea of an agricultural god in the popular sense has been largely conceived from a northern European point of view: a region with a very different climate than that of southern Europe and Asia, where the Dionysian current originates. Whilst the winter was often a time of hardship for those in northern Europe, in contrast the winter of the south was a time of rest and abundance for those who had survived the unforgiving heat and drought of the summer. Karl Kerenyi supports this argument when he writes, *'nature in the winters of the south does not evoke an image of dying, nor does it give the human spirit any reason to take part in sympathetic laments.'* The Dionysian festival cycle can at first seem confusing for those of us who have been practicing within a neo-pagan framework – our preconceptions have been built upon traditions that were originally designed for a northern European audience and climate.

However Dionysos was most definitely associated with viticulture – the production of wine from the vine plant all the way to the bottle – and in this way, some of the rites of Dionysos were associated with the solar year, albeit from a very different angle than a modern neo-pagan/northern European point of view. It is possible that the Dionysian festivals reflected part of the annual solar year which was associated with new growth upon the vine in the spring, the swelling of the fruit throughout the summer and the harvest of the grapes in late summer and autumn. But – the viticultural cycle

---

[164] Save perhaps his association with Demeter in the Eleusinian Mysteries

also relied upon darkness and rest; the process of fermentation, and aging.

Certain herbs, resins and flower essences were also sacred to Dionysos because of their use in flavouring wines such as strawberry, and ornate flowers in general were symbolic of excess, joy and luxury. Other plants added to wine during fermentation, such as the myrtle, were associated with the underworldly travels of Dionysos; the myrtle being the plant that Dionysos as Iakchos offered Hades in exchange for his mother. Fennel was often added to flavour and was of course associated with the thyrsus, his fennel staff.

"...Bacchus loves the ivy most..."[165]

But despite his popular association with grapes, it was not the grapevine but the ivy plant, or *kissos,* that was considered most sacred to Dionysos; and as such, Dionysos was often referred to by his epithet *Dionysos Kissophoros, 'the ivy bearer'.* Dionysos was often depicted on coins and other decorative paraphernalia of the period crowned with ivy wreaths, and sometimes sporting a bushy beard of ivy berries. The ivy berry itself is mildly toxic to humans, and may have been added to ritual drinks as an entheogenic ingredient to aid visions. And by some accounts, Dionysos carried a thyrsus rod made of ivy-wood, rather than fennel.

Dionysos also bore the title of *Perilionis, 'he who is entwined around pillars'.* This name refers to the ivy which wrapped itself around pillars sacred to the god, in particular the columns of Thebes (modern Thiva in Greece) where it is said the Thebans considered an ivy twined column sacred to the god. Elsewhere, ivy is also known to have adorned masked columns which was honoured as the embodiment of Dionysos himself. Depictions of the masked columns often show ivy creeping up the column and around the mask; this may have originated from earlier practices of hanging the Dionysian mask upon a living tree, where creeping ivy may have already been present. Other Dionysian items were also said to have been wreathed with ivy: the sacred mask of Ikarion (the location of an important Dionysian sanctuary) is also accounted to have been wreathed with ivy and

---

[165] *Fasti,* 3.767ff, Ovid, C1st BCE - C1st CE trans. Boyle)

throughout Greece the phalloi of street processions were wrapped with ivy during the Dionysian festivities.

Certainly, the ivy plant played an important part during the infancy of Dionysos – and there is no doubt as to why it is his favourite of all the plants. When his mother Semele burst into flames by the fires of Zeus, she was still pregnant with Dionysos; he would surely have died too, if cooling ivy creepers had not protected him from the heat that had consumed his mother. And after his birth, when his jealous stepmother Hera tried to track him down and murder him, Dionysos was concealed by the Nymphae within a wooden box which was screened with ivy leaves. In his youth Dionysos continued to admire the ivy, and legend has it that Dionysos was known to wander through the wild and misty forests where ivy and laurel grew.

The nature of ivy may also give us a clue as to the connection between this plant and Dionysos. The author Walter Otto describes ivy as *'twice born'* due to the nature of its growth; sending out shade-seeking creepers initially, and then adult leaves later which seek full sunlight.[166] This is a parallel which seemed symbolic of the duality of Dionysos – the liminal god who steps between the states of *Dionysos Meilichios*, the dark lord, and *Dionysos Bakcheus*, the manifest one. It is interesting that in general, ivy was actually kept away from temples in ancient Greece as it was considered an omen of death; yet another sign of how close Dionysos was considered to be to the ancestral underworld as the lord of souls.

The ivy is also connected to the snake, which appears throughout Dionysian cult and legend. The subject of the snake and its relation to Dionysos is discussed elsewhere in this study, however suffice to say snakes were considered the embodiment of him, and were often used as a symbol of his qualities. It is recorded that the cult rites of Dionysos often involved snake handling and wearing snakes as decoration upon the body, as well as a rather cruel custom which involved tearing venomous snakes to pieces as an offering. However more recent research suggests that it was ivy wreaths, and

---

[166] Dionysus Myth & Cult, Walter F Otto (1960) 1995: P.154

not real snakes, that were being destroyed.[167] This kinship between ivy and snake is further supported by the words of Nonnus in his epic *Dionysiaca*, when he writes that snakes, hurled by maenads against tree trunks, twined themselves around the trunks and became ivy plants.[168]

Dionysos was also associated with trees, and certain trees became considered as sacred to him. During the mysteries, he was also sometimes referred to as *'the branch'* and in the works of Nonnus, the troops of the Indian army complain of how difficult Dionysos is to defeat because his shape changed so often; one moment a lion, the next a panther, and even a tree. Certainly, his connection with branches and trees pointed to his association with growth and the natural cycles, but it also held a deeper meaning. Like the Magus depicted on the tarot card The Magician, Dionysos stood in the centre of all things – the *axis Mundi* with one tip of his staff reaching up towards the heavens and the other pointing down towards the chthonic underworld. This is similar to the Norse cosmology of the Yggdrasil or *'World Tree'*, *"with its branches reaching up to the sky and its roots reaching down through the earth"*[169] which illustrates the structure of the universe. Indeed, one of the possible meanings of the name Dionysos is *'He who impels the World Tree'.*[170] As a cosmogenic god or *world soul* (intermediary force between potential and material) Dionysos is certainly qualified to stand in this position. As *Meilichios*, Dionysos was honoured as a masked figure made of wooden cross-posts, which would be dressed in black robes or animal skins and would be considered the embodiment of Dionysos. It is likely that this custom originally began with hanging the mask and skins upon living trees, or hollow trees where honey had historically been found.

"Dionysos increases the nourishment of trees..."[171]

Several authors have suggested that the dismemberment of Dionysos Zagreus is comparable to the stripping of leaves from

---

[167] Dionysos: Archetypal Image of Indestructible Life, Karl Kerényi, 1996: P.62

[168] Dionysus Myth & Cult, Walter F Otto (1960) 1995: P. 155

[169] Craft of the Wise, Vikki Bramshaw, 2009: P.60

[170] Die Musik nach dem Chaos, Michael Janda, 2010: P.16-44

[171] Plutarch, quoting Pindar Vide inf. Sup.II ii. 1.(Source: The Great Dionysiac Myth Vol.1, Robert Brown, (1877) 2000: P.76)

deciduous trees during the winter, after which only the trunk or *'heart'* of the tree remains.[172] However, although this could be relevant to the Dionysian theme of presence and absence, I find it unlikely for several reasons – particularly because almost all of the plants and trees sacred to Dionysos (such as the fig tree, the grapevine, the ivy, the strawberry, the fennel, and the pine tree) are evergreens; i.e. they do not lose their leaves over winter. In many ways, Dionysos is perhaps more comparable to the nature of evergreen perennials: like Dionysos, they appear to live on, whilst all around them withers and dies. It truly is a symbol of indestructible life. However we should remember that the use of plants was more about what that plant symbolised, rather than being the focus of the Dionysian rites.

The evergreen pine tree was particularly sacred to Dionysos[173] and it frequently appeared in his myths and legends. As Spartan legend would have it, Dionysos was carried to safety across the sea within a box of pine as a baby; it was also within a pine box that Dionysos was concealed from the vengeful Hera in Euripides' *The Bacchae*. And Plutarch wrote *'...the pine ... it grows, so it was said, in warm earth, in those places where the vine prospered best also ...'*[174] Here we see a direct connection between the pine tree, the grapevine, and Dionysos. But why? To answer this question, we need only look to viticulture once more. Pine resin was used to conserve and refine wine; the *Pithoi* (fermentation jars) were sealed with pine resin and then opened at the Anthesteria which celebrated the birth of Dionysos. The baby Dionysos is symbolic of the newly opened wine. Incidentally, the pine-sealed *Pithoi* would have created a wine that tasted something like *Retsina*, a traditional Greek wine which is considered an *'acquired taste'* due to its overbearing pine flavour!! Certainly, Dionysos can be considered as an *'acquired taste'* himself.

The pine also appears in the legend of Pentheus, whose tale recalls the dismemberment of Dionysos and is also believed to have incorporated certain elements of Dionysian initiation. Other accounts of pine being used during the rites of Dionysos the ithyphallic *thyrsus* - a staff topped with a pine cone which was carried by Dionysian

---

[172] The Mythology of the Aryan Nations Vol.2, George Cox (1870) 2004: P.294

[173] Although arboriculture as a whole was of no concern to Dionysos

[174] Moralia, Plutarch, c. 100 CE

initiates. The pine cone was also sacred to *Sabazios*, one of the gods from whom Dionysos originates. Blazing torches were also made of pine and carried during nocturnal torchlight processions to Dionysos, whilst other accounts recall that the stumps of pine trees were dressed and worshipped as Dionysos in a similar way to the post-gods constructed for Meilichios.

Blood, Tooth & Horn : The Animals of Dionysos

"Appear as a bull or many-headed serpent or raging lion to see… throw a deadly noose around the hunter of the Bacchae as he falls …"[175]

Whilst Dionysos was connected with some aspects of farming and soil cultivation, his ancient origins meant that he was more closely associated with the raw materials that nature already had to offer: fruits, nuts, vegetables and meats that were gathered directly from a wild environment. He was also associated with the processes that would later be employed to transform those supplies from raw materials into goods and provisions. For instance mead, the very first sacred drink of Dionysos, was made from sweet honey gathered from wild bees which were found in caves and hollow trees; and even the domestic grape had a wild ancestor that was native to the Mediterranean region - a wild grapevine, whose fruit was gathered to create the very first fermented wine. The myths of Dionysos recall how he instructed mankind in the processes of creating both wine and mead for the first time.

However, some of Dionysos' most ancient associations lay not in seeds and leaves, but in blood and bone: the hunting of wild game for meat. Later, he also came to be associated with trapping wild animals for breeding purposes, and sport. He was the heart of the wild world, the beasts that lived within it, and the spirit of the hunter. Wild meat was an ancient produce that Dionysos came to be associated with, and indeed in one of his earliest forms Dionysos was the Hunter God. Depicted either bare-footed or wearing hunting boots, he symbolised the connection that could be forged between mankind

---

[175] The Bacchae, 1019-1020, Euripides, c. 400 BCE, trans. TA Buckley

and the natural world. However, he also embodied the force to overcome it. In comparison to the modern interpretation of the *'god of the wilds'*, the ancients perceived the nature gods as *controlling and dominating* nature; rather than an idealistic escape to nature, Dionysos aided the people to use nature to their advantage. He foraged for wild vines and taught his people to cultivate them; he captured wild animals and tamed them into captivity. Incidentally, Karl Kerenyi notes that a hunter who traps live animals is called a *'Zagreus'* in Greek; a reminder of some of the earlier Minoan origins of Dionysos.[176] It should be said that Dionysos was not the only deity to approach nature in this way; one of his most powerful consorts, the Phrygian goddess Kybele, was known for her ability to tame some of the harshest realities of nature to make the wild world an ally of mankind.

Certainly, many of the myths and legends of Dionysos, and the processes that were illustrated within them, described the transformation of something wild into something domestic. On a larger scale, these processes can perhaps be considered as symbolising the transition of hunter-gatherer societies into agricultural societies. This domination and domestication is perhaps one guise of the *'god of the wilds'* archetype that is often forgotten by modern neo-pagan interpretations; which instead suggest a somewhat idealistic (but unrealistic) idea of harmoniously being *'at one'* with nature. It is more likely that one of the earliest charges of the many *'nature gods'* from all across the globe was about containing and domesticating the natural world, which was often both cruel and bleak. This domination and domestication would later be interpreted in the myths as his control over those who denied his rule or who would harm his Bakkhoi, such as in the tales of Lykourgos. In such situations Dionysos was referred to as *'The Hunter of Men'*.[177]

Yet Dionysos stood in a place of liminality, between the domestic and the wild; he often symbolised the transition between states, rather than favouring one state or the other. And as time went on the appeal of rurality grew with the people inhabiting the polis, and Dionysos began to be invoked as a god of liberation. Just as

---

[176] Dionysos: Archetypal Image of Indestructible Life, Karl Kerényi, 1996: P.82
[177] The God Who Comes, Rosemarie Taylor-Perry, 2003: P.8

Dionysos had led the people in the control of nature, so too could those footsteps be retraced; freeing his followers from the trappings of modern life and civilization and leading them back into a primordial state of being in which his followers could be reunited with the memories of their ancestors - and the earliest origins of mankind.

"Bacchic god dwelling on mountain peaks..."[178]

With his influence, people abandoned the status quo and escaped from the towns and cities into the wilderness where they donned animal masks, and shapeshifted. Here they raved like beasts for Dionysos Bromios, *'the roarer'* in secret nocturnal rites. Leaving the boundaries of the city may have been symbolic of the breaking of boundaries on a psychological level: abandoning the ordered realm of the city and entering the liminal space of nature. They were his *Thiasos*, or band of followers. Animal masks were often used in the rites of Dionysos, and it is likely that the early depictions of satyrs and centaurs (as well as other half-man, half-beast creatures) are in fact depictions of the masked followers of Dionysos. Artwork also shows masked musicians and priestesses dressed up as animals or at least in animal skins, joining in with the sacred retinue. In Cyprus, whole bull skulls - complete with horns - would be cut to shape into masks and worn by the *Kerastai*, *'bull-horned priests'* in their rites to show their allegiance to the gods. It is possible that early cults used animal skulls exclusively for their ceremonies and processions, before man-made masks became popular. We also know of the Bassarai, who honoured Dionysos as *Bassarios 'Fox'* and worshipped him wearing fox skins. Legend has it that Dionysos punished the rebellious Thebans by setting a giant fox on them.[179] Usually depicted in a tunic or robe, Dionysos is often shown in the centre of his retinue, holding a drinking cup and ivy branch aloft. Behind him dance the Maenads dressed in leopard skins, and carrying snakes. After them came the goatskin-clad Satyrs, carrying the *keras*, or blowing horns.

---

[178] Oedipus Tyrannus, 1105, Sophocles, c. 429 BCE

[179] Description of Greece, Book 8, Pausanias (c. 200 CE) 1979: P.251 trans. WHS Jones

"Dance making swirl your fringe o' wooly skin … lead thou the dance … and play like a fawn."[180]

The animalistic features of masked Dionysian practice are likely attributed to Dionysos' association with the natural world, as well as his role as *Dionysos Eleutherios, 'the liberator'*. Behind the mask, Bakkhoi of Dionysos were set free from their identity and released from the ego. They were able to connect with the primordial self, rave and celebrate, free from their mundane day to day cares. The reveller became one with the wild beasts; to run, to feed, to procreate – man was reunited with his primal needs, and his ancestors. The particular animals which were chosen to be impersonated are also relevant: these animals, such as the panther, lion and bear which are described by the researcher Joseph Campbell as *'journeying gods'* were those who were believed to have the ability to traverse the worlds and petition the gods on the people's behalf for favours; and in particular, for immortality. A set of preserved wall frescoes at Villa dei Misteri – *'the Villa of the Mysteries'* located just outside of Pompeii in Italy show just one example of how shapeshifting and masked ritual was used: we see a female initiate in a scene of music and revelry as Satyrs play pipes and Silenus, the tutor of Dionysos, looks on. Here we see a suggestion of music and dance being used during initiation to change the consciousness and evoke a certain atmosphere for the initiate. The presence of the goat-like Satyrs, and Silenus (who was often depicted as half animal) suggests the use of animal masks and shapeshifting; the initiate is introduced to the bestial element of the cult and the animalistic part of herself.

Through masked dance and trance the followers of Dionysos transformed themselves into these animals which Dionysos was associated with. The animals were seen as the embodiment of the nature of the god, and therefore to become those animals was to unify oneself with the very spirit of Dionysos himself. When Dionysos appeared, he would often materialise as one of these animals: such as a lion, a bear, or a many-headed snake, but usually as a horned animal, such as a ram or a bull. After all Dionysos was known for his fondness of horned animals, having been born in his first incarnation as Dionysos Zagreus as the *'horned infant'*. Sacrifice

---

[180] Lysistrata, 1295ff, Aristophanes, c. 411 BCE, trans. J Lindsay

also played an important part in the Dionysian cult, and it is possible that the dance and revelry of the Bakkhoi of Dionysos was seen as being more effective should the revellers be dressed as the very animals they believed were sacred to Dionysos - those that were regularly sacrificed to him. Therein, the followers of Dionysos offered a doubly pleasing offering to Dionysos: the skin and blood of a wild animal, and the prize of a human soul.

Dionysos was the ecstatic, shamanic god who represented the dismantling of boundaries and the expression of desire which only the freedom of the torch-lit mountainside allowed. He was an antithesis of the world that mankind was now accustomed to living in: he led a rebellion against a society that revolved around consumerism and law and order rather than blood, sweat and bone; a culture which aims to isolate the individual from nature. This is one of the reasons that Dionysos is perhaps so relevant today: he helps us to reintegrate ourselves with the natural world, whilst remaining respectful of its strength and power. He is the embodiment of opposites and primal unity, breaking down false structures and boundaries and reuniting us with our primordial and bestial nature, which with it brings a sense of freedom, independence and creativity. Walter F. Otto writes:

"(Dionysos) brought the primeval world along with him. That is the reason why his onslaught stripped mortals of all their conventions, of everything that made them 'civilised', and hurled them into life which is intoxicated by death at those moments when it glows with its greatest vitality, when it loves, procreates, gives birth…"[181]

The animals associated with Dionysos are a testament to his unpredictable and paradoxical nature: those such as the bee, an insect which supplies sweet and nutritious honey yet administers a nasty sting if provoked. And the goat, a seemingly amiable creature which supplies inexpensive meat and nourishing milk to some of the poorest countries in the world - yet has a surprisingly cunning nature, reverting back to a wild existence with very little trouble if given half a chance. Dionysos was also associated with the bull: a creature which despite thousands of years of domestication alongside man, remains

---

[181] Dionysus Myth & Cult, Walter F Otto (1960) 1995: P.141

today as potentially dangerous and aggressive as the Auroch, its wild ancestor which is now sadly extinct.

The Goat

One of the animals most closely associated with Dionysos was the goat, and the male goat or *'horned buck'* was considered as one of the most loyal companions of the god. Hunted by our most ancient ancestors for both their meat and skins, wild goats were once native to the Phrygian mountains of Turkey[182] and became widespread across the Mediterranean and Asia. They would also be one of the very first species to become domesticated by man.

As a personification or embodiment of Dionysos, the goat is a classic example of the antithesis and opposition that played such an important part in the Dionysian cycle. On the one hand, the goat was one of his most favoured sacrifices: and in the Orphic Mysteries it was believed that an initiate could rise to a state of divinity (apotheosis) by the sacrifice and consumption of a goat kid. This is a likely reminder of the older origins of Dionysos Zagreus, the 'horned infant' who by using his therianthropic abilities assumed the form of a goat kid, amongst other animals, to disguise himself from Hera. Seeing past his disguise, Hera set the Titans upon him who tore him apart, boiled up his body parts in a cooking pot, and ate him up.

Echoing the symbolism of Dionysos within the cooking pot, in Delphi the bones of the sacrificial goat were placed within a kettle and then cast on the floor and read as a form of divination; whilst in Thrace the ashes of the sacrificial goat kid, akin to those of the Titans from which mankind was formed, would be spread upon the earth in honour of the dead god to the words *'euoi - blood, fire and dust will mix!!* [183] A set of Dionysian initiatory tokens found in Thessaly also mention the sacrificial kid as they read: 'From man (you have) *become* (a) *god; a kid* (you have) *fallen into milk.'* [184] This line perhaps reflects that the Bakkhoi had now undertaken the initiatory journey during which

---

[182] Linking them with Kybele, the Anatolian Mountain Mother, who can be considered as his consort

[183] Inscription from Perinthos, Thrace

[184] Pelinna Gold Leaves, c. 400 BCE

he becomes akin to the sacrificial goat, and through this sacrifice and ingestion has experienced a sense of apotheosis – a union with the god himself. The reference to the milk refers to the stewing of the goat kid in its mothers' milk during cooking, a form of sacrament to ancient Dionysian worshippers[185] and this ceremony was even later noted in the Bible where it was now accounted as a sin: '...*thou shalt not seethe a kid in its mother's own milk*'.[186]

On the other hand, whilst the goat was regarded as an embodiment of Dionysos it was also considered an enemy of him. Indeed, whilst domestic goats provided meat and milk, the wild goat was often considered a pest – especially by grape farmers, who watched the goats strip their crops of delicate young shoots. Due to its association with goats, the constellation of Capra (nanny goat) was also considered as detrimental to the growth of grapevines.[187] As the vine was considered as an embodiment of Dionysos, goats were sacrificed to Dionysos Aigobolos, '*the goat smiter*' as a form of retribution for their actions. In this case, the sacrifice was usually of an older billy goat which was at the end of its useful reproductive life, approximately the age of five years and performed during the period of Elaphebolion.[188] As legend has it, King Ikarios sacrificed a goat for eating his grapevines and made a bag from its skin which was filled with wine. This custom continued as a street game called the Askoliasmos or '*leaping on the wine skin*'.

Dionysos is described by Euripides as an experienced hunter as he pursues the blood of young male goats, and Virgil accounts that Dionysos was honoured as *Exarchos* '*choir leader*' imitating a goat whilst he hunted for them. Dressed in goat skins and performing their rites on the mountainsides, the Dionysian Maenads were themselves considered akin to the goat which '*leaps lightly, like a Bakkhe*' [189] and sometimes took the name of eriphe (nanny goat). They were said to imitate the bleating of a goat by issuing the Bacchic high-pitched cry,

[185] The God Who Comes, Rosemarie Taylor-Perry, 2003: P.15
[186] Exodus 23:9 34:26
[187] The Great Dionysiac Myth Vol.1, Robert Brown, (1877) 2000: P.134
[188] Savage Energies, Walter Burkert, (1931) 2001: P.8-9
[189] Imagines 1.19, Philostratus the Elder, c. 300 CE, trans. Fairbanks

eua! [190] The Satyrs who accompanied Dionysos as part of his thiasos were also depicted as goat-footed and goat-eared; both accounts point to possible links with mask-wearing and trancing by early Bakkhoi in order to shapeshift into the animals they were impersonating.

Like the Maenads who took the name of *eriphe* (nanny goat) his Satyr attendants were known as *tragos* or *'billy goat'*. This word is connected with the Greek word *tragodia* meaning *'the goat song'* and from which our modern *'tragedy'* finds its roots. The *tragodia* originated in the masked dances of the Dionysian revellers as they invoked the horned infant or goat god[191] they then lamented the sacrifice of the god in his goat-form. These rites later developed into more dramatised ritual and started to involve fictional characters and plots, but usually always revolved around a death – echoing the original meaning of the tragodia.

The goat was also associated with forms of fortune telling and the behaviour of live goats was studied as a form of divination. At the oracular sanctuary in Delphi – where Dionysos is likely to have held an important position before his usurpation by Apollo – goats had also once been held of great importance. Legend had it that a goat had discovered the oracular powers of the site by breathing in the prophetic fumes which rose up through the fissures in the earth.

Certainly, the goat often symbolised the darker aspects of Dionysos which were part of his nocturnal nature. One such epithet of Dionysos is *Melanaigis* which means *'of the black goat skin'* – and can refer to a man clad in black (a priest of Dionysos or a post-god figure dressed in black robes) or even a very dark red wine. Another interpretation for the term can be *'wrapped in dark storms'*. Melanaigis was also undoubtedly connected with *Dionysos Morychos 'the dark one'* who is accounted to have been honoured at the city of Syracuse, in Sicily. [192] Melanaigis was considered a capturer of human souls, as well as a guide to them as they travelled through the underworld.

---

[190] The Great Dionysiac Myth Vol.1, Robert Brown, (1877) 2000: P.134

[191] The Great Dionysiac Myth Vol.1, Robert Brown, (1877) 2000: P.136

[192] Dionysus Myth & Cult, Walter F Otto (1960) 1995: P.169

Associated with the dead, those who followed him were also deeply involved in ancestor veneration.

Dionysos Melanaigis would also be remembered in mythology. As legend would have it, an Athenian named Melanthos – the last descendant of Theseus – entered a duel with King Xanthos of Boetia to settle a border dispute between the two territories. As they advanced, Melanthos suddenly looked past Xanthos and perceived a figure; he shouted out that he saw a man in black goatskin stood behind Xanthos. When Xanthos turned around to look, Melanthos took the opportunity to kill him. Thereafter Melanthos took the throne as the next King of Athens, and the festival of Apaturia meaning *'deceit'* was held in honour of Dionysos Melanaigis as it was he who was perceived to have appeared to aid Melanthos win the dual. The festival of Apaturia would later come to also mark the coming of age and legitimacy of young men.

For some, this symbology of the dark goat god may conjure the image of Baphomet the *'sabbatic goat'* whose name was first mentioned in its present form during the inquisition of the Knights Templar. It was most popularly illustrated by the French occultist Eliphas Levi in the 19th century, in the classic *'magician'* pose: one hand pointing up to the heavens and the other pointing down towards the underworld. Upon its lap sat two snakes entwined around a rod, and between its horns shone a flame, which according to Levi symbolised *'the image of the soul elevated above matter, as the flame whilst being tied to matter, shines above it.'*[193] Historical accounts describe Baphomet as being honoured as a mounted goat skull or wooden mask in the form of a goat, dressed in black – strikingly similar to that of the Dionysian post god. Historically, the two gods cannot be connected by any common origin – but they certainly seem to share the same *'current'* in modern western magic. Incidentally, Levi called his Baphomet the *'Goat of Mendes'* who was recognised by the ancient Egyptians as the god Ptah in animal form. Certainly, Ptah and Dionysos share several similarities, including their roles in the matters of liminality, regeneration and cosmology.

---

[193] Dogme et Rituel de La Haute Magie Vol.1, Eliphas Levi, 1854

Big Cats

They say that a leopard was once caught in Pamphylia which was wearing a chain round its neck, and the chain was of gold, and on it was inscribed Armenian lettering: `the King Arsakes to the Nysian God.' Now the king of Armenia ... finding the leopard, let it go free in honour of Dionysos.'[194]

Big cats such as lions, leopards and tigers were considered as extremely sacred to Dionysos. This may have partly been influenced by his connection with the Phrygian goddess Kybele: the mistress of wild beasts, who was depicted with lions at her feet. As a consort of Kybele, she and Dionysos even shared a similar method of transport: both riding a regal chariot drawn by lions or leopards. However, it is likely that big cats were sacred to Dionysos in more ways than just those associated with Kybele; we find evidence of an older lord of wild beasts in Minoan art, the same culture where Dionysos finds so many of his roots - two lions flank him side by side. Incidentally, the panther was believed to love wine and it was said that shepherds would offer bowls of wine to try to prevent them from attacking their flock. And at Çatalhöyük, a Neolithic settlement in southern Anatolia (where we also find evidence of a bull cult strikingly similar to that of Minoan Crete) we find wall paintings of masked leopard men dancing around their prey, as they imitated the hunt of the big cats they observed in their environment. The Patron God of Argos, Heracles, was also depicted wearing lion skin or with a lions' face; he and Dionysos share many similarities and one of the most famous descendants of Argos, Alexander the Great had a special affinity with him. Certainly, several species of big cat were found wherever Dionysos was worshipped across the Balkan Peninsula and beyond[195] and even if certain species were not indigenous, trade and culture would have almost certainly brought them there.

The nature of the big cat is undeniably reflective of the nature of Dionysos, in particular his regal predatory disposition and his place as a god of the wild and untamed world. Wearing leopard skins about their shoulders, the Dionysian maenads said to have sprung effortlessly up the mountain ranges – something which the agile

---

[194] Life of Apollonius of Tyana 2.2, Philostratus, c. 200 CE, trans. Conybeare
[195] Dionysus Myth & Cult, Walter F Otto (1960) 1995: P.111

leopard will do with ease, as he silently pursues his prey across almost vertical rocky slopes.

Certainly, the wearing of leopard skins was likely to have facilitated shapeshifting. Similarly, upon these mountainsides the maenads are said to have torn at raw flesh with their teeth – in this condition the maenads were looked upon as predatory beasts, and in *The Bacchae* Euripides writes that Dionysos changed the women into panthers[196] before they tore his enemy Pentheus apart. In this form Dionysos was known as *Dionysos Omestes 'eater of raw flesh'*. And in Asia, one of the leopards' favourite prey items is the goat – the foe of *Dionysos Aigobolos 'the goat smiter'*, and as legend has it the leopard or lion was one of the forms into which Dionysos would choose to transform.

"If as a lion he shake his bristling mane, I will cry "Euoi!" to Bacchos on the arm of buxom Rhea, stealthily draining the breast of the lionbreeding goddess. If as a leopard he shoot up into the air with a stormy leap from his pads, changing shape like a master-craftsman..."[197]

Besides their hunter instincts, there are other reasons why big cats were associated with Dionysos; in particular his role as a god of duality and opposition. Many depictions show an ivy faced Dionysos together with a tiger or panther, which leaps up and snaps at the grapes he holds in his hands – perhaps as a demonstration of balance between his creative and destructive forms. Sometimes, the tiger has evergreen ivy around its neck, showing that the destroyer is an integral part of the nurturer. Indeed, big cats are known to be some of the most caring and attentive parents, something which may reflect the nurturing instincts of the Dionysian *thyiades* who as legend would have it cared for and protected the baby Dionysos. Nocturnal rites were held on the mountainsides as the thyiades searched for the baby Dionysos, and they concluded at the Korykion caves where he was awakened. Incidentally, many leopards will also prefer to give birth and care for their cubs within a dark and secluded mountainside cave, and prefer to hunt nocturnally.

---

[196] A general term in the ancient world for the feline genus which contains lions, tigers, leopards and jaguars

[197] Dionysiaca, 1.11, Nonnus c. 500 CE trans. Rouse

"She took the babes and laid them in the den of a lioness for her dinner. But a panther with understanding mind licked their bodies with her ravening lips, and nursed the beautiful boys of Dionysos with intelligent breast; wondering serpents with poison-spitting mouth surrounded the birthplace, for (Dionysos) had made even the ravening beasts gentle to guard his newborn children."[198]

Sadly, many subspecies of leopard are now critically endangered and close to extinction, such as the Snow Leopard and particularly the mountain-dwelling Amur Leopard – of which at the time of writing there are only about <u>35</u> animals left in the wild. Perhaps one of the best offerings to Dionysos you could give in this respect is a donation to the WWF, who work to preserve these amazing creatures. Please visit www.wwf.org.uk.

The Serpent

Snakes and serpents are a common motif throughout the cult and mythology of Dionysos. Snakes were often used during Dionysian rituals and processions, and evidence shows that they were handled during some of the very first Dionysian rites of Sabazios: the original god of the wilds of Eastern Thrace and Phrygia, from whom Dionysos partly derives. It was believed that all snakes belonged to Sabazios, and were sacred to him.

Indeed, the serpent is known to be one of the most primordial forms of the gods. An ancient symbol of opposition, the snake embodied both the creativity and the wrath of Dionysos; his role as an overseer of both fertility and destruction. The Caduceus of Hermes – a symbol made up of two snakes entwined around a rod – can in many ways be seen as a reflection of this opposition, and representative of Dionysos in animal form. Indeed one possible predecessor of Dionysos, the genderless serpent spirit known as *Agathos Daimon*, was often depicted together with the symbol of Caduceus – by some accounts, Hermes received the Caduceus wand from the Delphic Apollo, who is often identified with Dionysos. And as the Eleusinian Iakchos, Dionysos sometimes bore the name of *Bakkheios Hermes* – the chthonic guide.

---

[198] Dionysiaca, 48.240ff, Nonnus c. 500 CE trans. Rouse

The snake was symbolic of the natural cycle of life, death and regeneration – something which was depicted in the *ouroboros* (symbol of the snake eating its tail) and observed by the sloughing of its skin. Indeed, it was a symbol of the afterlife to the Greeks and echoed Dionysos' role as a symbol of indestructible life. Frequently the serpent was considered as a creature of the chthonic underworld realms and the Greek name for snake or serpent, *érpo* meant to '*crawl*' along or below the ground, equating the snake with the infernal depths of the earth.[199] Yet despite its chthonic nature the snake was also associated with energy, vital force and creation; it was considered a phallic form[200] and was associated with procreational rites.

Such was understood in the Eleusinian Mysteries, where a clay snake was passed under the table from lap to lap in a rite and referred to as the '*god through the lap*' during their inner rites; we also see a snake used as a symbol of the revelation of the mysteries within the *kista mystica*, the contents of which were seen as akin to the baby Dionysos. It was also the form of a serpent that Zeus took when he crept into the bedchamber of Persephone, impregnating her with the bull-horned infant Zagreus upon a '*dragonbed*'. In this way the snake embodied Dionysos in his role as a creator, the cosmogenic god who assisted in the creation of all living things – in both a cosmic and a corporeal sense. For as a prime mover of the vital forces of the universe, the serpentine Dionysos was also the embodiment of energy within the human body; the coiled serpent who could be awakened during states of trance and ecstasy. This force was channelled through the blood and released through sweat and breath during a state of ritual frenzy and trance. It can also be compared in some ways to the yogic practice of awakening the kundalini, the coiled force that rests at the base of the spine; this is achieved by way of comparable techniques and achieves similar results.

Both fictional and historical accounts alike compare the ecstatic dance of the maenads to the movement of serpents, and it is likely that this imitation was intentional. Certainly, it is known that real snakes were carried during processional dances to Dionysos, and dancing with a snake would probably have been seen as a most sacred

---

[199] Hekate Her Sacred Fires, edited by Sorita d'Este, 2010: P.79
[200] The Great Dionysiac Myth Vol.1, Robert Brown, (1877) 2000: P.126

union between the maenad and her deity. The later customs of the cult of the goddess *Bona Dea* (or the earlier *Angizia* from the Latin *Angius* meaning serpent) would echo the ancient dances of the maenads, with snake-handling and dancing taking place in honour of these liminal gods of above and below, life and death. The connection between Bona Dea and Dionysos is made quite plain in this funerary inscription for a young boy, which describes him as a priest of *'first, Bona Dea ... and of Dionysos Kathegemon* [201] – that is, *'Dionysos the Leader'* or *'Protector'*.

These ecstatic practices also helped to aid shapeshifting and were in a sense the very embodiment of the Dionysos the shapeshifter – namely *'the serpent of a thousand heads.* [202] In this way the serpent became connected to several other zoomorphic embodiments of Dionysos – in particular, the bull. Certainly, the bull and the snake are connected in Dionysian cult and mythology; the tauriform sun god was often represented as a serpent with horns, and several horned gods who can be identified with characteristics of Dionysos are depicted accompanied by a cunning serpent. And at Olympia, Dionysos was worshipped in the shape of a bull or a snake [203] interchangeably. He is even called upon for the purpose of a *'divine revelation'* in the *Greek Magical Papyri*, where he is named *'the serpent-faced god'* and given an offering of snake skin. [204]

Dionysian serpents are also known to be extremely protective: legend has it that snakes guarded the entrance to the cave where the baby Dionysos slept – and in Delphi Dionysos served to protect the earth goddess in his serpentine form. Historically, this protective role was imitated by Dionysian Bakkhoi known as *antrophulakes* [205] *'guardians of the cave'* who ceremonially guarded the entrance while rites were taking place and also acted as the caretakers or custodians of sacred space. It is here that we also find the *ouroboros* used again: the symbol is used as a protective charm in the *Greek Magical Papyri*. [206]

---

[201] Ancient Mystery Cults, Walter Burkert (1931) 1987: P.28

[202] The God Who Comes, Rosemarie Taylor-Perry, 2003: P.7

[203] Shiva and Dionysus: Gods of Love and Ecstasy, Alain Daniélou, (1979) 1992: P.115

[204] PGM 153 – 160

[205] Dionysos, Richard Seaford, 2006: P.67

[206] PGM VI 579 – 590

Snakes are widely exploited for the exotic pet industry, often wild-caught and imported into the UK, and the care they need is often greatly underestimated resulting in many being mistreated or abandoned; unfortunately, the plight of these critters is often overlooked by the general public. Our native snakes and reptiles are also at risk, due to their habitats being destroyed. Perhaps one of the best offerings to Dionysos you could give in this respect is a donation to your local exotic pet charity, or the Amphibian & Reptile Conservation Trust, who work to preserve these amazing creatures. Please visit **www.arc-trust.org**.

The Bull

By many accounts, Dionysos first appeared to the Greeks as a bull-formed sun god.[207] This is quite likely, as a large portion of the Dionysian current as we know it today migrated across from (and was influenced by) Minoan Crete, where the bull was a central theme of religion and culture.

It was also in Minoan Crete that the Bull of Dionysos was best known as associated with the Sun: in his bull form, Dionysos was often depicted with a solar sun disc upon his forehead and as such he was known as *Dionysos Karneios*, *'the horned sun'*. The name *Karneios* was later applied to Apollo and his festival of *Karneia*, but it was first used for Dionysos, in Thebes: the first of the Greek cities to receive the cult of *Dionysos Taurokeros*, *'the bull horned'*.[208] The Macedonian sunburst (similar to the one in the centre of the bull's head on the front cover of this book) was a popular decoration of the Temid Dynasty of Macedonia and some of its most famous family members (in particular, the immediate family of Alexander the Great) were known for their devotion to or connection with Dionysos. Both Alexander the Great and the official patron god of his family, Heracles, were depicted with solar tauriform imagery on coins, tableware and other decorative items from the period.

---

[207] Theatre of the Greeks, JW Donaldson, 1860: P.17
[208] The Great Dionysiac Myth Vol.1, Robert Brown, (1877) 2000: P.124

The cult title of *Karneios* or '*Karnos*'/ '*Keros*' (horn) [209] consistently appears throughout Greek mysticism and occult traditions alike in relation to the sun god bull or ox. It even featured in some early versions of the Witch's Rune, and is found in some of the original material of British occultist Alex Sanders in the form of *Karnayna*: '*...Eko Eko Karnayna ... Bagabi Lachi Bachanta ... Bachalyas Sabalyos...*' For many years it was believed that the Alex Sanders' *Karnayna* was simply a misspelling or alternative pronunciation of the more popular Latin *Cernunnos* of Gaul. However, this passage can also be found in an early French play called *Le Miracle de Theophile* (circa 1261) in which one of the characters conjures the devil by the same name; clearly, the name *Karnayna* has also been identified with the Horned One, and for much longer than the 1960's. And further, Professor Ronald Hutton has now identified that the word Karnayna finds common roots with the Arabic word *Karnain* also meaning '*horned one*' which can be found in the *Qur'an* and refers to Alexander the Great in his horned guise[210] as a battle hero of Islamic legend.[211] Ronald Hutton explains the use of this name by Alex Sanders as simply a '*pleasing pun*' however I am inclined to believe that Alex was quite aware of the Dionysian nature of what he was practicing - and pun and truth may have gone hand in hand. Indeed, Alex himself accounts that our ancestors revered: '*a horned deity, known as Cernunnos or Karnayna ... the other possibility is that of Pan, Dionysos, or Bacchus ...known to his Christian contempories as the Devil, and called by them Satan or Lucifer, 'Light Bringer'.*[212] Similar evidence exists in other words found in the passage, which was until recently believed to be simply a mixture of meaningless '*barbarous*' words. Incidentally, the word *Bachanta* means (in both Gaelic and Greek) '*muttering or drunken or inebriated chatter*' from which etymologists suppose the words *Bacchus* and *Bacchantes* are derived.[213]

Whilst the solar bull god is best known for his appearance in Crete, he is in fact an almost global phenomenon - and the Minoan interpretation of him could have well been influenced by a multitude of different cultures – including those of Egypt, Anatolia, Thrace and

---

[209] Cretan Cults and Festivals, RF Willetts, 1962: P.265

[210] The Triumph of the Moon, Professor Ronald Hutton, 1999: P.196, 331

[211] The Divine Thunderbolt, JT Sibley, 2009: P.99

[212] The Alex Sanders Lectures, Alex Sanders, 1984: P. 5, 8, 9

[213] Walter Whiter: Universal Etymological Dictionary, 1811

even India. To our ancestors the bull represented power, virility and kingship – all qualities which were associated with the strength and fertility of the sun. For instance in Sumeria, the bull was associated with Dumuzi the *Wild Bull*, a deity who was identified with Dionysos and embodied by the King during the rites of *hieros gamos* (sacred lovemaking) to bring wealth and fruitfulness to the community. And in Egypt, the Apis Bull was associated with fertility and kingship and associated in particular with Osiris, who in turn is closely identified with Dionysos. Offerings were made to Apis by each new Pharaoh as part of his coronation; something which Alexander the Great is known to have done as part of his instatement in Egypt. The bull or ox was also a symbol of creation; myths recall how a wild bull charged the egg of chaos and broke it with its horns, causing the beginning of all things. It was also known to be a sign of resurrected life, and by some accounts, swarms of sacred bees were seen to emerge from the body of sacrificial cattle and were believed to be the resurrected life force of Dionysos himself.[214]

Like the billy-goat, the bull was considered as both the embodiment of Dionysos and a pleasing sacrifice to him. From elaborate sacrifices carried out during public Dionysian festivals to more private nocturnal offerings, the sacrifice of the bull was seen as a symbol of the transition between this world and the next. For Dionysos in particular, young bulls were offered to the watery abyss of the Alkyonian Lake; it was into this same lake that according to myth Dionysos himself descended to find his lover Ariadne. And in the *Odyssey*, Odysseus uses the blood of cattle in order to create a gateway to the underworld[215] further supporting that the sacrifice of bulls and cattle was seen as a powerful way to create a portal and traverse the worlds. Bull blood was also believed to have the properties of purification in preparation for initiation, and one such tradition that developed from this belief was a bathing in bull's blood for regeneration. This practice involved the sacrifice of a bull upon a platform of wooden planks which were pierced with small holes, whilst the initiate would sit in a pit below and be showered with the blood. In Rome, the rite was known as the taurobolium and was held in honour of Magna Mater and Attis; this practice was recently

---

[214] Georgics, 4.538-58/425-28, Virgil c. 29 BCE
[215] Seidr: The Gate is Open, Katie Gerrard, 2011: P.182

portrayed in the TV series *Rome* when the niece of Julius Caesar, Atia of the Julli, takes part in the taurobolium to ensure the safety of her son Octavian. More anciently the practice may have originated in Anatolia (on a somewhat smaller scale) to Kybele and a Phrygian equivalent of Dionysos known as Attis.

The bull was considered a most worthy and fitting sacrifice to Dionysos. Not only did the sacrificial bull symbolise Dionysos' ability to travel between the worlds, it also represented his dual nature: his role as a deity of both creation and fertility but also of primal power and destruction, viticulture and hunting, and masculine and feminine natures. As such, a wide variety of Dionysian imagery depicts the unity of his viticultural and bestial aspects together with an image of the horned bull or ox – such as a wide variety of coin designs from Euboia which show the horned bull-god and vine-god together as two phases of one Dionysos.[216] In many occult traditions, horns are used to symbolise the two paths, or two different states of being; and certainly, this is no exception. As such, Dionysos was known in Samothrace as *Axiokersos* '*worthy horned god*' – and as his embodiment the bull was known as *Axio Tauros* '*worthy bull*'. In short, the bull was the god[217] either and in Samothrace, his female counterpart was known as *Axiokerse* '*worthy horned goddess*' a likely early guise or equivalent of Artemis.[218]

One tradition that was practiced in Minoan Crete and is believed to have been linked to both Dionysos, Artemis and duality was an acrobatic sport known as Bull Leaping - later known in Thessaly as the taurokathapsia '*touching of the bull*'. Many colourful wall frescos show images of bull leaping, during which a competitor would grab onto a charging bulls' horns and somersault right over the top of the bull in a display of athletic ability. Many theories have been made for the purpose behind bull leaping, but it is generally accepted that it held some sort of ceremonial significance – probably reminiscent of the hunting of cattle as wild prey before their domestication.

---

[216] The Great Dionysiac Myth Vol.1, Robert Brown, (1877) 2000: P.390

[217] Incidentally, the Germanic 'Gott' and English 'God' come from the Indo-European root, 'Go', meaning 'bull'

[218] Known as Artemis Taurike, or Artemis the Bovine

A similar tradition is known to have been carried out at Catal Huyuk in ancient Anatolia, where the bull was also held in great reverence and celebrated together with Kybele, the mountain mother. In many ways, bull leaping demonstrated both freedom and control – the false freedom of the bull as it charged around the ring together with the attempt of the leapers to conquer the bulls' fury and overcome or acquire the power of nature – just one of the many paradoxical traits of *Dionysos Dikerotes 'the two-horned one'* whose double horns seem to represent his double-nature. Another Dionysian feature which shines through in the depictions of the bull leaping is that of equality, or the dissolution of gender roles; images show both men and women participating in the games, with the women bearing a more flat-chested masculine form and the male athletes long-haired and fresh faced as *Dionysos Gynnis, 'womanly one'*. Indeed, the differences are hardly perceivable except for a few minor details, and men and women athletes appear equal; like Dionysos, they bridge the genders.

The primal energy of the bull was believed to be invoked during Dionysian rites in many ways other than sacrifice. One way would have been to have worn the horns of the bull, to aid shapeshifting during ecstatic trance: the ability to *'become'* an animal in order to take on its abilities, whilst perhaps using an instrument such as the *Rhombos* or Bull Roarer. This may have been used as a way of invoking the god into the priests wearing the disguise. Whilst striving to achieve god-possession or invocation is quite common today in modern mystery traditions such as Wicca, in ancient Greece this was almost entirely unique to the cults of Dionysos.

The Minotaur

'What two-formed monster, filling the labyrinth with his huge bellowings, has torn thee asunder with his horns?'[219]

The legend of the Minotaur is perhaps one of the most well recognised stories of Greek mythology. Usually depicted with the head of a bull and the body of a man, the Minotaur was the love-child

---

[219] Phaedra 1170ff, Seneca, c. 50 CE

of Pasiphae (the wife of King Minos of Crete) and a sacred White Bull.

Pseudo-Apollodorus writes how King Minos (then competing for the throne with his brothers) prayed to the god Poseidon that he might receive a sacred white bull to sacrifice in order to receive sovereignty from the gods. And so Poseidon delivered the bull – but it was such a splendid beast that the King disobeyed Poseidon, and killed another bull instead – keeping the pure white one for himself. Poseidon was so enraged that King Minos had tried to trick him, that he cursed the King's wife Pasiphae and caused her to fall in love with the white bull. Climbing inside the skin of a female cow, she allowed the bull to mate with her – and the result of their coupling was the Minotaur. When the boy was born, King Minos did not know what to do with this monstrosity – especially when it was discovered that the little boy would only eat human flesh.

King Minos consulted the Oracle of Delphi, who instructed Minos to commission a giant labyrinth which would contain the creature; and in order to satisfy the creature's hunger, King Minos declared that fourteen Athenian youths should be sacrificed to him every nine years. The Athenian hero Theseus swore to slay the Minotaur and accompanied by two other soldiers dressed as young girls, he tricked King Minos into sending him into the Labyrinth instead of the youths. After securing the assistance of Ariadne (one of the daughters of Minos) Theseus obtained a plan of the labyrinth – and by reeling out a ball of thread behind him, Theseus managed to find the centre of the Labyrinth. Here he destroyed the Minotaur, and then followed the thread to find his way back out again. After succeeding to the throne, Theseus built a temple to *Artemis Soteira* (saviour) to mark success over the Minotaur. And, in return for Ariadne's help, he promised to marry her; but he instead abandoned her on the island of Naxos, where Dionysos would later find her and fall in love.

It's worth noting that Ariadne plays a very important part in this tale: without her, Theseus could not have succeeded. Nonnus puts it well in his epic Dionysiaca when Dionysos says to Ariadne: *'Theseus shed the blood of the half-bull man whose den was the Labyrinth ... but you know your thread was his saviour: for he would never have found victory without a rosy-lipped girl to help him!!'* Indeed, Ariadne is known as the *'Mistress of the*

Labyrinth'. And as Cretan Star Goddess, she is a most fitting consort for Dionysos *Nyktelios* '*Night-Light*': the embodiment of the stars – who fell in love with her, raised her up to the heavens to sit beside the immortals, and placed the star constellation *Corona Borealis* upon her head as a crown.

The Minotaur is portrayed as a most vile and monstrous creature in this story. Of course, like so many of the Greek myths this tale is probably a relatively recent Athenian interpretation – a combination of ancient legend and modern political myth (in this case, indicative of Crete's defeat at the hands of Athens). The reinvention of how myth was used was also partly responsible – romanticising older legends in order to make more exciting plays for the Athenian crowds. However, if we look deeper we find that – whilst still a feared and respected creature – the Minotaur was also much loved and revered by our ancestors. Indeed, the Minotaur or *Minotauros* (the Bull of Minos) was originally known as *Asterion* '*Starry One*' from *Aster*, meaning '*Star*' associated with the constellation of Taurus and referred to as the '*Starry Bull of the Heavens*'. We also find *Iakchos* used as an epithet for Dionysos at the temple complex on Crete, which originates from the Minoan name for the star Sirius, where Dionysos was matched with Ariadne, the Cretan Star Goddess. Here we find a shining star as the centre of labyrinthine patterns on Cretan coins, seals and mosaics; another indication that the star was considered akin to the Minotaur.

The Minotaur's astrological placement marked the beginnings of summer and the promise of increasing sunlight, in the period of Thargelion which began with the present-day May New Moon. He was also the son of Pasiphae – the daughter of Helios, the sun – and as such he is *Dionysos Karneios*, the newly born bull-horned sun, and *Dionysos Bakcheus*, fire born encourager of heat. But as a creature of both above and below, his association with heat and fire was also connected with the '*nocturnal sun*'. Just like *Dionysos Zagreus* (embodied within the shining light which emanated from the darkness of ancient honey-caves) he was the spark of potential which was concealed in the underworld – at the centre of the Labyrinth. And so, just as new Mead fermented inside the skin of a dead goat at the centre of a cave, so the sacrifice of the Minotaur was necessary for renewal. The Etruscans certainly recognised this aspect of the Minotaur, where we find him depicted as a bull-headed infant upon the lap of Pasiphae –

in depictions which are very similar to those of Selene with the bull-headed infant Dionysos Zagreus upon her lap.

The Labyrinth

"You know your problem? You take too many things for granted. Take this Labyrinth: even if you get to the centre, you'll never get out again."[220]

The process of entering the Labyrinth and journeying to meet the Minotaur can in many ways be seen as symbolic of the cycle of life and death – and beyond. It is within the Labyrinth that we find the domain of the psychopomp, the Judge and Guide to the underworld; and the Minotaur as the embodiment of *Dionysos Euboulês, 'the chthonic guide'*. As *Asterion*, the *'Starry One'* the divine bull is both the goal of our journey and our most inner fear: death itself. Incidentally, the pseudo-historical King Minos was also named as an ordained judge of the underworld; Kings of Crete would have invoked and taken on the form of the solar bull god to reinforce their importance and position, and the sacrifice of the Athenian youths can tentatively be seen as parallel to Dionysos in his role as the feared chthonic Lord of Souls. In his bull-headed form Dionysos is an agent or intermediary in this process, consuming and separating souls and sending them on their journey to the afterlife. It is quite possible that Dionysian rites were held during which initiates recreated this serpentine journey into the underworld, either as a precursor to the journey after death. The same is evident within the Eleusinian Mysteries, which also contained a labyrinthine descent to the underworld.

Despite the descent into the underworld being a foreboding one, the overall journey itself was seen as positive and good. It was far from a descent into hell – moreover, it was a journey during which the initiate secured the longevity of one's soul. Karl Kerenyi writes, *'The Labyrinth suggested by meanders and spirals (of ritual dances) was a place of processions and not of hopelessness, even though it was a place of death.'*[221] Indeed, paradoxically the journey down into the underworld was also an ascent into the heavens. By journeying to the centre of the

---

[220] Labyrinth, 1986 Fantasy Film
[221] Dionysos: Archetypal Image of Indestructible Life, Karl Kerényi, 1996: P.94

Labyrinth the initiate reached *Asterion* the *'Starry Bull of the Heavens'*, the ascended *Dionysos Iakchos* who rose into the heavens before being reborn again to the underworld realms, who aided his initiates to reach higher levels of consciousness and epitomised the transcendental elements of initiation, trance and death.

One way we know our ancestors recreated the mythic journey to the underworld was through the medium of dance. Many researchers believe that the temple at Knossos on Crete was designed to resemble the Labyrinth from the legends of Theseus – but also as a dancing ground, where sacred dance would be performed.[222] Most notable is the *Geranos* or *'Crane Dance'* characterised by weaving, spiralling and interlaced movements. The *Geranos* was said to have been invented by the architect of the Creatan Labyrinth – and according to legend, the dance was first led by Theseus himself. [223]

   ... Theseus danced the Geranos around the Keraton, an altar made of horns...[224]

It is accounted that these labyrinthine dances happened during the period of Poseidon, the month beginning with the December New Moon. This period shares its name with the god who King Minos prayed to in order to receive the white bull which created the Cretan Minotaur.

We also know of the *Epilinios*, the *'Grape-Treading Dance'* which developed out of the movement of the grape-treaders' feet as they crushed the fruit. This later evolved into a circular dance, with steps that still appeared to imitate the wine pressing but also guided the dancers around the dance floor in a meandering, serpentine fashion. The connection between viticulture and the journey into the underworld is clear and has been discussed elsewhere in the book. Just like dance steps, the Labyrinth's meandering passages are often complex – but unlike a Maze, a Labyrinth has no dead ends; all paths

---

[222] Although no mosaic dance floor, as would be expected from this period, has yet been found

[223] The Craft of Zeus: Myths of Weaving and Fabric, John Scheid, 2001: P.102

[224] Plutarch Lives 'Theseus' Pt.21, c. 75 CE, trans. B Perrin

eventually lead back to the beginning; the epitome of the Dionysian *zöe* – the *'spirit of life' which suffers no interruption and permeates all things.*[225]

One further way the Labyrinth may have been viewed was as a symbol (or active tool) of ecstatic trance. In Shaivite practices (known for its parallels with ancient Dionysian practices) energy is raised via *'channels'* in the body, which are likened to the paths of a Labyrinth; the Shaivite *bhaktas* (who themselves bear a resemblance to the ancient Dionysian *thiasos*) believe that Ganesha guards the entrance to the Labyrinth and its meandering passages, which emanate from the energy coiled at the base of the spine.[226] In eastern mysticism, the energy centre at the base of the spine is known to be an active and fiery masculine force. We already know that Dionysian initiates used *orgia* (ecstatic rites) such as dance frenzy and intoxication to raise and channel energy through blood, sweat and breath to reach a state of *enthous* (possessed/inspired by Dionysos) and so it is quite reasonable to suggest that on reaching the centre of the Labyrinth the initiate finds union with Dionysos – and the inner bull, representative of one's inner self, and their power centre.

"When an initiate journeys to the centre of the labyrinth they find their own inner centre, the place of enlightenment or initiatory realisation."[227]

The Garlanded Bull

As always, this chapter was the result of a set of synchronicities. Dionysos loves synchronicities, because they confuse you so much that when things *do* start to add up, he looks even smarter. The first synchronicity was when I became aware of an exhibition named *Heracles to Alexander the Great*, which was held at the Ashmolean Museum in 2011. Other than my rudimentary knowledge of the relationship between Dionysos and Alexander the Great, I couldn't fathom why my internet browser kept taking me to the Ashmolean Museum website – so I thought I better visit their latest exhibition and see what all the fuss was about. What awaited me there was a

---

[225] Dionysos: Archetypal Image of Indestructible Life, Karl Kerényi, 1996: P.95

[226] Shiva and Dionysus: Gods of Love and Ecstasy, Alain Daniélou, (1979) 1992: P.122

[227] Symboles fondamentaux de la science sacrée, Réne Guenon, 1962: P.216

wealth of Dionysian symbolism and legend, which furthered my understanding and research for this book greatly. To the Ashmolean Museum, I give my thanks for creating such a wonderful exhibition and informative catalogue. The second synchronicity occurred when the painting was conceived for the front cover of this book, upon which the artist depicted the Macedonian sunburst which was beautifully illustrated in the Ashmolean's exhibition catalogue. I decided to take a photograph of the half-finished painting to send to Sorita d'Este, whilst it stood on the easel in our living room. On reviewing the photograph, I couldn't help but notice that I'd caught a frame from an episode of the old 1960's Batman series on the television in the background, with one of *Riddler's* crosswords splashed right across the screen: BANQUET, it read. What a perfectly Dionysian message.

"The bull is garlanded. All is done. The Sacrificer is ready."

This was the oracle that King Philip II of Macedonia – the father of Alexander the Great – received from a *Pythia* of Delphi just days before his daughter's marriage ceremony in 336 BCE. No one truly knows how he interpreted this oracle, but if he'd given some more thought about the spiritual history of his family, he might have taken it as a warning. On the eve of his daughter's marriage, Philip II commanded that a festival procession bearing statues of the twelve Olympian gods parade through the streets of Aegae. As a member of the royal line, Philip was considered a blood descendant of the gods; and as such he commissioned a 13th statue in his own image to be placed amongst the twelve Olympians. As he entered the town's theatre with a wreath of golden oak leaves upon his head (truly a *'Worthy Bull'*) he declared his birthright as a divine descendant of a god. It was at that moment that Philip was brutally murdered by one of his trusted bodyguards, and upon Philip's death Alexander the Great took the throne.

The Macedonians were believed to have been descendants of King Macednos, the *'horse-loving'* son of Zeus, who founded the city of Macedonia situated to the west of Thrace. The mother of Macednos was the goddess *Thyia*, who leant her name to the *Thyiades*: the Dionysian Maenads of the Delphic tradition. Thyia's name also means *'sacrifice'*[228] further connecting her with Dionysos and his sacred dismemberment. Certainly, Macedonia was home to a significant Dionysian following - something which is evident in its architecture and culture. Although Alexander the Great's family were originally from Argos, his family had integrated themselves into the local Dionysian culture of Macedonia and despite their devotion to their Argos-patron god Heracles (from whom it was believed they descended) the family was known for their devotion to Dionysos. The female side of the royal line was particularly devout to Dionysos, and Alexander's mother, Olympias, was well known for her exceptional loyalty to him. She was initiated into the service of Dionysos at Samothrace where the chthonic mysteries of Hekate-Brimo and her consort Dionysos/Sabazios were celebrated[229] and the sanctuary was thereafter taken into Macedonia's protection.

Certainly, there are some significant similarities between Heracles and Dionysos which may have allowed the Temid Dynasty to easily integrate the existing Macedonian culture within their own. Both Dionysos and Heracles were born to mortal mothers by Zeus. They also shared a wealth of Dionysian/Apollonian symbology and bestial imagery: such as big cats (like lions and leopards) and horned animals (such as bulls, goats and rams). Even the first city ruled by the Temenids in Macedonia was named *Aegae*, meaning *'the goat'*, and images of Heracles and Alexander the Great were used to decorate Macedonian coins. The significance of goats in the area, in particular their association with kingship, is particularly connected to Dionysos and the temples and ritual items of Heracles in Macedonia were decorated with Dionysian imagery including ivy leaves, mythological beasts, and even Satyrs and Maenads.

Another connection between Macedonia and the Dionysian current was horses. Like Sabazios, a god of the Dionysian current from Thrace and Phrygia, skilled horsemanship was an extremely important part of Macedonian culture and warfare. As a testament to their skills in horsemanship, the Macedonians were sometimes called the *Hippiocharmes,* which means *'expert horse rider',* or *'expert chariot*

---

[228] Ashmolean Catalogue: Heracles to Alexander the Great, 2011: P.1
[229] Hekate Her Sacred Fires, edited by Sorita d'Este, 2010: P.81

fighter'. [230] Alexander the Great was also known for his horse-whispering abilities, having managed as a child to mount and ride a wild black stallion, who he named Bucephalus. The horse remained with Alexander for the rest of its life, and was slain during the Battle of Hydaspes in 326 BCE where Alexander then founded a city in his honour named Bucephala.

Indeed Alexander the Great himself is often identified with Dionysos, and their stories conflated. Both would yearn to *overcome all obstacles and to transcend all precedents, to reach the end of the world* [231] - the *'great outer ocean'* of Homeric legend, which surrounded the earth. Like Dionysos, Alexander managed to conquer many kingdoms democratically (although not always without a skirmish) and was known to sacrifice in honour of foreign gods and integrate their cultures and traditions. He was willing to break the *'status-quo'* to achieve his goals. Indeed in his later years, Alexander the Great also declared himself the embodiment of *Zeus-Ammon*, a favoured god of Sparta[232] who also absorbed elements of the Phrygian Sabazios.

Orphism was also popular in Macedonia, and may well have originated in the region. It is interesting to note that there are connections between Dionysos and Alexander's family here, too: Queen Eurydice (the grandmother of Alexander the Great) shared her name with the wife of Orpheus, who according to legend was the first *mystes* (initiate) of Dionysos. Orpheus was accredited with inventing the Dionysian mysteries, and although we now know this not to be true, it is likely that Orphism held within it several concepts that were already being used in older Dionysian cult rites and belief systems from the region. When Queen Eurydice died, her funerary pyre remains were wrapped in purple cloth and put inside a chest which was placed upon a throne within her underground tomb. The throne was decorated with images of Persephone's abduction by Hades, a myth which Orphism imitated in its legend of Eurydice's descent to the underworld.

---

[230] Ashmolean Catalogue: Heracles to Alexander the Great, 2011: P.2

[231] Ashmolean Catalogue: Heracles to Alexander the Great, 2011: P.23

[232] Description of Greece, 3.18, Pausanias (c. 200 CE) 1979 trans. WHS Jones

The Cockerel

One animal known for its association with Dionysos is the Cockerel. The Cockerel is depicted together with Dionysos on many reliefs, coins, mosaics and pottery – sometimes with two Cockerels flanking Dionysos either side, or simply shown with one as his companion.

A known sacrificial animal to Dionysos, the Cockerel was held sacred for its ferocity and strength and was especially protective of its females. Accounts are given of annual cock-fights being held in the Theatre of Dionysos Eleutherios in Athens[233] where cock-fighting is depicted on a marble throne reserved for the Priest of Dionysos. With legs carved in the shape of lion's paws, the back of the chair shows two Satyrs carrying grapes and the arms show two boys setting two Cockerels to fight. The spilling of the Cockerel's blood after the fight was believed to appease the spirits; a similar rite known as the Tabuh Rah is carried out in Balinese Hindu practice. Its blood was also believed to ward off disease if scattered around vineyards[234] linking the Cockerel to Dionysos through viticulture.

The Cockerel was also associated with the role of Dionysos as Guardian of Boundaries: as a creature that declared the rising sun with its call, the Cockerel was seen as marking the liminal threshold between night and day.[235] This theme of change and transformation was also signified in how the Cockerel was sometimes depicted in ancient Greece: for instance, the Cockerel was occasionally shown as a *'hybrid'* or fusion of two or more different animals (such as the Hippalektryon – a creature with the wings and legs of a Cockerel but the head and tail of a horse. The Hippalektryon was mentioned by Dionysos in Aristophanes *Frogs*). Also, the Gnostic archon Abraxas (identified as a possible synchronisation of Iao-Osiris-Dionysos, linked with the Sun God guise of Dionysos and his role as a cosmological prime mover) was often depicted with the head of a Cockerel. In the *Greek Magical Papryi*, we find one invocation petitions the Sun God as Abraxas with distinctly Dionysian offerings: calling

---

[233] The Attic Theatre, AE Haigh (1898) 1969: P.177

[234] Greek Religion, Walter Burkert (1931) 1985: P.82

[235] Cockfights, Contradictions & the Mythopoetics of Ancient Greek Culture, Eric Csapo, (lecture) 2006: P.16

upon him as *'earth shaker'*, the ritual involves presenting a Cockerel to the sun together with 12 pinecones and an offering of milk and wine, whilst holding the skin of a snake.[236]

The Cockerel was also connected with the comedic ithyphallic aspects of Dionysian theatre. Masked followers of Dionysos would carry figwood phalli through the streets shouting lurid obscenities at the crowd; the slang word *'cock'* is believed to have partly originated in the strutting and fertile Cockerel, and Dionysian reliefs show a Cockerel whose head and neck has been replaced by a phallus, clearly indicating the link between the Cockerel and regenerative abilities. Indeed, the Cockerel is also known to have been a popular lovers' gift in ancient Greece, especially between male same-sex partners.[237]

The Gryphon

"The Gryphon is a quadruped, like a lion; it has long claws of enormous strength … it has a beak like an eagle … its eyes are like fire. It builds its lair among the mountains … and guards the gold in those parts." [238]

Gryphons (or *Gryps*) were legendary creatures with the head, forelegs and wings of an eagle and the rear, back legs and tail of a lion. Sometimes, they are described as being spotted like a leopard (another of Dionysos' sacred animals). The Gryphon was frequently depicted alongside Dionysos, who was often shown either riding a Gryphon or in a chariot drawn by them. In some cases, his chariot was drawn by several of his sacred animals (such as a Lion, a Bull and a Gryphon all together).

By many accounts Gryphons guarded divine places, and hoards of treasure. They were a symbol of divine power; messengers of the gods, and guardians to secret places. Indeed, the Gryphon was a creature of liminality; like the Cockerel, its hybrid appearance symbolised the notion of transformation and the abolishment of boundaries. The beast is beautifully depicted in wall frescos at the

---

[236] PGM III 633-731

[237] The Twilight of Ancient Egypt, Karol Mysliwiec (1993) 2000: P.207

[238] On the Characteristics of Animals, 'Two Beasts of India' IV 27, Aelian, circa C2rd CE

palace/temple complex of Knossos on Crete, where many links to Dionysos are found.

As God of Moisture

Dionysos, according to Greek belief, was the lord and bearer of all moisture.[239]

Dionysos was firmly connected with natural bodies of water such as rivers, lakes and oceans. As a god of foreign origin, common belief held that Dionysos was carried across the ocean to Greek shores from a distant and exotic land; and certainly, the arrival of luxurious goods from abroad marked his epiphany and were considered akin to him. For instance, it is very likely that the skill of wine making arrived in Crete from across the sea — most likely from Libya. The industry quickly spread through Crete and into mainland Hellas where it began to be made and exported. Therefore both the knowledge of viticulture and the exportation of it became an embodiment of Dionysos: the foreign god who was integrated into the culture of Greece. Indeed, the Athenian playwright Hermippus wrote of the many fine things that Dionysos brought back to Greece with him on his ship following his voyage across the sea; and one decorated *cylix* (shallow drinking cup) depicts Dionysos sailing upon the ocean, his ship stocked with goods and his ships' sails overgrown with grapevines[240] echoing the ancient legends. In Athens, his arrival by sea was honoured during the month of Anthesterion when an icon of Dionysos was carried through the streets of the city in a wooden boat, as his adventures at sea were recalled and his journey celebrated.

In one such adventure, Dionysos is captured by pirates but frees himself with ease, transforming his captors into dolphins; these dolphins are also depicted on the decorated cylix. Dolphins were associated with both Dionysos and Apollo, and their arching movement in and out of the water may have been seen to represent the course of the sun as it rose and set upon the horizon. And as a boundary between above and below — the here and the beyond — the

---

[239] Dionysus Myth & Cult, Walter F Otto (1960) 1995: P.156
[240] Cylix of Exekias, circa 540 – 30 BCE illustrating a scene from the Homeric Hymn to Dionysos

horizon would have been held as particularly sacred. Indeed according to some forms of Greek cosmology there existed a vast river at the edge of the world which surrounded the earth and to which all rivers and seas ran; the *'Great Outer Ocean'* that Alexander the Great himself was determined to explore. So the legends of Dionysos' journey across the sea were not just symbolic of the import and export of the goods which embodied him - they also demonstrated the ability of Dionysos to traverse the worlds, even defying death itself and returning to the world of the living after an initiatory period as *Meilichios* the nocturnal and *'absent'* god. In earlier times, the sea god Poseidon may have been celebrated in a similar way as he was also originally associated with coming across the sea on a journey like Dionysos[241] he also shares several epithets and attributes with him.

This initiatory absence was also implied in the stories of his journey to the oracular sanctuary of Dodona, when Dionysos employed two mules to carry him across a watery abyss to reach the sanctuary in order that he might regain his sanity. Just like many modern western mystery traditions today, the ancient Greeks considered water a liminal, otherworldly substance; a gateway to the otherworld which could be found in the unexplored depths hidden beneath the waves. It was this boundary between the worlds, this horizon between above and below, that Dionysos broke when he descended into the bottomless Alkyonian Lake to find Ariadne – the same lake into which offerings of lambs were historically cast to Dionysos. The Alkyonian Lake was also known as Kingfisher's Pool, perhaps forging a similarity between Dionysos and this bird of the air which plunges into the depths of water for its survival. In neo-paganism, the kingfisher is sometimes used as a symbol for the wounded hero the *Fisher King* who finds his roots in the Celtic *Bran the Blessed* – and like Dionysos, Bran was associated with a cauldron of resurrection. The River Hebros was also known for its connection with the worship of Dionysos as the *'wounded god'*, into which the body parts of Orpheus were thrown by the frenzied Maenads who tore him apart.

---

[241] The Great Dionysiac Myth Vol.1, Robert Brown, (1877) 2000: P.255

"... brekekekex koax koax .... marshy children of the waters...let us sing my sweet song, koaxkoax, which for Nysian Dionysos, son of Zeus, we sang at Limnae... "[242]

Certainly, whilst Dionysos was connected with the ocean he was also associated with lakes, springs and marshlands. Unlike the ocean, these were usually considered as feminine in nature, perhaps once again recalling his androgynous form. The Satyrs of Dionysos were known to preside over these bodies of water, and a prophetic Satyr named Silenus (by some accounts the tutor of Dionysos) was said to have given Dionysos the moisture he needed to make grapes juicy, and mead refreshing. Indeed, Dionysos also hydrated trees with his revitalizing waters and Plutarch states that the ancients considered Dionysos as not only the creator of wine but also of liquid and life-giving moisture as a whole.[243] The *Etymologicium Magnum* (c.1150 CE) gives an account of Dionysos as *Dionysos Huês* meaning *'moist nature'* or *'rainy'*, because rain was often seen as a sign that sacrifices should be made to him. The Greek orator Demosthenes also mentioned the epithet *Huês* in his account of Dionysian ritual cries: *'euoi saboi, huês attes, attes hues!'*

---

[242] *Frogs*, 209ff, Aristophanes, c. 400 BCE, trans. M. Dillon
[243] *Moralia*, 745a, 757f, Plutarch, c. 100 CE

Chapter 5

Sacrifice, Dismemberment & Rejuvenation

Dionysos is a diverse character with a multitude of roles, masks, responsibilities and facades. However, one particular theme can be found running through almost every aspect of his nature – that of sacrifice, dismemberment (or *sparagmos*) and rejuvenation.

In many ways, this aspect of his nature came hand in hand with his involvement with hunting. The type of hunting that Dionysos was known to aid included both blood and bloodless sport – both hunting to kill and live capture. For instance, many manhood rites of the *ephebeia* (youth training institutions with links to Dionysos) included hunting with a net to bring the quarry back alive.[244] In a similar sense, many followers of Dionysos were known for devouring bloody raw flesh, whilst many others were strict vegetarians. Suggestive of Dionysos' paradoxical nature, this was also reflected in the role he was known to play during the actual hunt. Because, whilst Dionysos was known for his role as the savage hunter (*Anax Agreus*, or *Agrionios*) he was <u>also</u> identified with the prey animal itself. The humble goat is a good example of this paradox: the goat was known as the enemy of Dionysos for its destructive grazing on grapevines, and sacrificed to him in a form of divine retribution. However, it was also seen as the embodiment of him, and in this case sacrificed as a symbol of his regeneration. Indeed it was said that from the blood of Dionysos Zagreus, the first grapevine grew.

The male goat (or by some accounts, a ram) was of particular importance in the Dionysian legends of rejuvenation. In the Orphic Mysteries, an initiate was known to rise up to the realm of the gods

---

[244] Ashmolean Catalogue: Heracles to Alexander the Great, 2011: P.78

by sacrificing a goat – a belief which probably originated in the legend of how Dionysos Zagreus was torn apart by the Titans, and his body parts were boiled up in a cooking pot and eaten. When Zeus discovered what the Titans had done, he struck them down with a thunderbolt and they turned to ash; from this ash the human body was formed. By sacrificing and ingesting the goat in a similar way, the initiate reaffirmed the state of the human body; a form which was both Dionysian and Titan – the older gods, who were the children of Gaia. He or she was transformed from one state to another. Dionysos was also reborn into a new incarnation after he was murdered, further forging the connection between destruction and recreation.

The theme of Dionysian regeneration also made an appearance in the legends of Medea: the enchantress and priestess of Hekate, who owned a rejuvenative cauldron of her own. Jason had finally completed his quest to retrieve the Golden Fleece in order to claim the kingdom of Iolcus; but when Jason brought the ram's fleece to King Pelias and tried to claim his throne, the old King refused to stand down. Medea – who was in love with Jason – decided to intervene. She called the daughters of the elderly King together and showed them the fantastic regenerative powers of her cauldron. She slaughtered an old ram (or goat) cut it into pieces, and threw it into her cooking pot, boiling the parts up. Almost immediately the ram sprung back out of the pot, now a youthful lamb, full of life. She did the same with the nurses of Dionysos, and they too all sprang back to life – youthful, refreshed and rejuvenated. Medea was also well known for offering the Bakkhoi of Dionysos their youth back as well as using her knowledge of magic for healing purposes. So convinced of the cauldron's powers, the daughters were certain that it could restore their fathers' youth; foolishly, they set upon him and ripped him to pieces, dismembering him with their bare hands. But when they placed the parts of his body into Medea's pot, nothing happened - the spell had failed to work. They had been tricked by Medea – their father was dead, and Jason claimed his rightful place as the King of Iolcus. A piece of pottery found in Italy circa 460 BCE clearly illustrates Medea's regenerative cauldron. Medea is shown wearing an ivy-wreath (the crown of Dionysos) in her hair, as she leads an old man towards a cooking pot which is sat upon a tripod; a young boy is also shown, symbolic of the result of the spell.

Medea's connection with themes of dismemberment didn't end there. After it was discovered that Medea had been instrumental in the old Kings' death, Medea and Jason were forced to leave their new home in Iolcus and flee to Corinth with their children. But whilst they were there, Jason met another woman and left Medea for her. Furious, Medea ripped apart her own children and murdered them in a state of frenzy – similar to that of the women of Argos, who were accounted to have devoured the flesh of their own children in a state of madness induced by Dionysos after they disregarded him. Incidentally, Corinth is known to have been the location of a temple and a number of sacred caves dedicated to *Dionysos Omadios 'taker of sacrifices'.*

Sacrifice and dismemberment was common in Dionysian legend – and the act of dismemberment was often used to illustrate these myths, just as the myths illustrated the ritual act. Just like the women of Argos who ripped apart and devoured the flesh of their own animals and children, Pentheus (the King of Thebes) was also dismembered by Dionysian maenads for opposing Dionysos. He too was restored to physical completeness – but not being a Dionysian initiate, his dismemberment led to permanent death rather than rebirth! Orpheus, the pseudo-historical poet identified with Dionysos and Sabazios was murdered by Maenads after he refused their advances, and his body parts were thrown into a river. King Lykourgos of Thrace chased Dionysos out of his city and was driven insane; murdering and dismembering his son. Later, he was dismembered himself after a Delphic oracle proclaimed he should be sacrificed to bring fertility back to the land. And a Greek hero named Acteon was turned into a stag and ripped apart by his own hunting dogs after coming across Artemis whilst she bathed; Artemis was of course identified with Sabazios and Dionysos and often worshipped alongside them.

"... they swooped down upon the herds of cattle ... a single woman with bare hands tore a fat calf, still bellowing with fright, in two ... There were ribs and cloven hooves scattered everywhere, and scraps smeared with blood hung from the fir trees. And bulls, their fury gathered in their horns, lowered their heads to

charge, then fell, stumbling to the earth, pulled down by hordes of women and stripped of flesh and skin ..." [245]

Briefly returning to the story of the Golden Fleece, we find another interesting dismemberment story. According to legend, Jason had to plough a field and plant the land with dragon's teeth; these teeth immediately grew into soldiers who Jason had to defeat. This story finds its origins in the older myth of Kadmos, another character closely associated and identified with Dionysos, who slew an earth serpent who protected a sacred lake. Athena instructed Kadmos to plant the serpents' teeth, from which the *Spartoi* grew – a tribe of ancestral warriors known as *'sown men'*, *'children of the serpent'*, or *'soil-sprung'*.

"... gliding down out of the sky, Athena appears and bids him plough the soil and plant the serpent's teeth, from which all future people should arise ... with his plough (he) *opens wide furrow, then across the soil scatters the teeth, the seed of mankind. The* (soil) *began to stir : first points of spears were seen, next helmets ... then shoulders, chests, and weapon-laden arms arose, a growing crop of men ..."* [246]

In their new-born confusion they destroyed and dismembered each other, except for five men who became the comrades of Kadmos. The links of this story with Dionysos are numerous. According to some accounts the earth serpent was sacred to Ares, the half-brother of Dionysos who is often identified with him. The serpent of this story is also protecting a sacred site; reminiscent of the earth serpent of Delphi – Dionysos in serpent form. The parts of the serpent are scattered upon the land and new life is born; reflecting the importance of Dionysos within the cycle of regeneration, and reminiscent of the Orphic legends of how mankind was created from the ashes of the god. The men born are believed to be the ancestors; reminiscent of the connection between Dionysos and the spirits of the dead, or the *chthonioi*, *'earth-people'.* [247]

---

[245] The Bacchae, 735-746, Euripides, c. 400 BCE, trans. W Arrowsmith

[246] Metamorphoses, 3. 101 ff, Ovid C1st BCE - C1st CE, trans. Melville

[247] Themis - A Study of the Social Origins of Greek Religion, Jane Ellen Harrison (1912, 2010: P.292

Purpose, Meaning & Method

Sacrifice was an important part of Greek religion, but its meaning and nature would often vary depending on who the deity was and for what purpose the sacrifice was being made. In Dionysian rites, it was often used to symbolise or encourage the return or rejuvenation of the god, the theme of resurrection. As part of this, the sacrifice also demonstrated his ability to traverse the worlds; above and below – this life and the next. Indeed in the *Odyssey*, Odysseus uses the blood of cattle in order to create a gateway to the underworld[248] a good example of this principle. And during the Festival of Awakening (when the Thyiads of Delphi ceremonially searched Mount Parnassos for the reborn Dionysos) secret sacrifices were made in the temple of Apollo[249] – one life assured by the sacrifice of another, a common motif in both myth and religion.

Offerings were made of oils, perfumes, wine, fruit and other fine things – but for very important rites, animal sacrifice was particularly popular. The subject of animal sacrifice is highly controversial and in **no way** do I condone such an act for ritual or magic today. Because – besides being unethical – it is also rather irrelevant: to our ancestors, animals were some of their most precious commodities. To give us a very rough idea, a small piglet was worth around three drachmas – which in ancient Greece was about three days' wages for a middle class worker – so perhaps £150 modern English Pounds. Aristophanes writes, *'lend me 3 drachmae to buy a young pig; I wish to have myself initiated before I die.'*[250] And indeed it was not piglets, but *Cattle* – inordinately more precious in ancient Greece – which were seen to be one of the most fitting sacrifices for Dionysos. In addition, the animals being sacrificed would have taken time, effort and money to keep – accounts are made of bulls being at least six years of age before being sacrifices, therefore this would have been an offering of wealth and time as well as blood. Then, depending on the nature of the sacrifice once the rite was complete the animal parts would be divided, cooked and eaten. Looking at this evidence, it is not difficult to see that an animal offering is simply not relevant to our lives today;

---

[248] Seidr: The Gate is Open, Katie Gerrard, 2011: P.182
[249] Dionysus Myth & Cult, Walter F Otto (1960) 1995: P.190
[250] Peace, 361ff, Aristophanes, c. 420 BCE, trans. Eugene O' Neill, Jr., Ed.

but having identified what our ancestors' idea of a sufficient offering was, it sets the bar rather higher for our own offerings (which in my experience of the modern western tradition quite often ranges from the inadequate to the downright insulting!)

How sacrifices were made would also vary, but in general for a sacrifice to a chthonic deity such as Dionysos, the sacrifice would have been made into a pit in the earth either a man-made cavity or a natural chasm. By some accounts[251] a circle would be drawn around the sacrificial space with a knife, which would have segregated the sacred space off from the crowd who were witnessing the rite. If an animal was being sacrificed, the head of the animal would have been turned down towards the earth when it was sacrificed, unlike the Olympian gods for whom the head would have been turned up towards the sky. Sacrificial tools were also important: the spear was often used for sacrifice, but the double headed axe (reminiscent of the *keraunos* axe of the bull cults of Minoan Crete) became particularly associated with sacrifices to Dionysos – and the three-headed double bladed axe became a popular decoration cast in bronze during the Temid Dynasty in Macedonia.[252] In a particularly Dionysian fashion, wine would then be poured upon the earth next to the blood of the animal after the sacrifice in libation[253] and finally any tool used during the sacrifice was cast into a body of water, as it was believed that the sin of the person who had slaughtered the animal (and therefore the god himself) would be bound to the blade that they used.

But what of human sacrifice? Certainly, human sacrifices were made to Dionysos at one time and they have been accounted, particularly on the islands of Chios and Tendos where they were offered to *Dionysos Omadios 'eater of raw flesh'*. Some modern researchers believe that human sacrifices would have originally been preferred, and that animal sacrifice was only brought in later as a substitute to human sacrifice. However for a deity like Dionysos I tend to disagree, particularly if we consider how important the animal form of Dionysos was to his followers. Indeed, there are accounts made of a Dionysian Priest in the Greek village of Chaironeia who started to

[251] Ashmolean Catalogue: Heracles to Alexander the Great, 2011: P.77
[252] Ashmolean Catalogue: Heracles to Alexander the Great, 2011: P.97,98
[253] The God Who Comes, Rosemarie Taylor-Perry, 2003: P.79

perform human sacrifices, but suddenly died of a mysterious disease; this was taken as a bad omen from Dionysos and thereafter human sacrifices were prohibited there.

Eating Raw Flesh – and Vegetarianism

Consuming sacrificial food items was actually quite common within the worship of most deities in ancient Greece and beyond, and it was customary for sacrifices to be divided up and eaten amongst by the celebrants. Usually it was grilled or boiled first and then handed out afterwards. But the rites of Dionysos were different. Although meat is known to have been cooked within Dionysian rites, Dionysos is well known for his association with the consumption of raw meat (known as *Omophagia*) and as such he was known as *Dionysos Omestes*, *'eater of raw flesh'*.

An inscription from Miletus in Phrygia suggests the eating of raw flesh dates back to 276 BCE at the earliest, but it is probably much more ancient than that. Why the practice was carried out is uncertain. One possibility is that the flesh was seen as the body of Dionysos himself, and therefore by eating the meat the initiate would become part of the god. Whilst a valid theory for the consumption of meat as a whole, it doesn't explain why the meat would have to be raw; and surviving accounts detailing the consumption of raw meat do not seem to make any reference to the raw meat being the body of the god.[254] We also know that several particularly ancient Dionysian legends make reference to the importance of boiling up the god's flesh in a cooking pot as an extremely important part of his transformation from one state to another, so again, this doesn't make sense. According to legend, when King Lykourgos was dismembered (a character often considered akin to Dionysos), his limbs were put into a tripod basin before burial which was fashioned in a shape reminiscent of the oracular tripod of Delphi; this perhaps suggests links between the alchemy of the cooking pot, transformation, and oracular messages; the inevitability of death and rebirth and occult implications of resurrection for Dionysos and his initiates. Certainly, eating the meat of the animals seen to embody Dionysos was a way

---

[254] Dionysus Myth & Cult, Walter F Otto (1960) 1995: P.132

for the initiate to unify with the god through the consumption of his body; just as drinking wine was the consumption of his blood. But this doesn't explain why the meat had to be raw.

A possible reason for the consumption of raw meat in particular, was that the practice was a part of entering the ecstatic domain and becoming set apart from everyday society. Indeed it is known that in classical times, the eating of raw meat was in fact *an act of defiance against state-sanctioned rules of worship*[255] and it was with this final act that the initiate stepped over the threshold and into a truly *'wild world'*. Here, the Bakkhoi joined the spirit of the hunter and the untameable beasts of the wild: such as the leopard and the serpent. By the reversal of the norm and the abandonment of rationality, the Bakkhoi was delivered into a state of ecstatic frenzy where he or she was liberated from the constraints of humanity. The Christian writer Clement of Alexandria wrote that the Bacchants *'excited their madness'* by eating raw flesh suggesting that this indeed aid the initiate to shapeshift: running through the night and swaying like a serpent, or leaping like a leopard. It is no wonder that Maenads (responsible for consuming raw meat by most accounts) so often wore leopard skins; and at other times the skin of a fawn – the prey.

Curiously, a number of accounts describe how the consumption of raw meat during rites of a Dionysian nature was actually *part of a rite of vegetarianism* within that cult. Indeed a number of accounts describe how raw meat was eaten as part of an initiation rite which was followed by a long period of vegetarianism, as the initiate abstained from meat of any kind. This may have been practiced as a form of purification, and may also have focused on the duality of the god:

'... *having fulfilled the life of the night-wandering Zagreus and the raw flesh eating feasts, and held up the torches of the Mountain Mother and having been purified, Bakchos of the Korybantes I invoked. Clad in white, I fly the race of mortals ... and I have been guarded against the eating of live food ...* '[256]

---

[255] The God Who Comes, Rosemarie Taylor-Perry, 2003: P.15

[256] Kretes, Porphyry (Source: The Great Dionysiac Myth Vol.1, Robert Brown (1877) 2000)

The practice of vegetarianism eventually became integrated into Orphism and later Pythagoreanism; Pythagoras himself being an initiate of the Orphic Mysteries.

There is of course a good reason why humans don't normally eat raw meat; all raw meats are susceptible to quickly becoming contaminated with potentially fatal bacteria and parasites which cause food poisoning, gastroenteritis, salmonella – and worse. It is possible that the ancient Greeks had stronger stomachs, perhaps a greater immunity – or perhaps they were just lucky. But even a rare *'blue'* steak is flash-fried both sides in order to kill off any potential bacteria; and so I would not recommend the modern practitioner to introduce any kind of *Omophagia* into their practice! However, it is possible to alter your food choices to become more in line with the Dionysian way of thinking. Choose more organic and unprocessed foods, and try eating vegetables such as carrots raw instead of cooked, and drink fresh fruit juices instead of tea and coffee, or even vegetarianism. Whilst this might not seem quite as radical as eating raw flesh, you'll be surprised what a change this can be – and how it will liberate you from the supermarket shelves.

Chapter 6

Dionysos as Liberator: Eleutherios and Liber

The figure of the Liberator, found in the Hellenic epithets: *Eleutherios 'liberator'* and *Lysios 'of release'* or *'releasing'* is one of prime importance when studying and connecting with this far-reaching divinity. This is even more apparent when you examine the name of his Roman equivalent the god Liber, whose name came to mean *'free'* in Latin. *'Liber'* is the root of many modern English words relating to freedom such as *'liberation'*, *'liberator'*, *'liberty'* and *'liberal'* and therefore it would be reasonable to suggest that he is a guise of Dionysos that has never truly left us - even if remaining only for the most part in our language.

Dionysos the Liberator is a comprehensive guise of the god, and one that is related to many different forms of liberation. This can be from freedom from actual imprisonment, to spiritual liberation sought through ecstasy, to freedom from the constraints of the polis and society, and even liberation from the very laws of nature, bursting the bonds that regulate the cosmos.[257] By removing restrictions, we tap into the powers of primordial chaos; we return to the creative origin of all things.

Freedom from imprisonment

"And the Bacchae whom you shut up, whom you carried off and bound in the chains of the public prison, are set loose and gone — they are gamboling in the meadows, invoking Dionysos as their god. Of their own accord, the chains were loosened from their feet, and keys opened the doors without human hand."[258]

---

[257] Tearing Apart the Zagreus Myth, Radcliffe Edmonds, 1999
[258] The Bacchae, 444-450, Euripides, c. 400 BCE, trans. TA Buckley

Here, in Euripides' *The Bacchae*, we have an example of the first type of liberation to which Dionysos can be attributed to: that of freedom from actual imprisonment. Here the Maenads, who had been imprisoned by King Pentheus of Thebes, managed to escape without help from any mortal hand for their fastenings loosened and the locked doors swung open, freeing them as if by magic. In the cases of King Pentheus and also with Lykourgos, it is Dionysos who frees his Maenad followers; removing their chains and unlocking their prison doors, which seems to occur without visible cause. There are several other legends which seem to parallel the Lykourgos story: in the myth in which he is captured by Tyrrhenian (Etruscan) pirates he frees himself with ease, and transforms their ship into a great vine tree and his captors into dolphins. Here, he reveals himself as *Eribromos 'loud-shouting'*. By this time, the shy boy who needed Zeus' aid when he was driven into the sea is now *Agrionios 'the savage'*[259] a form in which he was greatly celebrated.

This is a motif that appears amongst several Dionysian myths; and a reoccurring theme that is all too apparent in narratives describing his arrival to new cities and territories. Dionysos and his followers arrive at this new city or locale, where they immediately face opposition from a ruling king and rival divinities who refuse to acknowledge the god's divine status. Subsequently Dionysos or his Bakkhoi are thrown into a jail, or repressed, until Dionysos decides to free them. This liberation and consequent triumph over his captors led to an establishment of his cult within that given centre. This hints at the power of the cult of Dionysos, at least in archaic and classical times – one that was far too prevalent and powerful to be repressed or denied. Any successes the leaders have in driving Dionysos out are short-lived, and usually followed by a complete triumph of Dionysos over their city. This is a powerful symbol of the Dionysian spirit: one that is free and uncompromising, and cannot be imprisoned in rigid structures but must be allowed to grow and manifest.

---

[259] The Great Dionysiac Myth Vol.1, Robert Brown, (1877) 2000: P.27

The Liberation of Spirit

"Everything that has been locked up is released. The alien and the hostile unite in miraculous harmony. Age-old laws have suddenly lost their power, and even the dimensions of time and space are no longer valid. The ecstasy begins – in the mythical sphere – at the moment when the god enters the world."[260]

An important area in which Dionysos Eleutherios was connected was the ecstatic domain: a sphere that led to spiritual liberation and a freeing of the soul as participants shifted their consciousness and entered the realm of the gods. This they did through collective song, cathartic dancing, shamanistic bestial rites, orgiastic mania and Dionysian spirit possession – the domain of *Dionysos Epaphios*, *'god who inspires frenzy'*.[261] He is the associate of Kybele, the bronze-rattling Phrygian goddess of ritual frenzy, and the loud-shouting god of pandemonium, the inciter of orgiastic ritual accompanied by horns, drums, salpinx and cymbals. Dancing amongst them, Dionysos *cleansed their minds of their troubles*[262] and caused a change in consciousness. These ecstatic initiatory rites, coupled with a connection to the chthonic realm with which they wished to attune themselves, allowed them to free their souls and venture into Dionysos' divine realm; entering a state in which invocation, spirit possession and oracular messages were possible. As Madame Blavatsky writes:

"…before an initiate could see the gods in their purest light, he had to become liberated from his body; i.e., to separate his astral soul from it."[263]

Of course another way to achieve this spiritual liberation, and one to which Dionysos is most infamously and intimately connected, was the consumption of drugs or alcohol in order to help free the soul from the body. This was a practice that was particularly characteristic of Dionysos' orgiastic worship, the belief being that the drunkenness induced by wine consumption helped participants to

---

[260] Dionysus Myth & Cult, Walter F Otto (1960) 1995: P.96

[261] The God Who Comes, Rosemarie Taylor-Perry, 2003: P.9

[262] See Classical Antiquity 17, 'Dionysos and Katharsis in Antigone', Scott Scullion, 1998: P.96-122

[263] Phaedrus, Plato c. C3rd BCE Source: Isis Unveiled Vol. 2, H.P. Blavatsky (1877) 2008: P.143

free themselves from their material cares and to prepare themselves for *perceiving higher realities*.[264] A modern day parallel can be found in the Hindu *Tantra Raja*, where it is said:

"Those who have known supreme liberation and those who become or strive to become adepts always make use of wine."[265]

Despite making an appearance in several modern mystery traditions (including the early Wiccan rites) the use of intoxicating substances such as drugs and alcohol to change the consciousness and aid trance is something that has come to be frowned upon in modern magical and religious practice, and as a result has been *'written out'* by many working groups and modern authors. However I believe that this is an area that should not be entirely dismissed. Certainly, I do not - and never will - promote the use of illegal drugs (or an unprescribed excess of legal drugs or alcohol) for *any* purpose. However, the consumption of alcohol played an important part in many ancient mystery cults, and so to dismiss it entirely without analysis would be a mistake. As we have already indentified, alcohol was not consumed in large quantities for the majority of it was mixed with water. Rather, in small quantities, it worked as a catalyst to help shift the consciousness of practitioners, removing them from their ordinary states of consciousness.

"The rational faculties are clouded by...drink, and the animal nature, liberated from bondage, controls the individual – facts which necessarily were of the greatest spiritual significance."[266]

Lastly, Dionysos would become representative of the free and untamed spirit at the heart of all mankind, and even the mystery gods themselves - who despite their described appearances, were not in fact limited to their proscribed forms. Jane Harrison explains it beautifully when she writes:

---

[264] Shiva and Dionysus: Gods of Love and Ecstasy, Alain Daniélou, (1979) 1992: P.154

[265] Tantra Raja (VIII)

[266] The Secret Teachings of All Ages, Manly P. Hall (1928) 2008: P.275

"They are caught, fettered for an instant in lovely human shapes; but they are life-spirits barely held; they shift and change. Dionysos is a human youth, lovely with curled hair, but in a moment he is a wild bull and a burning flame. The beauty and the thrill of it!"[267]

Oppression & War

"You, and you alone, shall suffer for this city."[268]

More often than not, the city-state rulers who were seen to reject the Dionysian cult are portrayed as being tyrants and oppressors, hinting at another expression of Dionysos Eleutherios: that of the liberator of people from oppressive rule, the protector of those who deserve mercy, and the conquest of other societies in the name of culture. It is here that we also see Dionysos' connection with democracy - an association that was celebrated in the city of Athens, which was a strong proponent of the democratic way. In this guise, Dionysos was associated with bringing civilisation and a sense of liberation to the people. This could have been actual liberation (as we can see with the myths of King Pentheus and King Lykourgos). This justification for invasion could also be seen as being an early equivalent of the view taken by the Roman Empire: (something that again resurfaced with the major European powers during the Colonial Era) the belief that primitive nations were better off under the control of civilised empires than they were on their own, and that the imperial powers were bringing civilisation to the ignorant masses. A very recent equivalent could be found in the Iraq War (which incidentally was known as *'Operation Iraqi Freedom'*) where the coalition's stated goal was to *'bring democracy'* to the Middle East nation; liberating its people from Saddam Hussein. Whether this was indeed the case is of course a matter of dispute, but one that is still comparable to Dionysos' mythic invasions.

However, it could have been a justification for conquering other nations and territories. This was certainly true of the Dionysian myth

---

[267] Myths of Greece and Rome, Jane Harrison (1927) 2007: P.74
[268] Dionysos to Pentheus - The Bacchae, 963-966, Euripides, c. 400 BCE, trans. TA Buckley

regarding the invasion of India, where invading forces were said to have taught the indigenous population religion and to have *'civilised'* them. This seems likely to be a mythological version of Alexander the Great's invasion of India, for Alexander and Dionysos were often identified with one another in myth and legend and their stories conflated. Alexander the Great was sometimes referred to as being *'the new Dionysos'* and it is probable that his real invasion of India was an influence on Dionysos' mythic one. The conquest of India is just one of the many accounts of *Dionysos Lyaios '(deliverer) under arms'*, and there are several battles which feature throughout the myths of Dionysos. Many of these battle accounts probably find their origins in the introduction of the cult of Dionysos to new shores - conquests in which the god himself would have been considered as the *'leader'* at the forefront of the occupation. To the Bakkhoi of Dionysos and his converts he would have indeed been seen as a liberating force and his conquering of cities and territories would have fit Dionysos' connection with the removal of boundaries - in this case the borders of various nations, tribes and societies. This greater unified empire then could have been seen as a Dionysian ideal: one without boundaries and without end. A relatively modern equivalent could be found in the USSR and with communism, which removed many of the cultural and economic boundaries throughout its extensive empire and that promised (even if it didn't always deliver) equality for all.

Dionysos Deliverer Under Arms

The role of Dionysos as a god of war is often understated: indeed, even some of the sacred objects of Dionysos were actually instruments of war and invasion. For instance the Salpinx trumpet, an instrument which is described as having an unmelodic shrill or piercing sound, and which was often depicted being played by his satyrs in their festival choruses. This instrument in fact used by soldiers on the battlefield to command their troops, and was described by Aristotle as an instrument with which **not** to make music; but of course, the piercing and somewhat chaotic nature of the Salpinx would probably have created a fitting cacophony to accompany the raving revels of Dionysos. Even a dance which was sacred to Dionysos (and performed during the City Dionysia) was associated with movements upon the battlefield; it came to be known as the Military Square.

It is important to relate however, that many of the mythological battles between Dionysos and rejecting kings and city-states were more likely symbolical confrontations rather than actual skirmishes. This was likely representative of the original rejection of the Dionysian cult and the eventual acceptance through time and the proselytisation of citizens. There wasn't quite the same religious persecution that we see in the world today; in the domains of ancient religion - foreign equivalents were usually identified with regional deities rather than entirely condemned or demonised. Certainly, rival gods had contests with one another – and these contests often found their way into their myths and legends. But ultimately, there was usually a union of rituals and symbology with both cultures integrating something from the other. It has even been suggested that his role as *Dimetor* (born of two mothers) could be related to the fact that his cult was not entirely conceived within Greece herself, but also from the '*outerworld*' – in other words, foreign lands.[269] His cults were embraced by Greece and nurtured within the cults already there. This would have given Dionysian followers ample opportunity to spread their orgiastic cult throughout the Hellenic world with very little physical resistance. Mythological narratives like those of Lykourgos and Pentheus could have spoken of some opposition, indeed from the higher rungs of society, though it is interesting to note that it does not come from religious leaders and the priesthood but from the civic leadership: the king of the city-state. This shows that indeed the major threat that Dionysianism posed was not a religious revolution but a social one, one that threatened to deny power to tyrannical leaders and monarchic powers. Perhaps this then explains why he held such prominence in the city of Athens, where democracy, and not monarchism, ruled.

So what threat did Dionysos pose to absolute rulers and the aristocracy? Why were the tyrants so threatened by the Dionysian cult? This brings us to another domain of Dionysos Eleutherios, that of civic or social liberation.

---

[269] The Great Dionysiac Myth Vol.1, Robert Brown, (1877) 2000: P.31

Social & Civic Liberation and Equality

A reoccurring motif of orgiastic cults is the abolishment of social barriers. This is a characteristic that appears throughout Dionysian mythology and in accounts of the cult of Dionysos: the belief that Dionysos was the god of the people, and that within his worship all people were treated equally. All people ate together during Dionysian festivals and they danced, sang hymns and marched in Dionysian processions together. On Dionysian feast days roles were often reversed and slaves could order their masters about; something that was echoed throughout the ancient world and was apparent in the middle ages in Western Europe in Ireland's Beltane celebrations and England's May Day. A modern equivalent can still be found in the Indian spring festival of Holi, a festival which is celebrated around the same time as the ancient Greater Dionysia would have occurred, where artisans and servants have the right to insult and ill-treat their masters, the nobles and even priests.[270] The inversion of roles and duties found in ordinary civic life allowed for participants to embrace the wilderness and their own wilder natures: for, *it is through trickery and the perverse, irrational rites of the mysteries that both heaven and earth can be conquered.'*[271]

The high status afforded to slaves and poor workers in the cult of Dionysos further reflects his position as a *'god of the people'* - a view that was distorted and overturned in subsequent cults such as Orphism which took a much more elitist view; this view was not shared by earlier adherents of the Dionysian current. To them, Dionysos was a god of those who lived on the fringes of society – of those who were otherwise looked down upon or oppressed, and those who followed alternative lifestyles. He embodied the empowerment of those who might otherwise be marginalized, such as slaves and the poor – and women, who were held in high regard within *thiasos*. In early Dionysian cults it was only women or transsexuals who could participate.

---

[270] Shiva and Dionysus: Gods of Love and Ecstasy, Alain Daniélou, (1979) 1992: P.71

[271] Shiva and Dionysus: Gods of Love and Ecstasy, Alain Daniélou, (1979) 1992: P.90

Indeed, male celebrants are usually only found to participate in early Dionysiac revels when dressed in a woman's clothing (or dressed as animals). This can be found in Euripides' *The Bacchae* when Dionysos says of Pentheus: *"first drive him out of his wits, send him upon a dizzying madness, since if he is of sound mind he will not consent to wearing women's clothing, but driven out of his senses he will put it on."*[272] Here we perhaps have a connection with a primal ecstatic form of Dionysianism, one that is akin to shamanism and to some branches of Hindu mysticism such as Shaivism: the belief that when dressed in women's clothing a male mystic can bridge the gap between male and female, the *anima* and the *animus*[273] and by doing so, can journey between the worlds. Dionysos is also often depicted wearing the *peplos* (the dress/robe of a woman) together with the *zoster* (the warrior belt of a man) again, bridging the genders and placing himself in the centre of all things, as the *axis mundi*. Dionysos was often depicted in this particular costume along with other cosmological attire, portraying him as a prime mover in the creation of the universe – perhaps suggesting that this balance of male and female was seen as being of primary importance to the demiurge. Many aspects of Dionysos' worship were about role reversal. Even his birth demonstrated a stark reversal of the usual way of things; instead of a woman giving birth to him he was born from the thigh of Zeus, a male deity. And by some accounts, he was raised in a womens' gynaecaeum where he was dressed in female garments to hide him from Hera. Aiskhylos called Dionysos *Gynnis*, 'womanly one', and Euripides described him as *'the womanly stranger'*.[274] This position within the *'marginal realms'* was the domain of the mystic who must journey between the worlds; and it was likely for this reason that members of the transgender community were considered privileged within a Dionysian society.

Nor was it unusual to be bisexual or homosexual during the Classical and Hellenistic periods. Dionysos himself was known to have an affection for young men (and why *should* he choose one gender over another, when he stands in a *'place between'*!!) In turn, it was quite common for Kings to have male companions in addition to

---

[272] The Bacchae, 851-854, Euripides, c. 400 BCE, trans. TA Buckley

[273] Craft of the Wise, Vikki Bramshaw, 2009: P.112

[274] See Euripides & Alcestis, Kiki Gounaridou, 1998 P.72

their wives – something which both Philip II and Alexander the Great of Macedonia are believed to have enjoyed. Certainly, the value of a man was not judged by his sexual preference, demeanour or even his appearance. By 400 BCE, Dionysos had already developed a new image – in the shape of a *'clean-cut'* attractive and effeminate youth. This sort of appearance had become very popular for many of the deities in the Classical era, something which becomes obvious when we start to look at statues of the gods from this period of time: youthful, smooth-faced and the body of an Adonis.

Of course, Dionysos had always possessed two opposing faces – that of the young god, and that of the older *'bearded'* god, who was a stark contrast to the effeminate youth and who was still seen depicted on pottery and mosaics in 600 BCE. Of course, Dionysos could move between these two states; and it was only with the Classical era that the older, bearded Dionysos began to be phased out and he began to remain in his classically feminine form. The Romans would later develop this image even further in their own interpretation of the god: Bacchus.

Chapter 7

God of Possession & the Oracles

"Then, looking down at the earth, the god gave a loud hiss and the earth was opened ... It gave birth to a creature of its own, the Pythian serpent, who foreknew all things..."[275]

The modern English word *enthusiasm* has its origins in the Greek *enthousiasmos*, from *enthous* *'possessed by a god, inspired'* (based on *theos* *'god'*) and describes the Dionysian expression of zöe: the spirit of life, through the liberation of the spirit and unification of mortal with god. An archaic meaning of the word is *'religious fervour'*, supposedly resulting directly from divine inspiration - typically involving *'speaking in tongues and wild, uncoordinated movements of the body'.*[276] Dionysian initiations also often involved speaking in riddles, to intrigue and confuse the initiate during the rites. The English word *ecstasy* also has its origins in Greek, from the word *ekstasis* *'standing outside oneself'* perhaps referring to the feeling of absence from the physical body which is experienced during a spirit/deity possession. A secondary meaning in modern English is *'an emotional or religious frenzy or trance-like state, originally one involving an experience of mystic self-transcendence.'*[277]

"The union of man with God came regularly through Ekstasis—the soul must get clear of its body—and Enthousiasmos—the God must enter and dwell inside the worshipper."[278]

---

[275] PGM XIII 343 – 646

[276] Oxford English Dictionary

[277] Oxford English Dictionary

[278] Five Stages of Greek Religion (studies based on a course of lectures, 1912) Gilbert Murray, 1955: P.144

These two words, enthusiasm and ecstasy, lay at the heart of Dionysos' connection with trance-possession and hearkened back to an earlier form of this archaic god - one that was ancient even to the classical Hellenes themselves. This was the god of *orgia* (ecstatic rites) whose worship was celebrated with energetic dance, intoxication, and often simply unrestrained frenzy: one of the most primal of all religious practices which employed the channelling of energy through the blood and releasing it through sweat and breath; much like the practice of Seething in Norse mysticism.[279] In this way the initiate also became *'tabula rasa'*; (a blank slate) –the self had been removed to such a degree that their bodies became a direct channel of a divine force and the deity could reside within (and merge with) the body of the celebrant. This is a method that is still found today in many primitive communities, mystic practices and even in more established religious traditions such as Voudou and Hinduism. Whilst *'riding'* the body of the celebrant the deity might even speak or prophesise, and there are countless tales of mortals having received divine information from the gods. For instance in *The Bacchae*, a priest offers the mysteries of Dionysos declaring that he has received the *orgia* directly from the god himself.

"But she, foaming at the mouth and twisting her eyes all about ... was possessed by Bacchus ... seizing his left arm and propping her foot against the unfortunate man's side, she tore out his shoulder, not by her own strength, but the god-gave facility to her hands."[280]

This passage from Euripides' play, *The Bacchae*, gives us a good description (albeit an exaggerated one) of someone in the grips of Dionysian spirit possession: that is, becoming possessed by the spirit of Dionysos. The characteristic rolling of the eyes, rigid gaze, staggering or shaking movement and inhuman strength is a common motif found within extant ecstatic trance and spirit possession today, such as those found in the animistic faiths of West Africa and the Caribbean, amongst others. Such accounts of inhuman strength also point to another factor which may be in play here: adrenaline, a by-product of the excitement of the Dionysian rites which would have provided a boost of energy to the celebrants and allowed them to

---

[279] See Seidways: Shaking, Swaying and the Serpent Mysteries, Jan Fries, 2009
[280] The Bacchae, 1124-1129, Euripides, c. 400 BCE, trans. TA Buckley

move with a seemingly inhuman resistance to exhaustion. A similar Dionysian state can perhaps be witnessed in today's clubbing and rave music scene: a powerful atmosphere of loud trance-enducing music of successive repetitive beats intensified by heat, intoxication, and adrenaline-fuelled physical exertion.

> *"This is my church ...*
> *Content in the hum ...*
> *Between voice and drum ..."*[281]

A similar account of spirit possession is also found in the *Vishnu Purana*, an important Hindu text in which Ananta (one of the names of Vishnu) is described to: *"roll his eyes fiercely, as if intoxicated"*.[282] Here, we have another comparable example that binds together the Dionysian twin dominions of alcoholic intoxication and spiritual possession, two aspects of the god that are intrinsically linked - for Dionysos is a divinity that reigns over all ecstasy, whether caused by enthusiastic ritual, the consumption of drugs and alcohol, or music and dance. This is not to say that possession could not have occurred without the use of alcohol; but that like any other ritual tool (such as repetitive drumming, or sensory deprivation) it would have aided the Bakkhoi achieve the state of trance and possession. A series of sensory changes and external influences can achieve different levels of trance and changes to the consciousness; and a combination of many causes a deeper (although not necessarily a more beneficial) state.

As well as becoming possessed by the spirit of Dionysos himself, the celebrants would also have been able to open themselves up to a different kind of spirit possession: that of the spirits of the dead, or the *chthonioi*, *'earth-people'*.[283] As a cult that revered its ancestors and emulated the journeys of the dead, spiritual mediumship through spirit possession may well have occurred. Possession by both gods and ancestral spirits is common in many other shamanic trance traditions, such as Voudou and Norse mysticism – the last being the

---

[281] God is a DJ, Faithless, 1998

[282] The Vishnu Purana Book 2 Ch.5, c320CE, trans. HH Wilson

[283] P. Themis - A Study of the Social Origins of Greek Religion, Jane Ellen Harrison (1912) 2010: P.292

domain of the Norse god *Odin* who like Dionysos is also described as mad and ecstatic, a lord of souls, a wanderer,[284] and an initiator. As a psychopomp - with one foot in the world of the living and one foot in the world of the dead - Dionysos aided ecstatic trance methods which initiated a state of *'death'* for the practitioner who having traversed the worlds had like Dionysos endured and overcome death. This concept is reflected in the legends of Dionysos in which he was only considered a complete being (in his case, a complete god) after he had made both the descent into the underworld and returned - having both experienced and transcended death.

The quote from *The Bacchae* also reveals another important aspect to Dionysos' connection with ecstatic-trance and trance-possession: the importance of the *thiasos*, his mystical group of followers. For it is often only within the structure of the thiasos, a group of people working towards one goal, that we hear of ekstasis and enthousiasmos - divine ecstasy and possession. Jane Harrison, a classical scholar of the early twentieth century theorised that this was of great importance when approaching the ecstatic nature of Dionysos, writing that: *"Dionysos is the god of ecstasy, but it is ecstasy of the group, not the individual."*[285]

"Then the adept was rapt away in bliss, and the beyond of bliss, and exceeded the excess of excess. Also his body shook and staggered with the burden of that bliss and that excess and that ultimate nameless. They cried, he is drunk or he is mad or he is in pain and about to die; and he heard them not."[286]

Ecstatic trance, chaotic music and revelous dance stood in distinct contrast to the sober prayers and hymns with which most of the Olympian pantheon came to be worshipped, and it is likely for this reason that the Hellenes were so keen to label him a foreign god of *'barbarian'* origin. This is made clear by Herodotus, who accounts the wide scope of peoples worshipping Dionysos (or a god akin to him) from the Thracians of what is now known as Bulgaria to the Arabians of the Middle East, the Ethiopians of East Africa, the Egyptians/Libyans of North Africa and even the Scythians of what is

---

[284] The God Who Comes, Rosemarie Taylor-Perry, 2003: P.8

[285] Myths of Greece and Rome, Jane Harrison (1927) 2007 P.73

[286] Liber LXV, Aleister Crowley, 1919: Part II Lines 45-47

now the Ukraine.[287] Dionysos' mythic invasion shows that he was even seen as being worshipped as far east as India, and indeed everywhere that the ancient Greek chroniclers travelled they found this far-reaching god of ecstasy.

The myths of Dionysos repeatedly indicate both the benefits and the very real dangers of possession and trance. Like alcohol, the use of this method to change the consciousness is a paradoxical technique, which can result in either the *'right'* or the *'wrong'* kind of *'madness'*. Even today, there remains a fine line between the benefits and disadvantages of working with the spirit world – a thin boundary between *'spiritual advancement'* and *'madness'*. There seems to be a popular new-age trend right now which suggests that in order to advance spiritually, we must become disconnected from the mundane trappings of life and instead participate in an idealistic and sanitized (yet impractical and unrealistic) vision of the world. I would suggest that this is not only flawed but also dangerous. It is true that those of us working with the mysteries must learn to open our minds - perhaps more than ever before - in order to achieve liminality and step across into the otherworlds. Yet we must also have the ability to keep both feet firmly on the ground, and remain in touch with the physical and logical world that keeps us of sane mind – without compromising our intuitive abilities which allow us to cross the hedge and traverse the worlds.

Masked Possession

Euhai, Euhoi! – Ritual Dionysian cry

Dionysos' connection with masks and masked rites may have added to his ubiquity: the idea being that wherever these rites were being performed, Dionysos could be found by simply presenting the mask. This was especially true of the Bacchic masked revels, in which the donning of masks together with rites of an ecstatic nature went hand in hand - the wearing of masks was likely used as a tool to separate the individual from their normal everyday persona. When donning an animalistic mask this would have been even more so, by not only removing the celebrant from their everyday persona but also

---

[287] See *Histories*, Herodotus, c. 450 CE

putting them in touch with the wilder aspects of themselves and with the untamed nature of this god. In this sense the bacchant would become both male and female, both human and animal, and both mortal and god in one. It is also possible that the satyrs and centaurs who are often depicted in art accompanying the *thiasos* were in fact Dionysian revellers, wearing masks and trancing in order to shapeshift into the animals they were impersonating. This sort of animal possession is also believed to have originated in Africa – the same continent where wine, and perhaps even the Dionysian cult itself, originates. Certainly, Dionysos himself is associated with shapeshifting – he too had the ability to turn himself into any form he wished, and particularly favoured an animal form. Many images of initiation show masked Maenads and other followers of Dionysos using trance as a way to shapeshift, taking the name of *eriphe 'the goat'* a scene which is often accompanied by a *kista mystica* (a basket of sacred objects, often present at initiation) with a snake inside. Those dressed as animals are also reported to have screeched, bellowed and hissed like animals, and this is something which may be reflected in some of the techniques in the Greek Magical Papyri which involve bellowing and hissing as part of their magical operations.

The thiasos themselves would channel the god and become one with his divine essence by the use of masks. This is something that can be found today with the Shaivite *bhaktas*, who themselves bear a striking resemblance to the Bakkhoi of the ancient Hellenic world.[288] It was these masked rites, alongside the singing of the dithyramb, that helped give birth to drama and specifically to tragedy: from the Greek *tragodia, 'the goat song'* which originally involved donning a goat mask in an anthromorphic guise of the god but later involved participants taking on imaginary personalities of mortals, and performing fictional deaths. It is also likely that the dithyrambs themselves were originally improvised song and dance, which was improvised in the midst of Dionysiac ecstasy.

---

[288] Shiva and Dionysus: Gods of Love and Ecstasy, Alain Daniélou, (1979) 1992: P.101

The Unique Practice

"Homage to thee O'night prowler, O'great liberator, bull-horned and bull-faced Lord of the Mound...."[289]

The practice of god-possession was almost entirely unique to Dionysianism in ancient Hellas, and was not usually found in the worship of any of the other Olympian deities. People would pray and make offerings to Apollo or Zeus, or Hermes, Aphrodite or Hera, but they would not seek to *'become them'*. In fact, this was something that was considered as quite distasteful, for the gods acted in extremes. *"Strive not thou to become a god,"* says Pindar; *"the things of mortals best become mortality."* [290] It is no wonder why this cult seemed so alien and outlandish to Greek and Roman sensibilities. His worship was an ecstatic one, which aimed to merge man with the divine in the most primal way - something that was foreign to Athens, but quite at home in ancient Egypt and Mesopotamia, for instance: just some of the geographical regions from which the Dionysian current is believed to have originated. Even his legends recall how Dionysos was not originally of Hellenic soil; he had to earn his place amongst the Olympian gods of Greece by undertaking challenges.

In the Dionysian path, participants would enter trance-like states in order to project - as a group - the divine essence of Dionysos. Achieving ecstatic states was no simple task, however, and possession by Dionysos was not considered to be open to all his followers. This was expressed by Plato when he wrote: *many are the wand-bearers, few are the bacchants.*[291] That is to say, many people performed Bacchic rites but very few managed to possess and project his true spirit. This too could be said of modern pagan movements, in which there are many followers but very few actual initiates in comparison.[292] To achieve this ideal it would have likely taken a lot of hard work and preparation such as intensive periods of fasting, and possibly the ingestion of

---

[289] The Book of Ways, PJ Ralls & V Bramshaw, Private Unpublished Text, 1999

[290] Myths of Greece and Rome, Jane Harrison (1927) 2007 P.73

[291] Phaedo, 69c, Plato, c. 360 BCE, trans. B Jowett

[292] Here it is important to stress that I do not simply refer to lineaged initiates such as those of the Gardnerian and Alexandrian rites but to all those who engage actively in the mysteries rather than just its theatre alone.

drugs or alcohol. This would not have been a path for the fainthearted, by any means.

According to several accounts divine ecstasy and spirit possession was in fact required for a mortal to even be able to *see* the god - to those not in this state, Dionysos remained invisible. This *'invisibility'* of Dionysos is accounted in *The Bacchae* when Pentheus, the King of Thebes, could not perceive the god in his true shape until he himself was possessed by Dionysos Bakcheios, *'exciter to frenzy'*. It was only in that state that he could truly acknowledge the god, seeing Dionysos in bull form. Indeed, the philosopher Philo also wrote that the Dionysian initiates practiced ecstatic possession until they *'saw'* an epiphany (manifestation) of the thing they desired – in many cases, a manifestation of the god. These visions are often explained by academics as hallucinations which were brought on by a mixture of lack of sleep and intoxication, but having worked with the otherworldly realms I can most definitely say that this is not the case! The scholar Walter Burkert put it beautifully when he wrote that too much rationality *'closes the doors of the secret, rather than revealing it'*.

The Oracle of Delphi & Apollo

"Dionysus, our Thracian prophet, told me so."[293]

The connection between Dionysos - who Euripides called *Mantis* – meaning *'Seer'* or *'Prophet'* – and the art of divination and prophecy was widespread in the ancient world and predated the more well-known oracular gods, Apollo and Zeus, by some time. In fact, many of the oracle sites associated with these two latter gods had shrines to Dionysos, or else other markers that showed that Dionysos may well have been one of the original deities present at the site. Nowhere is this more apparent than at Delphi, where Dionysos had a great degree of importance and was originally seen as presiding over the oracle throughout the entire year – his nocturnal face ruled during the three months of winter and his bright face ruled during the remaining nine months. Later as Apollo grew in popularity, Dionysos would come to only preside over the three winter months whilst Apollo

---

[293] Hecuba, 1273ff, Euripides, c. 424 BCE, trans. ED Coleridge

came to take the remaining nine months - until the importance of Dionysos was moved aside altogether and Apollo came to be identified with the fierce summer heats of June and July. But literature would not forget Dionysos: Plutarch wrote that Dionysos had *no less property in Delphi than Apollo himself* [294] indicating that in the prophetic realms, Dionysos and Apollo were hardly distinguishable. And several later *paeans* (songs/poems) addressed both deities as one *'... laurel-loving Bacchius* (Dionysos) *paean Apollo, player of the lyre'.* [295] However, this does not mean that these two deities are *'the same'.* To consider Dionysos and Apollo as two distinct deities may first appear foolish to the neo-pagan, as in general we are conditioned to consider deities as identified with one another to the point where *'all gods are one god'.* This phrase was used by Dion Fortune in her novel, *The Sea Priestess* in the early 1900's - a view which as influenced so many other writers and pagans' alike but has been sub-consciously influenced by the leftovers of a fairly rigid monotheistic culture. Whilst we must accept the undeniable historical fact of syncretism, we must also remember that the gods were usually seen by our ancestors as completely literal (not allegories or archetypes of any kind). Robert Brown writes that their *'forms sprung up together and independently ... no Hellene of the early ages would ever have considered that Dionysos and Apollo were identical.'* [296]

The set of steps which led up to the Delphic tripod (the elevated seat where the pythons of Delphi delivered the oracles of Apollo) was referred to as the gravestone or *'tomb'* of Dionysos. The myth of Apollo slaying the enormous serpent Python, and the presence of a *'tomb'* of Dionysos at Delphi, presents us with some rather interesting questions such as: is Python really Dionysos in serpent form? Was this myth representative of Apollo usurping a cult site of Dionysos? And was it symbolic of the change from a more corporeal and chthonic oracle site of Dionysos and the Great Mother to one that focused more upon the heavens, and that had a more transcendental view of divinity? Indeed Erwin Rhode[297] writes that there was an *'earth spirit'* at Delphi, who was conquered by Apollo. This allows us

[294] Source: Plutarch's Morals, G Bell, 1889: P.182

[295] Lykymnios fr.480, Euripides, c. 400 BCE (Source: Dionysos: Archetypal Image, Karl Kerényi, 1996: P.233)

[296] The Great Dionysiac Myth Vol.1, Robert Brown, (1877) 2000: P.57

[297] Psyche (Vol 6) Erwin Rohde (1925) 2006: P.97

to speculate that there was indeed a strong connection between these two figures, and that they may in fact have been two names for the same deity that presided over the oracle before the arrival of the Olympian Apollo.[298] This myth would then represent the shift from the ecstatic power of Dionysos and Rhea to the more orderly oracle of Apollo.

"O Dionysodotes, bestower of the God within, thou who giv'st the God of life and death, your darkened and wild twin. Aigletos, shining flame of knowledge, come we pray. Enliven our minds as Dionysos enlivens our hearts."[299]

Another element pointing to Apollo's usurpation of Delphi is the modern theory that the site is thought to have originally been presided over not by male gods (like Apollo or Dionysos) but by female goddesses (such as Themis, Gaia, Phoebe and Nyx). Dionysos' parallels with Near Eastern deities such as Attis and Adonis, and the presence of a dominant *'mountain-mother'* cult in Minoan Crete and beyond, prompts us to tentatively suggest that Dionysos' presence at Delphi was originally as the consort and protector of an oracular mountain-mother, such as Kybele (the goddess of the Phrygian mountains) who originally presided over the oracle and was identified/conflated with the goddess Rhea of Minoan Crete. By some reports[300] the sacred stone named the *omphalos* was purported to represent the *'navel'* or *'centre'* of the earth, which the Python was said to protect with its life. This navel or centre could be symbolic of the Great Goddess; and incidentally, the word Delphi comes from the same root word *delphys* meaning *'womb'*.

We can find evidence of Rhea's prophetic role in *Dionysiaca*, in which Rhea relates a prophecy to Dionysos Zagreus about how to construct the first wine press; and other sources account how *theophoretoi* (being *'carried'* by the god) was practiced together with *'seductive rites of the cymbals'*[301] during the rites of Kybele. The fact that

---

[298] Python A Study of Delphic Myth and its Origins, Joseph Eddy Fontenrose (1959) 1980: P.376

[299] The Book of Ways, PJ Ralls & V Bramshaw, Private Unpublished Text, 1999

[300] Tatian, Adv.Gr8.68 (Source: Python A Study of Delphic Myth and its Origins, Joseph Eddy Fontenrose (1959) 1980: P.376)

[301] In Search of God the Mother - The Cult of Anatolian Cybele, Lynn Roller, 1999: P.168

the Pythia of Delphi was always female could strengthen this theory, as well as the fact that Delphi - like many oracles - is situated high in the mountains. There are strong parallels here with a Thracian tribe, the Satrians, who were described by Herodotus as being: *"they who possess the Oracle of Dionysos ... on their most lofty mountains... a prophetess who utters the oracles, as at Delphi..."*[302]

There are other markers at Delphi which show that Dionysos may indeed have pre-dated Apollo's worship there - such as the belief that goats discovered the Delphic oracle by ingesting gases that rose up through fissures on the cult site. In fact, there is no evidence to suggest that these gases actually existed: it is more likely that this legend arose from the use of hallucinogenic incenses, and that the goat represented Dionysos or perhaps a human incarnation of him. Other legends said the physical body of Python (likely Dionysos in serpent form) was the origin of the prophetic fumes: when Apollo slayed Python, he fell into the fissure where his body burned and created the smoke which caused inspiration. Goats were also sacrificed during Apollonian rites at Delphi on the 7th day of the Delphic month of Bysios (Athenian month of Anthesterion) which according to some marked the birth of the *'second born'* Dionysos; therefore, also the death of the first. This cult act is particularly Dionysian in its meaning and origins (goats were considered both an enemy and embodiment of Dionysos). It has also been suggested that the *'sacred lots'* (divination bones) which were kept in a kettle by the Pythia at Delphi were in fact the remains of Dionysos himself – a belief that was perhaps a reminder of the dismembered body of Zagreus which was boiled up in a cooking pot and eaten by the Titans.

"... this god is a prophet, for Bacchic revelry and madness have much prophetic skill. For when the god enters a body in full force, he makes the frenzied foretell the future."[303]

We could also draw a parallel with the Bacchic Maenads, showing perhaps that the Pythia at Delphi was a descendent of such a group - only one that had been *'civilised'* by the touch of Apollo, and

---

[302] Histories, Vol2. 102-103 Herodotus, c. 450 CE

[303] The Bacchae, 299-302, Euripides, c. 400 BCE, trans. TA Buckley

by the civic authorities present. As we can see from the quote above, taken from Euripides: *The Bacchae*, Dionysos' ability to inspire prophetesses and prophets was not simply limited to specific oracular priests and priestesses, but would have been possible to all those that were possessed by his vibrant spirit. The practice of a mortal prophesying or being *'ridden by'* a god form is not limited to Dionysian rites, either; it also appears in Norse Seidr, as well as African/Caribbean Voudou - both of which possess the more shamanic ritual form which was almost exclusive to the Dionysian cult (in that part of the world) at that time. Therefore, we can assume that in the grips of divine ecstasy, his Maenads were also bestowed with such ability.

Delphi is not the only place where Dionysos is known to have presided over the oracles. Accounts are found from all over the ancient world, and particular examples include scrying in vessels of liquid and mirrors (such as that depicted on wall frescos at the Villa dei Misteri – *'the Villa of the Mysteries'* located just outside of Pompeii in Italy). There are also accounts of a sort of divination known as *oenomancy* and *kottabos* which was carried out by the ancient Greeks by interpreting the colours and patterns of the sediment left at the bottom of a goblet of wine (or spilt wine).

Liminality, Initiation & the Underworld

The worship of Dionysos came to mean many different things to many different groups of people; however one theme remained prevalent throughout and was reflected in almost all Dionysian rites and festivals, regardless of the geographical region. That theme was that Dionysos occupied the spaces of betwixt and between: the state of liminality. Stood on the threshold between the worlds, Dionysos dwelt in a state between the composed and the ecstatic, the captive and the free, the sane and the insane - and even life and death itself as he acted as an initiator and mediator, a portal between the worlds for both the living and for the dead.

By the very nature of his worship, Dionysos facilitated his initiates and followers to achieve the state of mind and being that was required to traverse (journey between) the worlds, and undergo initiation. His orgiastic rites of opposition and duality, masked dance and ritual trance (and the many other trance-inducing methods of worship as discussed in this book) all functioned as tools (*'keys'* or *'doorways'*) which aimed to change the consciousness on a very real level; releasing the spirit from the earthly realms and allowing it to travel between realities. Travelling between the worlds was considered an incredibly important element of both ritual worship and initiation.

The state of being that was created by a change in consciousness allowed the Bakkhoi to access visions; achieve possession and invocation, and reveal prophecies - and of course, practice effective magic. In order to make any sort of real change with ritual or magic it was thought necessary to change the consciousness and travel to the otherworlds to perform those rites in the spiritual realms; for it was believed that nothing real could be achieved on the physical plane. Therefore celebrants would transform between two states of being (the mundane and the trance state) particularly at liminal places (such as lakes and caves) which were considered as entrances to the otherworlds, and at liminal times (such as dusk or dawn).

The Dionysian rites were largely chthonic in nature: focusing on the journey after death, the underworld, the promise of renewal - and they involved both the celebration of life and the liberation of the spirit in death. For the followers of Dionysos, the deceased Bakkhoi was promised *'the eternal banquet of the blessed'*, in the realm of Elysium at the end of their journey.[304] On the whole, the initiations of the Dionysian cults seem to have imitated the process that they believed they would encounter after death – to assure the continuation of consciousness after their present physical life had ended. A single initiation created changes for the initiate on a variety of levels. The first stage for the initiate was the physical initiation into a group. The second was a personal initiation – an ability which developed over time to connect with Dionysos on a deeper and more meaningful level, learning how to traverse the worlds and ritually change the consciousness during life. And then, there was the final stage of initiation - the eventual passage of actual death.

To the Bakkhoi, the spiritual path and initiations had a direct effect on the path that the initiate would take beyond the grave. By

---

[304] Ashmolean Catalogue: Heracles to Alexander the Great, 2011: P.167

learning how to traverse the worlds in life, the Dionysian initiate ensured the passage of his or her soul after death to join the spirits of the dead – the *chthonioi*, or *'earth-people'*. Incidentally, there was an established necromantic culture in ancient Greece, particularly in the cults of the chthonic gods such as Dionysos. It was believed that the undead were able to return to the upperworld, and there are accounts of ghouls terrorising the living – as well as being called up during necromantic rites.

There are several accounts of necromancy in the myths of Dionysos. One story tells of how an army of the undead rose at Dionysos' command to march with the Athenians against Persia: one thousand dead men, who drove fear into the hearts of the Perisan soldiers. Another myth is that of the soil-sprung *'sown-men'*, the ancestral warriors who were reanimated under the earth but in their new-born confusion they destroyed one another. Even Dionysos himself is known to participate in necromantic activities, descending into the underworld to retrieve souls and reanimating them, and of course he himself was the result of a kind of resurrection, when Zeus ate the bloody heart of Zagreus so that Bromios could be born.

There is also evidence to show that necromancy was part of the historical cult worship of Dionysos. As Lord of the Dead, Dionysos presides over restless souls and is known to guide them between the worlds: and during the festival of Anthesteria in Athens, the dead were invited to return to the world of the living for three days for celebration and possession before being driven back into the underworld with a cacophony of noise.

"There awaits men when they die such things as they look not for or dream of ... that they rise up and become the wakeful guardians of the quick and dead ... night-walkers, magians, bakchoi, lanai, and the initiated...'[305]

The theme of an initiatory transition between two states is common in Greek mythology. In the tale of Dionysos and Hypolinus, Dionysos sought out the entrance to the Underworld: a portal between the upperworld of men and the chthonic realms of Hades. He also makes a transition between two states when he descends into

---

[305] Herakleitos of Ephesos, fr.122-124, c. 500 BCE

the sea, to seek refuge with the sea goddess Thetis: as he dives through the waves he makes a transition from dry land to the watery depths of the ocean. The concept is also reflected in the more widely known tale of the Ferryman, who gave passage to souls across the River Styx in order that they might cross into the otherworld. All these legends indicate a transition between two states, which ultimately symbolised the passage between life and death. In ritual, an individual was able to enact this journey to the afterlife by way of a series of challenges and experiences, all of which caused a transition between normal consciousness and trance, and culminated with the individual becoming a fully initiated *mystai*.

In many cases it was believed that those who had not undertaken the sacred initiations would be refused entry to the underworld. Tokens were often given to the initiate to mark their initiation and assure their entry into the afterlife, such as the Dionysian Bone Plates, which were found at Olbia in Italy. These plates stated that the Bakkhoi was fully initiated - and as such, should be allowed to travel beyond the physical realm and into the domain of the gods. Part of the inscription upon the plates further supports Dionysos' association with the sequences of life, death, and rebirth, and the deeper mysteries which revealed sacred truths and knowledge to the initiate:

'Life. Death. Life. Truth. Dio (nysos)'. [306]

The Pelinna Gold Leaves, a set of funerary inscriptions found in Thessaly, are believed to be similar initiatory tokens: this time marking the final journey of a Dionysian initiate beyond death, and offering them a guide to the afterlife. Dionysos is mentioned in the inscription as the *'mediator'* between the two worlds who is guiding the initiate on their journey to the underworld and bargaining with Hades. Procedures then follow to ensure the initiate safe passage into the otherworlds. Stating the name of the deceased, together with their title as *mystes* (initiate) the text goes on to state: *'Now you have died and now you have been thrice blessed, on this day tell Persephone and Bakkhios (Dionysos) himself have released you.'* [307] Although the Gold Leaves are

---

[306] Olbia bone plates, c. 500 BCE
[307] Pelinna Gold Leaves, c. 400 BCE

often ascribed to the later Orphic mysteries, it is likely that they are in fact from an earlier, pre-Orphic Dionysian cult.[308]

Like Dionysos (who could only achieve full god status after he had descended to the underworld and then ascended to the heavens afterwards) the initiate could only achieve spiritual accomplishment by travelling both Above and Below. Through initiation, by way of a feigned pseudo *'death'*, the initiate travelled to the underworld and entered the heavenly realm of the gods *before* his or her mortal life had ended. In Dionysian ritual, the initiates' face was smeared with white clay or ash to give them a deathly appearance, further connecting them with the realms of the dead. Fennel and Poplar, two sacred plants of Dionysos, may also have been used during the initiatory rites of Dionysos. According to some the White Fennel was symbolic of the manifest god, present in the upper world of men - but also of the Probationer, who had not yet undertaken their initiation. The Black Poplar was symbolic of the nocturnal Dionysos - the absent god of the underworld, and the fully initiated *mystes*. According to other sources, the initiate was crowned with the Black Poplar as he entered initiation and symbolically descended into the underworld, and was crowned with the White Fennel when he returned to normality, after the rite had ended. It is quite possible that the two plants were used interchangeably in this way, for the initiate in the underworld must return to the upper world of men just as surely as he or she descended. Dionysos was both the beginning and end of the initiatory journey.

One of the clearest examples of Dionysian initiation comes to us from a set of wall frescoes at Villa dei Misteri – *'the Villa of the Mysteries'* located just outside of Pompeii in Italy. Constructed in approximately 62 CE after the previous building had been destroyed by an earthquake, the Villa is believed to have been the private residence of a wealthy and influential family from the area. It was a large property which incorporated private baths, grand courtyards and walkways, and even its own bakery within its walls; as well as a room put aside for wine production. Dionysian worship had become very organised by this time and it was not uncommon for a *thiasos* (ritual

---

[308] Dionysos in the Underworld - An interpretation of the Toledo Krater, Stian Sundell Torjussen, Masters Thesis University of Tromsø Nordlit 20, 2006: P.93

group) to be funded by a local beneficiary, who would hold ritual meetings for the privileged on their own property (despite the ban of Bacchanalian rites in Italy, which was set in force at least 200 years before, the cult persisted in both the upper and lower classes). It is believed that The Villa of the Mysteries was one such place. Within a small room at the back of the property lay what has come to be termed The Initiation Chamber: a hall decorated with colourful wall frescoes depicting the stages of a Bacchic initiation. It is likely that the hall was used as a living room or dining room, but it has been argued by some that this room may have actually been used for ritual and admissions into the cult. This we may never know – but at the very least, the owners of the house must have been privy to the initiation rites and had a fond association with them to decorate their walls in such a way. Perhaps it is more likely that this was somewhere that the fully initiated met to eat and socialize together - for it seems unlikely that a probationer would have been allowed to view the frescoes which outlined the procedures of the initiation in such detail. The wall paintings are remarkably well preserved, and stretch all around the room depicting the process of an (albeit later) Dionysian initiation, in detail.

Oscillation

Just like many mystery traditions today, the ancients believed that in order to travel between the worlds and communicate with spirits one must change the consciousness and enter a trance state. A popular way of doing so was by ritual oscillation: swinging, spinning, and shaking. As identified earlier, the Latin words *spiritus* (spirit) *animus* (the mind) and *thymos* (soul/desire) all come from Sanskrit words meaning to *blow*, *rush* and *shake*; perhaps suggesting that spiritual and magical practices can be aided or encouraged by movement – in particular by moving things through air, or the motion of air itself. Several ritual and magical methods are known to have been used in the ancient world to make use of the element of air, and imitate the movements of the breeze. One such method was a Dionysian practice called *aletis*: swinging back and forth on a swinging seat, which led to visions and prophecies. The sacred swings were set up in close proximity to where the *pithoi* (wine fermentation jars) were stored half buried in the ground, and during the festival of Anthesteria young Athenian girls would use the swings during the opening of the jars.

"They instituted the practice of swinging themselves on ropes, with bars of wood attached, so that one hanging could be moved by the wind. They instituted this as a solemn ceremony ..."[309]

It was believed that as the jars were opened, the spirits of the dead would rise from the underworld and enter the upper world of men. Dionysos was also believed to have ascended from the pithoi at this time and so it is possible that the ritual swinging - which lulled a sense of otherworldliness into the person upon the swing - was also seen to aid the transition of the spirits from one world into the other. Other sources account that the pithoi were sometimes buried at the banks of rivers and marshes[310] and that young girls swung above them in a similar way. The location of these pithoi would have been particularly poignant due to Dionysos' connection with water, and the element's qualities in relation to trance states and otherworldly journeys.

It is likely that the practice of swinging seats was associated with the legend of the harvest maiden Erigone, daughter of King Ikarios. The legend goes that Dionysos showed the King how to create wine, but underestimating its effects King Ikarios served the wine to the men of his court. Having never felt the effects of wine before, they believed he had poisoned them and brutally murdered him. On finding her father's body, Erigone hung herself (swung) from a grapevine which had grown from the corpse of her father. Another tradition may have emerged from this custom: a children's competition called the *eiresione* that became popular during the festival of *Oschophoria* in which children were invited to decorate olive branches with swinging decorations - this time to mark the return of Theseus from Crete. A similar bough was created during the month of *Thargelion*, which marked the departure of Theseus.

"Eiresione for us brings figs, and bread of the richest,
and brings us honey in pots, and oil to rub on the body,
Strong wine, too, in a beaker, that one may go to bed mellow."[311]

---

[309] Astronomica, 2.2.4, Pseudo-Hyginus, c. 100 CE, trans. M Grant
[310] The God Who Comes, Rosemarie Taylor-Perry, 2003: P.58
[311] Plutarch Lives 'Theseus' Pt.22, c. 75 CE, trans. B Perrin

Another folk custom involved hanging small faces or so-called *'little mouths'* of Dionysos, named the *Phallos* (or *Oscillim* in Latin) from the branches of trees. This custom was particularly prevalent near vineyards, and pine trees were usually chosen as they were considered as sacred to Dionysos. As the small masks swung in the breeze, they were believed to send fertility in every direction they faced. As the Roman poet Virgil wrote, *'they* (the people of Italy) *put on hideous faces carved from bark, invoking you, Bacchus, with glad refrain, and to you they hang the benignant oscilla from the lofty pine.'* [312]

The rites of Eleusis – which recognised Dionysos as guide and assistant to the Mysteries – also used methods of ritual oscillation. Accounts are given of a magical wheel called the *Rhombos* meaning *'spinning top'* (related to the words *Rhembō, 'to turn round and round'* and *Rhembein, 'to whirl'*).[313] Many researchers believe that the Rhombos was a 3-dimensional object that could be spun on its axis - much like a child's spinning top toy (which was one of the *'sacred playthings'* of Dionysos Zagreus). The Rhombos was spun in a circular motion during the Eleusinian rites, and was believed to imitate the movement of the stars.[314] However most accounts describe the Rhombos as a flat object which was whirled on the end of a single rope - much like the instrument more commonly known as the *Bull Roarer.*

Other liminal deities, who share similar roles with Dionysos, are also known to have been invoked or petitioned by similar hypnotic spinning. Hekate was invoked by the spinning of the *Strophalos*, an object which acted as a vehicle to alter the consciousness and assisted the practitioner to communicate with otherworldly beings. Decorated with symbols and characters and with a sapphire in the middle[315] the Strophalos was spun in the air to create hypnotic whirring sounds during invocations. Like the Rhombos, there remains some ambiguity on the shape of this object. Some accounts describe the Strophalos as a spoked-wheel, instead – sometimes called an *Iynx* which shares its title with a bird of the same name, more commonly known as the

---

[312] Georgics ii.388, Virgil c. 29 BCE (Source: The Great Dionysiac Myth Vol.1, Robert Brown, (1877) 2000: P.231)

[313] A Greek to English Lexicon 1940, Liddel & Scott (on Perseus)

[314] The Great Dionysiac Myth Vol.1, Robert Brown, (1877) 2000: P.108

[315] Byzantine Magic (edited by Henry Maguire) 'The Theory & Practice of Magic' John Duffy, 1995: P.85

Wryneck. Attached to a circular frame, one part of the bird would have been selected to create each spoke of the wheel (neck, tail and wings) and as the wheel was spun, the sounds that the bird made would be interpreted as a form of divination. There might be one other connection between the Iynx and Dionysos: the Wryneck's feathers are mottled or spotted – and so like several of the creatures considered sacred to Dionysos, this bird also shares a leopard-print coat. Sadly, the Wryneck is now globally threatened and close to extinction. Perhaps one of the best offerings to Hekate or Dionysos you could give in this respect is a donation to the RSPB, who work to preserve these amazing creatures. Please visit www.rspb.org.uk

Katabasis (Descent)

"Under the earth, you have to expect the unexpected."[316]

Dionysos' absence from the upperworld of men marked a period of mourning for the people, as well as festivals and rites to encourage his return. But where was their god during his absence? The *Orphic Hymns* stated that Dionysos slept in the House of Persephone (the underworld) whilst he was absent from the mortal world. Indeed, as the son of Persephone (in his Zagreus incarnation) there is perhaps no place more fitting for him reside; he truly is *Dionysos Chthonios, 'of the underworld'*. The Greek tragedian Aeschylus even equated him with Hades him, calling him *'the underworld Zeus'* and it is possible that this was the mystery that was revealed to initiates in Dionysian rites, which were integrated into the Eleusinian mysteries in Hellas. The two gods also shared the ability to bring trance and states of rapture to their followers. The philosopher Heraclitus wrote that, *'Hades and Dionysos, for whom they go mad and rage, are one and the same*[317] and Euripides referred to the followers of Dionysos as *'the bacchants of Hades'.*[318]

Whilst Dionysos acted as a guide and mediator for others travelling between the worlds, he also gathered many of his own legends, too: as he himself journeyed toward and dwelt within the

---

[316] Journey to the Center of the Earth, 1976
[317] Herakleitos of Ephesos, Frag.15, c. 500 BCE
[318] Hecuba, 1077, Euripides, c. 424 BCE, trans. ED Coleridge

netherworldly depths. The most famous of all the tales is that of Dionysos' quest to retrieve his lover Ariadne (or by other accounts, his mother Semele) by descending into the bottomless Alkyonian Lake - the gateway to the land of the dead. The exact location of the lake is not known, although the geographer Pausanias states that it was at Argos, where nocturnal rites had been performed every year since in memory of Semele. By other accounts the lake was at Lerna, where similar rites were held: here, the local people would call Dionysos from the deep prior to the festival marking his return to the world of men, making offerings of lambs to the sound of trumpets concealed inside thyrsus-staves.[319] The Lake of Lerna is also mentioned in the tales of Perseus, who opposed the Dionysian cult and forced Dionysos and his retinue to seek refuge in the Lake of Lerna with Thetis, the sea goddess. This story was recalled during the festival of Agriona held during the Athenian month of Munychion. Water itself was associated with the spirit world (and still is, in many modern occult traditions) and therefore was associated with both life and death, and travel and transformation (for initiates, a journey between the mundane state and the trance state). Conversely, water was also associated with the birth of Dionysos, such as the Spartan account of his birth in which the baby Dionysos was washed up onto shore in a wooden chest with the body of his dead mother. Herein this story lies yet again the greatest of Dionysos' mysteries: the intimate relationship between life and death.

> *"Heracles: Why, you rash fellow, will you dare to go?*
> *Dionysos: Which of the roads will bring us quickest down to hell?*
> *Heracles: You'll see ten thousand snakes and terrible wild beasts...*
> *Dionysos: Don't try to frighten me, or make me scared.*
> *You won't turn me aside."*[320]

Other wet environments were also believed to be gateways to the underworld: liminal places where Dionysos descended, and where people would gather to call him back to the world of the living. Such a place lay just outside of the oracular sanctuary of Dodona – a dangerous swamp, which Dionysos had to cross in order to find a cure for the insanity which Hera had brought upon him. The task

---

[319] The Great Dionysiac Myth Vol.1, Robert Brown, (1877) 2000: P.264
[320] Frogs, 116, Aristophanes, c. 400 BCE, trans. M.Dillon

seemed impossible, for crossing the swamp meant certain death. But Dionysos did manage to cross the swamp, by employing two mules to carry him across. In this tale, we see Dionysos undergoing a transition between the states of sanity and madness, and overcoming death itself: the two main aims of the Dionysian initiation. Dodona was an important oracular centre, second only to Eleusis and dedicated to the goddess Dione, who can be identified with Rhea (or Kybele) and Demeter, the mother of Dionysos Iakchos. Other swamps were also considered liminal portals to the netherworldly depths, such as the swamp adjacent to the temple of *Dionysos Limnaios* (meaning, Dionysos of the Marsh) outside of Athens. An air of mystery surrounded this temple of Dionysos, which was closed to all except the fully initiated. The name Limnaios lives on in the modern Greek word *'lake'* but also *'libido'*,[321] for the marshes would also be the setting for *hieros gamos* (sacred lovemaking) during the Dionysian festival of Anthesteria.

The mule itself is symbolic of a liminal *'place between'*: being a cross-bred creature which is neither donkey nor horse - the result of which breeds a creature that is much hardier and stronger than the horse, and more willing and larger than a donkey. The mule was the preferred mode of transport for both the ancient Hellenes and Romans, making it an important and valuable asset to both the average person and the nobleman; perhaps then, a fitting mount for a god whose worship transcended the boundaries between the rich and the poor. Yet for all its benefits, the mule was also infertile. By reproducing and giving birth to new life, in a way our own immortality is ensured through our offspring. But with the infertility of the mule, who cannot continue its line, comes a sort of finite mortality: and therefore in many ways, it can also be considered as symbolic of death, or endings. The donkey was also associated with Dionysos, who was often depicted being carried upon its back particularly in scenes relating to his descent into the underworld.

Water was not the only medium that could be used to enter the underworld; caves were also popular in Dionysian rites and journeying. Already associated with the mythology of Dionysos, they served as places of transformation and initiation. One such sacred

---

[321] The God Who Comes, Rosemarie Taylor-Perry, 2003: P.46

cave existed near the temple of *Palaimon-Melikertes* in the ancient city of Corinth, which was probably built there for the purpose of being in close proximity to the cave. Dedicated to *Dionysos Omadios 'taker of sacrifices'* this particular temple made use of another medium for communicating with the underworld: chthonic fire pits. Excavations at the site discovered three burning pits in the temple foundations that still held the ashes and bones of bulls which had been sacrificed during the nocturnal rites.[322] In magical theory, it is often considered that out of the five *'classical'* elements, fire and water are the two elements considered the most direct mediums through which the underworld can be accessed (mainly because they are the most powerful elements with which to enter a trance state).

The underworld itself was an intriguing and often confusing place, an environment which would be recreated by several mystery traditions throughout history to bamboozle their initiates during the initiations. Plato[323] writes that Socrates described the underworld as a labyrinthine landscape of twists and turns, and three-way intersections (forked crossroads). No matter whether the traveller was a living soul traversing the worlds, or a ghost of the recently departed, the maze-like qualities of the underworld challenged them to make a decision at every turn. The architecture of the underworld symbolised the transitory and mazelike journey of life, death and rebirth. The 'round dances' or *geranos*, which were held during the festivals, recreated the movement of the soul as it travelled through the netherworlds, and was particularly associated with the tales of the Minotaur, and Ariadne. As the dance spiralled into the centre it represented the passage into the underworld and death, and as it spiralled out it represented the journey out of Hades, and into new life. In other initiations, the initiate was enthroned whilst others whirled around them in dance to create a similar sense of confusion.

Again, wall frescoes at Villa dei Misteri – *'the Villa of the Mysteries'* in Italy show just one example of katabasis in the Dionysian mysteries. We see the initiate gaze towards the next scene with a look of fear in her eyes; it is this part of the painting that suggests the

---

[322] Gnosticism & the New Testament, Pheme Perkins, 1993: P.35
[323] Phaedo, 108A, Plato, c. 360 BCE (Source Dionysos: Archetypal Image of Indestructible Life, Karl Kerényi, 1996: P.93)

initiate must now begin her descent into the underworld. The prophetic Silenus, who appears in this scene, perhaps hints at the next element of the wall painting. He holds a bowl which may hold water, whilst a Satyr gazes into it: the Satyr perhaps enters a trance-like state as he scries into the bowl for visions. Another Satyr holds up a mask, which could also be reflected on the surface of the water in the bowl. There are several accounts of mirrors being used during Dionysian initiation to confuse the initiate and create an intriguing atmosphere; the reflective surface of a scrying bowl may have been used in a similar way, reflecting the mask which was held up behind them. Perhaps this was symbolic of the initiate meeting their shadow self or alter-ego; or perhaps, the Dionysian spirit within them. It is also here that the initiate meets Dionysos, the lord of souls.

Lord of Souls

"Mysterious dedications called him the Lord of Souls."[324]

Naturally, as a chthonic deity of the underworld (who, part-mortal, had himself made the transition between life, death and rebirth) Dionysos was considered as close to the shades and spirits whose journey he guided: *Eleuthereus Melanaigis 'black goatskin'* the dark guise of Dionysos. His followers were also considered as being intimately associated with the souls of the dead, and the Dionysian rites often embraced an element of *'shamanic'* ancestor worship and ancestral trance and mediumship, to communicate with the spirits of the otherworld. As Zagreus, Dionysos was the *'capturer of wild animals'* and so too was he the capturer of mortal souls, who made their way to the underworld for judgment and rest.

Sources show quite clearly that the two cults – *"that of Dionysos and that of the dead – were inherently related and amounted basically to one cult"*.[325] Indeed, it was believed that the ancestors were present at many of their descendants' central moments – such as birth, marriage, and ritual initiations – and their annual festivals and celebrations. Unlike modern ancestor worship (which in the western mystery tradition is often a solemn affair, and usually carried out during the

---

[324] Dionysus Myth & Cult, Walter F Otto (1960) 1995: P.49
[325] Dionysus Myth & Cult, Walter F Otto (1960) 1995: P.118

dark half of the year) the ancients often involved spirits in their spring and summer festivals. The festival of Anthesteria, which was held in early spring and marked the opening of the first barrels of wine, celebrated Dionysos' return from the underworld and was also therefore an *'all-souls festival'* which honoured the spirits who had followed Dionysos up into the mortal world of the living. The ancestors were invited to join in with the festivities; mediumship was used to communicate with them, and they joined their descendants during the feasts. Initiates' faces were smeared with white clay or ash to give them a ghostly appearance, further connecting them with the realms of the dead. However by their nature these spirits were also feared, and rites would also be held at the end of the festival in order to encourage the spirits to descend back into the chthonic depths of the netherworld.

> *'...the crash of unseen drums clamoured, and fifes and jingling brass resounded, and the air was sweet with scents or myrrh and saffron ... the hanging cloth grew leaves of ivy, part became a vine ... bunches of grapes were seen, matching the purple with their coloured sheen ... suddenly the whole house began to shake, the lamps flared up, and all the rooms were bright with flashing crimson fires, and phantom forms of savage beasts of prey howled all around.'* [326]

Besides human souls, other underworld deities were also considered *'under the spell'* of Dionysos Chthonios, such as the chthonic vengeance spirits the *Erinyes*. The Erinyes were sometimes identified with the goddess Lyssa - also of the realm of Hades - who was associated with canine madness and frenzy. According to some accounts, it was the madness of her dogs which possessed the women in Euripides *The Bacchae* to attack the rebellious Pentheus and tear him to pieces, a story which is believed by some to be indicative of elements of the Dionysian initiation.

---

[326] Metamorphoses, 4.389, Ovid, C1st BCE - 1st CE trans. Melville - The daughters of King Minyas turning into bats

Chapter 8

Dionysos as Lord of Hieros Gamos

"Give way, make room for the god! For it is his will to stride exuberantly erect through the middle!!"[327]

As a deity concerned with earthly matters, Dionysos is well known for his association with fertility and sensuality. Indeed, this is commonly believed to be one of his most significant aspects: however like his association with wine, this is also one of the most often misunderstood aspects of his nature.

Certainly, Dionysos was known as a god of virility and the beliefs behind his cult were known to both acknowledge and satisfy the physical needs as well as the spiritual needs of his followers. The gifts of the natural world were seen as keys – used to access and embrace the forces of the physical and facilitate spiritual advancement. Dionysos was seen as the origin of these keys: food and drink, song and dance, sexuality and procreation. In contrast to later cults which strived toward salvation from the material world, the mysteries of Dionysos held an acknowledgement of the sacredness of the physical world close to godliness. To embrace the pleasures of the physical was to acknowledge the authority of the Fertile God: the animating force. Indeed to *thyein*, 'rave' with *Dionysos Bakcheus* was to release the spirit and leave behind all boundaries and cares. One way of doing so was through erotic ecstasy: the peak of *zöe*.

Paradoxically however, Dionysos was also a patron god of homosexual relationships – which cannot be connected to the creation of new life in the conventional sense, and yet were held as

---

[327] Semo's Song of the Phallophoria in Athenaios XIV 622B

incredibly sacred to Dionysos. This indicates that his connection with sexual rites was not entirely concerned with fertility per-se, but sexuality as a force in its own right – and the power of sexuality in all its forms to raise energy, and create change and transformation. As such, he was a symbol of sexual and phalloric pride.

The image and symbolism of the Phallus is a constant companion of Dionysos; however, it is interesting to note that although the phallus is seen carried and worn by his Satyrs and celebrants, earlier depictions of Dionysos do not usually show the phallus actually being worn by the god himself. On the whole it was much later depictions which showed Dionysos, usually as the Roman Bacchus, as an ithyphallic god and in fact Dionysos is usually shown dressed quite modestly in comparison to his accompanying Satyrs. Moreover, the encounter with the phallus was symbolic – or used for comedic light relief during ritual processions and theatrical performances. In a ritual sense, the phallus was seen to mark the arrival of Dionysos: usually starting from the seaport, a wooden phallus was carried through the streets to mark the *'coming'* of Dionysos; but the Phallus was not actually seen as Dionysos himself. It was during this time that songs were sung to Dionysos as *Phales* – the Satyr associated with Dionysos in his role as fertility-giver.

"Let the basket bearer come forward ...hold the phallus erect behind the basket bearer and I, following, will chant the phallic hymn. O' Phales ... fellow reveler, night-rambler-around, seducer ..."[328]

A similar rite was held to mark the departure of Dionysos in which a large wooden phallus was carved, painted in bright colours and given wings. Known as the *'Phallus-Bird'* it was put into a wagon which was then driven into the sea. As the wagon sunk, so the Phallus was seen to float up and away on the current. Another way that the Phallus was used in conjunction with the mysteries of Dionysos was as one of the sacred objects in the *liknon* – the willow basket of the Eleusinian Mysteries which held items that revealed certain secrets to the initiates. The initiate would be commanded to lift a cloth which covered the basket and reveal the sacred objects – one of which was believed to be a carved phallus and which partly symbolised the soul

---

[328] The Archanians, 241ff, Aristophanes, c. 425 BCE, trans. anon

of Dionysos. Other accounts tell of how the initiates performed a rite of sexual unification known as *'God through the Lap'* by passing the carved phallus (or perhaps a snake) from lap to lap under the table.

Although the theme of sex and sexuality was an important factor in Dionysian myth and practice, and Dionysian Phallic rites and processions were commonplace in the ancient Greek world, actual sexual acts were actually not as common as most would believe. Most accounts of Dionysian rites are not actually sexually gratuitous, and the presence of sexual symbology is just that – more symbolic than actual. The fact that so many rites to Dionysos were held at night (and in secret) probably helped fuel the suspicion – and in *The Bacchae*, Dionysos points out to Pentheus how flawed this suspicion is.

Neither were the Bakkhoi of Dionysos required to take part in sexual rites: indeed many images show the lustful Satyrs trying to woo the Dionysian Maenads, but the Maenads ward off their advances. Although sexual *'orgies'* are known to have occurred as part of Dionysian practice, Dionysos himself was never depicted as actually taking part in the sexual acts; moreover he seems to be the facilitator of the act, the origin of desire that causes it. Indeed, the word *'orgy'* is an interesting one: coming from the Greek word *orgazein* meaning *'celebration of life'* and originally used in ancient Greece to describe any ecstatic form of worship such as dance, sacrifice, feasting and revelry. Rosemarie Taylor-Perry[329] gives an English approximation of the meaning of the word, *'celebration of the physical expression of energy which animates the soul'* – suddenly the function and meaning of the orgy seems very different. Certainly as the Dionysian practice became integrated into the worship of the Roman equivalent *Bacchus* (and his Bacchanalia) the meaning of the sexual rite became more about self-gratification and excess rather than a way of achieving ecstatic union with the god. But on the whole, the sexual rites of the ancient Greeks were carried out to achieve *heiros gamos* or the divine marriage: unification between two mortal souls and the divine, in which the people involved would be identified with gods.

One such rite of Dionysian origin was the *hieros gamos* of the King and Queen of Athens, the *Archon Basileus* and the *Basilinna*.

---

[329] The God Who Comes, Rosemarie Taylor-Perry, 2003: P.14

Considering that Athens founded the world's first democracy in 683 BCE (and the concept of a monarchy had been considered of very little importance for a long time even before that, with non-hereditary elected magistrates favoured instead and whom adopted the name of *Archon Basileus* to continue the tradition) a ritual based upon a monarchy must have been quite ancient indeed. The rite occurred during the festival of Anthesteria when the King (or substitute dignitary) known as the Archon Basileus, was filled with the presence of Dionysos and performed the sacred marriage with his Queen the Basilinna at the *Boukoleon* sanctuary or *'bull stable'* – where the Queen reaffirmed the King's position as the mortal personification of Dionysos, by his unity with the most important woman in the city. Incidentally, the King was likely to have also been the Hierophant – and as such the Hierophant is referred to as the *Boukoloi.*

It was a grand affair and depictions show the Queen being anointed with fragrant oils and pouring offerings upon the fire while she prepared for the ritual. The wife would then go to the Boukoleon where her husband awaited; and during the rite they would symbolically conceive Dionysos Meilichios who would be born nine months later at the *Festival of Awakening.* This rite appears very similar in nature to the sacred marriage rites of the Sumerians, where the King was deified as the horned god Dumuzi and addressed as the *'Wild Bull'.* As the personification of Dumuzi, the King performed hieros gamos to bring fertility to the land.[330]

How literal this union really was is debated. Some believe that it was symbolic at best, with the Basilinna perhaps opening a *liknon* (winnowing basket) and simply observing a sacred mask, or a vinewood phallus. However whilst this rite may have been imitated in a symbolic way during mystery rites, I am inclined to believe that this union was originally very real – particularly considering how *'literal'* the presence of Dionysos was believed to have been during this time of year. The terminology used by Aristotle in his *Constitution of the Athenians* also indicates that these rites were of a very carnal nature: he described the rite as *symmeixis* (higher unification) through *gamos* (physical bodily union).

---

[330] VS: Duality & Conflict in Magick, Mythology & Paganism, edited by Kim Huggens, 2011

Whilst he was known to have loved many women and men alike, Dionysos was a god of fidelity at heart: ascending to the heavens with his one true love, his wife Ariadne. In a similar way, Dionysos was considered a guide to brides on their wedding day, which in itself was considered a passage of initiation. He was also known to bless marriages and bestow them with good luck and fertility: one of the earliest surviving images of Dionysos shows him offering up a kantharos (drinking cup) and bunches of grapes to Peleus and Thetis on their wedding day.[331] And in his guise as Hermes the Psychopomp, he is depicted as holding a folded bedsheet – a common wedding gift and symbol of consummating wedlock. An interesting set of scenes from the Dionysian Villa of the Mysteries in Pompeii shows a female initiate undertaking a number of challenges. In the first scene we observe the initiate being scourged: a process of suffering (or perceived suffering) was common in the mysteries, and followed by liberation and the unveiling of sacred knowledge. In the second scene we see another priestess, a Maenad who dances and plays the cymbals and represents the joy of the Dionysian mysteries, and the attainment of full initiation. And in the third scene, we see the initiate taking part in her marriage ceremony. Many researchers have interpreted this fresco as a depiction of a bride's preparation for marriage – but I would argue that it may also be a depiction of the process of Hieros Gamos, the figurative *'marriage'* of sacred lovemaking between an initiate and a representive of Dionysos.

The Women of Dionysos

'To the mountain! Where the throng of women waits, driven from shuttle and loom!' [332]

Dionysos was historically known for his fondness and respect of women, who made up a large number of his followers and were portrayed as some of his most trusted and faithful companions. Far from shrinking violets, they were also known to be brave warriors, and Polyainos describes them in his *Strategems of War* as *'brandishing their thyrsuses instead of spears, and with wreaths concealing their faces'*

---

[331] By the Attic potter and vase painter Sophilos

[332] The Bacchae, 115-120, Euripides, c. 400 BCE, trans. R Lattimore

referring to the Maenads protecting a temple of Dionysos from the invading Taulantii.

From an early age Dionysos was nurtured and defended by women, and all three of his mothers – Persephone, Semele and Demeter – were fiercely protective of him. In terms of cult worship, Dionysos was often worshipped together with his mother and their mysteries presented side by side (such as the Mysteries of Demeter, Iakchos and Dionysos and Eleusis, and the earlier rites of Phrygian Kybele) and he was often shown surrounded by goddesses in depictions of the revel rout of Dionysos. [333] His worship is also known to have been connected to some very notable women: Olympias, the mother of Alexander the Great, was a devout follower of Dionysos, and the Queen of Aegae (Macedonia) is accounted to have performed Dionysian rites on the hillsides of the Pierian mountains, near Mt. Olympus. [334]

Indeed, Dionysos had quite an affinity with the mother figure: whilst the common image of the Maenad is a younger woman, IM Lewis[335] suggests that older, married women with fully-grown children were also considered as suitable candidates. At this stage in their life, they would have been seen to have fulfilled their obligation to their family having undertaken the full initiation into womanhood, and had the benefit of an already established social status. Indeed, the cult of Dionysos was very compatible with married life for women, especially those whose families were involved with, or had an interest in, political concerns.

It is clear when reading academic sources that the role of women in the Dionysian cult has been a difficult subject for many researchers to approach in the past. Many of the theories about Dionysos were put together in the late 1800s and early 1900s: a time when the independence and self-expression of women was still discouraged in many ways, and this seems to have had a direct influence on how their role in the cult was interpreted by researchers of the time. Indeed as Dionysos Gynaimanes, Dionysos has been described by

---

[333] Dionysus Myth & Cult, Walter F Otto (1960) 1995: P.134

[334] Ashmolean Catalogue: Heracles to Alexander the Great, 2011: P.95

[335] Ecstatic Religion, IM Lewis (1971) 2003: P.171

interpreters as both the *'inspirer of women'* and also *'he who drives women insane'*. The same sort of opinion was given to the ecstatic rites and prophecies of the Dionysian women, who have been described as *'insane'* or *'inspired'*. These two diametric translations of his epithet go some way to show how differently the role of Dionysos, and his gifts of ecstatic ecstasy, has been interpreted by different researchers depending on their individual viewpoints. As such, the way the material has been interpreted has perhaps been more of a reflection of what society deemed appropriate at the time of writing, rather than what it meant to our ancestors. Indeed, the experiences of women during the rites of Dionysos were often described by researchers from the turn of the century as being quite shameful, something for women with very little or no class. It was even said that the very nature of women, their naïveté and their fanaticism was responsible for the mad ramblings that ancient people had believed were genuine prophecies. The possibility that the prophecies were actually real, or inspired by spiritual rapture, was not often considered. What the thiasos really offered women was something very special; an alternative to the patriarchal polis, the civic sphere in which women and others like them had so little sway. To quote Walter Otto in his study first published in 1960, *'to burst the bonds of marital duty and domestic custom in order to follow the torch of the god over the mountain tops and fill the forests with wild shrieks of exultation – this is the purpose for which Dionysos stirs up women'.*[336]

It is a modern misconception that the Classical world was a time of tolerance, and that women were afforded much greater freedom than in the subsequent monotheistic societies which followed - this was not always the case. Ancient Greece (which was not yet unified) was made up of many different districts of ruling, which often had vastly different laws and cultures. For instance, *'respectable'* Athenian women were kept in gynaecaeums (women's quarters) whilst only prostitutes and slave women were permitted to walk the streets alone.[337] What a different perspective we have today. And during the later history of ancient Athens, it was only within a Dionysian thiasos that women were allowed the freedom to mix with men in religious

---

[336] Dionysus Myth & Cult, Walter F Otto (1960) 1995: P.179

[337] This was not the case all over Greece: in Thessaly it was considered acceptable for women to ride on horses, and in Sparta they even competed in sporting events.

setting or even drink wine: they were discouraged from both these things in Athens. [338] However, almost all women were entitled to take part in women's cults which gave them a certain amount of prestige and some of these cults were originally run by women, for women. It is believed that the original thiasoi had no specific hierarchy, although as the cult grew some structure developed in some branches of the cult, in which a Hiereia (Priestess) and later, a Hieros (Hierophant) led the rites. The thiasos allowed women a sense of power, education, and training in what we might now describe as occult practices, as well as a liberation from the status quo – as Plato puts it, a relief from hardship. [339] In return, women propagated his cult throughout the ancient world, and helped make his cults one of the most successful in history.

"All were asleep, their bodies relaxed, some resting their backs against pine foliage, others laying their heads at random on the oak leaves – modestly, not as you say drunk with the goblet… your mother raised a cry … to wake their bodies from sleep … one took her thyrsus and struck it against a rock from which a dewy stream of water sprang forth. Another let her thyrsus strike the ground, and there the god sent forth a fountain of wine. All who desired the white drink scratched the earth with the tips of their fingers and obtained streams of milk, and a sweet flow of honey dripped from their ivy thyrsoi.' [340]

Descriptions of the Dionysian women are detailed, descriptive and evocative. They are described as frenzied, distraught, shrieking and possessed - their behaviour may well have accompanied the specific mythos that they were celebrating during that rite (such as the desperate searching for the baby Dionysos upon the mountainsides of Mount Parnassos during the Festival of Awakening). They are also described as crawling, scratching and devouring raw flesh: half human and half animal, perhaps reflecting how Dionysos bridges the gap between man and beast and cannot be contained by physical form. And yet, the Maenads are also described as stately, proud and often silent: to me this implies that the women of the Dionysian cult were not clinically insane (as other researchers have suggested) but chose their moment for divine madness – this was very intentional ecstatic

---

[338] The God Who Comes, Rosemarie Taylor-Perry, 2003: P.28

[339] Socrates in Plato's Phaedros

[340] The Bacchae, 680-710, Euripides, c. 400 BCE, trans. TA Buckley

trance. Indeed, Euripides' *The Bacchae* describes how a far worse insanity awaits those who do not accept the Dionysian ecstasy – and it is usually those women who demonstrate a far more extreme behaviour, such as infanticide.

'Our greatest blessings come to us by way of madness ... which indeed is a divine gift.'[341]

They are also known to have performed impossible feats, such as drawing milk, honey and wine from rocks, and communicating with animals. It was also said that fire would not burn them, and no weapon could harm them. In many ways, we could say that these women are being described as having occult powers: this would have only added to the mystery and legend that surrounded them.

Whilst the title of Maenad is familiar to most, there was more than one title given to these female devotees of Dionysos: the word Thyiad is also used to describe these women. Although generally considered to be synonymous with one another, the roles carried out by these titles do seem to have subtle differences. Whilst the Maenad is described as being fierce in character – associated with actual sacrifice, ecstatic rites and changing the consciousness – the Thyiad is tender in character and associated with personal sacrifice, awakening, renewal and nurturing. The different roles of the Maenad and Thyiad seem to reflect the different faces of Dionysos (Bakcheus the Ecstatic One and Meilichios the Mild One) and it is possible that one woman could take either role and title.

According to legend the name of the Thyiad was taken from Thyia, the daughter of the river god Castalios, at Delphi who first gave sacrifice to Dionysos there. [342] As the nurturer of Dionysos, the Thyiad acted as both Nursemaid and Mother to Dionysos as an infant, furthering his affinity with women of this nature: it was to them that Zeus placed the baby Dionysos for safekeeping. This role of nurturer and safekeeper was extended to the rituals which revolved around the rituals of the leather sack on the slopes of Mt. Parnassos,

---

[341] Socrates in Plato's Phaedros

[342] The Harvard Theological Review Vol.72, 'Ecstasy and Possession', Ross S Kraemer, 1979: P.66

where they cared for the mead (identified with Dionysos) fermenting inside in the Korykion antron. The Thyiads also played a part in the caring of the Liknon (grain winnowing basket) which held the sacred objects in the Mysteries of Eleusis. In return for looking after Dionysos, legend has it that the nursemaids of Dionysos were put amongst the stars by Zeus: they are the Hyades, a star cluster in the constellation of Taurus, found between the horns of the Starry Bull. Of course, the title given to the women of Dionysos also varied depending on geographical location or specific cults, and are too numerous to list here; but some include the mythic female warrior followers of Dionysos the Korybantes of Anatolian origin, the venerable women-elders of Athens the Gerairai, and the title of Bacchae which lends its name to Euripides' play and simply means *'female worshippers of Bacchus'*. [343]

---

[343] The Harvard Theological Review Vol.72, 'Ecstasy and Possession', Ross S Kraemer, 1979: P.57,58

Chapter Ten

The Dionysian Calendar

When studying the Dionysian festivals, we first have to consider how their calendar year was arranged. Unlike our modern year - which is split into twelve months with a predictable number of days in each month - a year for our ancestors would have depended upon geographical location, political pressures, special events and a whole host of other external influences. Unlike today, there was no international method of calculating time: days, months and festivals were determined locally, and in keeping with local climates and trades. Time is something that is rigidly adhered to in our modern world, but for the ancient Greeks it was something that could be manipulated to suit what was going on in the world. It was not uncommon to add in an extra day – or even an extra month – for agricultural, social, religious or political benefit.

And let us not forget that Dionysos was worshipped far and wide all across the Mediterranean and beyond; what happened in ancient Greece is only one tiny piece of a much bigger picture. Indeed whilst the Athenian calendar is relatively well recorded, many of their practices originated elsewhere – influenced by earlier mystery cults of the Phrygians, Thracians, Mycenaeans and Minoans, amongst others. To add to confusion, besides his own festivals Dionysos was also often involved in the celebrations for other deities – such as those at Eleusis in which Dionysos was an important part of the rites but was not always considered as the central figure. It can also be argued that Dionysos was honoured in the guise of other deities with whom he had been conflated or usurped by; this is particularly evident in the rites of the Cretan Zeus and Zeus Meilichios. All these factors only add confusion when trying to piece together an accurate Dionysian calendar – the sheer diversity alone makes it almost impossible to create a definitive record of when, how or even why his rites were celebrated. Therefore, the rites of the Athenian festival calendar are sometimes described as being impure in form; partly because they are relatively recent and therefore may be distorted from the original rites but mainly because the Athenians were known to draw from many different sources and shoehorn them into their festival year. However, the Athenian twelve month calendar is also one of the most widely researched of all the ancient calendars and definitely one of the most inclusive – for these reasons, I have used the Athenian calendar as a framework for this chapter.

So how was the Athenian year constructed? The Athenian New Year began in the month of *Hecatombia* which began with the present-day July New Moon.[344] This month marked the height of summer and hottest point in the year; it was also marked by the rising of Sirius, the brightest star in the night sky. Like today, one year was determined by the period of time the earth took to orbit the sun: approximately 365 days. Calendar months were determined by a *'lunisolar'* cycle: that is, the position of both the moon and the sun were considered. A single calendar month was determined by one complete lunar cycle - from new moon to new moon – and just like us today, the Greeks named twelve months (moon cycles) in one solar year. However this caused a problem in the long term, because the length of time that each moon cycle actually varies very slightly; and so after some time, it would appear that the seasons had 'drifted out' of their appointed months. Nowadays this is overcome by ignoring the length of each lunar cycle and giving a set number of days to each month. But in the ancient world, they solved the problem by adding in an extra month every two years, to bring the calendar back in harmony with the solar year.

The Trieterica

And for her they will set up many statues in temples
As he cut you into three pieces in triennial feasts
Men shall always sacrifice to you unblemished Hecatombs
So hail, Dionysos Eiraphiotes, and your mother Semele …[345]

---

[344] Although it should be noted that other cities in ancient Greece may have marked their New Year in different seasons.
[345] The Homeric Hymns, Hymn to Dionysos Frag.1, Apostolos Athanasskis, 1976: P.1

The Athenian festivals were usually carried out on an annual basis, and as such Dionysos was often considered a Year Daimon: that is, a cyclical annual deity in tune with the solar year. However the rites of Dionysian revelers *outside* of Athens and beyond may have been very different. For example, one celebration held in Delphi in honour of Semele's ascent from the underworld was held only every eight years. But of particular interest are the *trieterica*, or *'triennial feasts'* which were said to have been established by Dionysos himself upon the mountainsides of Nÿsa. This *Orphic Hymn to Dionysos* (45) was inscribed as dedicated to *Dionysos Bassareus Trieterikos*, in whose honour the trieteric festivals were held:

"Come, blessed Dionysos, various-named, bull-faced, begot from thunder, Bakkhos famed. Bassaros God, of universal might, whom swords and blood and sacred rage delight: in heaven rejoicing, mad, loud-sounding God, furious inspirer, bearer of the rod: by Gods revered, who dwellest with humankind, propitious come, with much rejoicing mind."

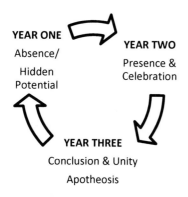

YEAR ONE
Absence/
Hidden
Potential

YEAR TWO
Presence &
Celebration

YEAR THREE
Conclusion & Unity
Apotheosis

The structure of the trieteric festivals is still largely unknown, although it is supposed that the first two years may have represented the paradoxical nature of Dionysos – the first year representing the hidden or absent god (*Meilichios*) and the second year representing life and presence (*Bakcheus*) and one concluding third year which marked the unity of opposites, and the renewal of the cycle of Dionysos. It was here that one cycle concluded, and another began; a place of apotheosis and rebirth. In this concluding year, life, death and rebirth found its *culmination and end*.[346] This was a festival cycle of highs and lows; in comparison to the Athenian festival calendar which celebrated death and rebirth within one solar year, the trieteric festivals celebrated the cycle of transformation on a larger scale, over a longer period of time. One could argue that this cycle is also evident in the tales of Nonnus,

---

[346] Dionysos: Archetypal Image of Indestructible Life, Karl Kerényi, 1996: P.197

reflected in the natures of *Zagreus* and *Bromios* and of course *Iakchos*, the third incarnation of Dionysos and spark of eternal life.

> *"And when you rouse anew the yearning for the triennial festival, you begin the song in the midst of your female attendants, the beauteously girt ones, who gives voice to the shout of joy and excite the choruses to the dance..."* [347]

As time went on it is likely that many of the older rites of the trieterica became integrated into the Athenian festival cycle, which came to embrace both sides of the God and his unity within a twelve month calendar year. It is also possible that the trieterica continued in a traditional way outside of Athens during and despite partial integration into the Attic festival cycle. Either way, the trieteric festival practices were preserved in the accounts of writers and countless others must have been integrated into the Athenian festival calendar, their true origins now forgotten.

One such trieteric rite that has been preserved by literature is the Delphic *Festival of Awakening*. During the first year of the cycle, a symbol or icon of Dionysos was *'laid in state'* as if in a tomb; whilst the second year marked his reanimation and rebirth. During this *'awakening year'*, the Thyiads of Delphi rushed up Mount Parnassos, seeking the reborn Dionysos. Their search would conclude at the Korykion Antron (cave of the leather sack) where the sacred fermentation sack was found and opened, marking the rebirth of *Bakcheus*. The year that followed, the third year, would likely have been seen as a period of celebration and glorification of the unified god. It is likely that the Awakening ritual is particularly old; originally, the fermentation sack would have held mead which hearkened back to some of mankind's oldest hunter gatherer skills and primal foods and would have been held at the conclusion of the forty day period of mead making. Later, the sack came to hold wine, and the festival coincided with the clearing of the first wine of the year. This festival eventually came to be integrated into the Athenian festival year during the period of Maimakterion (beginning with our modern-day November New Moon).

---

[347] Dionysus Myth & Cult, Walter F Otto (1960) 1995: P.82

Several legends attempt to explain the origin of the trieterica. Some say they were instigated to celebrate the return of Dionysos when he returned home after three years in India. Others say they were started by Dionysos himself when he eventually reclaimed his kingdom from the mountain god Nysos (who he had allowed to rule for three years) whilst others claim that Theseus was responsible for the beginnings of these festivals. But outside of legend, it is quite possible that the trieteric cycle finds its origins in the processes of mead making and wine making. Dionysos' period of *'lying in state'* his *'hidden potential'* during the first year may well reflect the period of aging and fermentation. Mead can take anywhere between three months and twelve months to brew, meaning that a particularly sweet mead may have been left in the fermentation sack for up to a year before it was opened. In this way, the first year of fermentation would have represented the first nocturnal *'hidden'* Dionysos, whilst the second year which marked the opening of the mead would have represented the appearance of Dionysos in the world. The third year represented the unity of things, and the ending of one cycle and the beginning of another. Like Mead, good wine is also a labour of patience; whilst wine can be made very quickly (fermentation itself can take as little as two weeks) a better wine can be made by allowing it to age, with many wines tasting no more superior after a year's aging. Although the Hellenes were known to drink recently cleared wine, aged wine would have been a much more sought-after commodity. The trieteric festivals may also have been symbolic of the agricultural method of leaving land *'fallow'* – that is, leaving a field unseeded for one year so that it might regain its natural balance of moisture and nutrients which would otherwise become depleted by constant farming. Although Dionysos was rarely associated with agriculture in general, as attendant to Demeter he was sometimes involved with her grain and harvest cycles. During this period the fallow land falls quiet, barren and rested: a symbol of death but also potential for new life. In Delphi, this two-year agricultural period was marked with the ritual *'tearing'* of the god at harvest time and in the winter, and the burial (or *'sowing'*) of his parts during the spring.[348]

Indeed, the trieteric festivals are believed to have sustained some of the earliest Dionysian dismemberment rites – a theme which

---

[348] Greek Mysteries, Michael Cosmopoulos, 2003: P.231

would be embraced by the later Orphics, who were influenced in part by the mystery rites of Delphi and Crete. A method of divination carried out in Delphi reflected the dismemberment myths of Dionysos, and is believed to have originally been part of the trieteric festival cycle. A sacrificial bull calf was slaughtered and divided into either three or seven parts; the parts were then boiled up in a sacred cooking pot (originally called a kettle) until only the bones remained. The bones were declared the sacrificial remains of Dionysos; and they were then cast upon the floor, and read as an oracle. The bones were used to conduct the divination during the first year of the cycle which honoured the chthonic and absent Dionysos (Meilichios) but during the second year the literal presence of the reborn ecstatic Dionysos (*Bakcheus*) was considered so strong that it was sufficient to fill the kettle with the spirit of Dionysos only - in this case, oracles were given by more direct means such as prophetic vision, and by talking to the god directly via the initiates who were possessed by him. The Orphic legends of the young Zagreus who was murdered, dismembered and boiled up in a kettle seem to reflect this Delphic rite; another reason to suggest that the Orphic legends have preserved several elements of mysticism from much earlier forms of the Dionysian current.

Several other festivals embraced by the Athenians are considered to have originally been part of the trieteric festivals, including the *Agrionia* which was held in honour of *Dionysos Agrionios*, '*the wild*' during the month of *Munychion* (beginning with the New Moon of April). This festival also possessed the theme of presence and absence, as well as highlighting the ability of Dionysos to punish those who betrayed or denied him or his cult. The offering of Hecatombs (100 sacrificial cattle) at Mount Nÿsa, the mountainside birthplace of Dionysos, are also believed to be of trieteric origin.

Athenian Month	Rites & Practices
Hekatombion	*Rites of Sirius. New year rites with emphasis on coolness and harvest. Hecatombia sacrifices. Dismemberment & Soul Transference. Rites to mark beginning of grape harvest & mead making.*
Metageitnion	*Petition return of Meilichios. Rites of balance between polarities. Processions to temples where contact with spirits is made, and oracles given. Prepare to enter the underworld.*
Boedromion	*Festival/rites to Ariadne. Complexities of life and death. Rites of joy and revelry followed by sorrow.*
Pyanepsion	*Harvest celebrations. Grape Treading Dance. Masked rites. Shapeshifting. Offerings of grapevines, animals, chorus and waterside rites. Contact with the underworld via liminal mediums, water/fog.*
Maimakterion	*Torchlight processions & Feasts. Invitation to Meilichios. Figwood Phallus rites of indestructibility. Lying in state and then awakening. Visiting mountainsides for chorus & trance. Opening the sack.*
Poseidon	*Celebrations of fruit, wine and grain stores. Balance of sustenance and death/dormancy. Divination. Oracle and sacred lots. Sweeping of temple spaces and spiral dances of the Cretan labyrinth.*

Gamelion	*Divination and prophecy in particular bone divination (sortilege) recalling the dismemberment myths. Recognition of ancestors. Petition return of Bakcheus. New wine and sunlight representing return.*
Anthesterion	*Icon/ mounted masks brought into temple to represent return. Mix water and wine to trumpet blasts. Water: journeying and initiation. Wandering spirits, Sexual union & fertility. Communality.*
Elaphebolion	*Theatre and mummery. Processions, dance and song. Spirit reincarnation. Sexual union. Vinewood Phallus rites of indestructibility. Festival/ rites of remembrance for Semele. Goat sacrifice*
Munychion	*Recollection of rebellions against Dionysos and rites to his wild and unforgiving side. Flogging, and blood offerings to the statues.*
Thargelion	*Rites of Bakcheus. Purification and Scapegoating. Music and dance competitions and offerings of cooked vegetables.*
Skirophorion	*Divination from the sounds of the sacrificial bull. Sacrificial blade cast into water. Petition for cooler months and harvest.*

Calendar

Athenian Month	New Moon	Agri / Viti	Summary	Festivals	Observations
Hekatombion	*July (New Year) Nm*	*Hottest Point Of The Year*	*Acknowledgement/ Rites Of Bakcheus*	*Hecatombia*	*27° Rising Of Sirius*
Metageitnion	*August Nm*	*Harvesting & Mead Making*	*Preparation For Descent/Absence Bakcheus*	*Initiatory Processions*	*27°*
Boedromion	*September Nm*	*Harvesting & Mead Making*	*Preparation For Descent/Absence Bakcheus*	*Torchlit Ceremonies*	*23° Autumn Equinox*
Pyanepsion	*October Nm*	*Wine Pressing*	*The Veil Is Thin. Descent Of Bakcheus*	*Oschophoria*	*19°*
Maimakterion	*November Nm*	*Pruning*	*Advent/Birth Of Nocturnal Dionysos/Meilichios*	*Festival Of Awakening*	*15°*
Poseidon	*December Nm*	*Leafless Canes*	*Acknowledgement/ Rites Of Meilichios*	*Haloa*	*11° Winter Solstice*
Gamelion	*January Nm*	*Leafless Canes*	*Consultation With Meilichios*	*Rural Dionysia/ Lenaia/ Theoinia*	*10°*
Anthesterion	*February Nm*	*First Wine Opened*	*The Veil Is Thin. Arrival/Birth Of Bakcheus. All Souls*	*Anthesteria/ Agrai*	*10°*

Elaphebolion	*March Nm*	*New Shoots Appear*	*Marriage/Heiros Gamos Of Bakcheus*	*City Dionysia*	*12° Spring Equinox*
Munychion	*April Nm*	*Buds Swell*	*Legends Of Dionysos Recalled*	*Agrionia*	*15°*
Thargelion	*May Nm*	*Climate Hotter – Fruit Swells*	*Acknowledgement/ Rites Of Bakcheus*	*Thargelia*	*19°*
Skirophorion	*June Nm*	*Climate Hotter – Fruit Swells*	*Acknowledgement/ Rites Of Bakcheus*	*Bouphonia*	*23° Summer Solstice*

I have indicated each *New Moon* that marked the beginning of each Athenian month. So for instance, the first day of the Athenian month of Hecatombia can be most closely aligned to the New Moon of our modern month of July. So for example in 2011, the period of Hecatombia began on approximately the modern 14th July and ended on approximately the modern 12th August. It should however be noted that modern calendars now use the term *'New Moon'* to refer to the point when the moon is dark, and hidden from sight. However to the ancients, the *'New Moon'* was taken as *the first sign of the crescent moon*, which would have occurred two or three days *after* the dark of the moon. The shaded months indicate *Dadophorios* (the three winter months) that the Mild Dionysos ruled over with the Ecstatic Dionysos ruling over the remaining hotter and lighter part of the year.[349]

Hekatombion

The period of Hekatombion began with the present-day **July New Moon**. It also coincided with the rising of Sirius (the brightest

---

[349] Later, Apollo would usurp the lighter part of the year, leaving Dionysos with the three winter months only.

star in the sky) and was considered by the ancient Greeks as their New Year.

The climate was at its hottest at this time, and Dionysos Bakcheus – the bright and ecstatic fire born god – was alive and manifest in the world. Yet the Solstice, which had occurred during the previous month of Skirophorion, had also marked the promise of shorter days. From now on, the days would become cooler and the nights would become longer. For those in the Mediterranean, the promise of a cooler climate would have been a welcomed relief from the heat of the summer. They longed for Dionysos Meilichios: the dark and cool 'shade-face' of Bakcheus - to return from his period of rest in the underworld. The *Hecatombia* was celebrated during this time: a sacrifice of one hundred cattle which were then dismembered, placed on a fire and doused with red wine; the meat was then consumed.[350] According to some accounts, the Hecatombs were offered to Dionysos at his birthplace on Mount Nÿsa, although this particular place is more likely to a place of fantasy, a combination of different mountainside sites where the cult of Dionysos was practiced and he was believed to have been born. Offerings at any mountainside would have been sufficient for Dionysos and would have come to be considered as the local 'Nÿsa'. This rite is usually considered as a festival of the god Apollo[351] but author Rosemarie Taylor-Perry[352] suggests that the nature of the rite implies that this sacrifice may also have been in honour of Dionysos: the word 'Hecatome' meaning '100 segments' which could indicate that it was associated with the dismemberment myth of the bull-formed nocturnal Dionysos Zagreus, who was torn apart and eaten by the Titans. After his dismemberment, the soul of Zagreus was reconceived by his second mother, Semele, as Bromios. The sacrifice of one thing to birth another was a common theme in Dionysian thought - a sort of soul transference from one physical form to another - and the ritual dismemberment of sacrificial animals and their consumption (either cooked or raw) emulated the legend of Dionysos' rebirth. The occurrence of this rite during the period of Hekatombion could have been carried out to mark the 'birth' of the New Year: the end of one

---

[350] The Iliad, II.428ff, Homer, c. 800 BCE, trans. AT Murray

[351] It is therefore likely that the 'Apollo' of the Hecatombia was Dionysos usurped

[352] The God Who Comes, Rosemarie Taylor-Perry, 2003: P.40

year and the beginning of another. The sacrifices of the Hecatombia may also have marked the beginning of the Season of Opora, the season of grape harvesting and mead-making, which started now (roughly our modern-day mid-July) and would last until Boedromion (roughly our modern mid-September).

Metageitnion

The period of Metageitnion began with the present-day **August New Moon**. The grape harvesting and mead making that had begun in Hekatombion continued during this time, and initiates of Dionysos continued to petition for the return of the mild and nocturnal Dionysos of the wintertime months. This time of year represented a tip in the balance between the two paradoxical faces of the god: between life and death, and the blazing sunlight of the summer sun and the coolness of winter.

It was also during the month of Metageitnion that initiates began to prepare for an important part of the Eleusinian Mysteries: a procession from the sanctuary of Dionysos in Athens to Eleusis, which concluded with a necromantic nocturnal rite held there. Smearing white clay, ash or fleshy wine lees upon the face to give themselves a deathly appearance, the established mystai (initiates of Dionysos) would dress up as underworld souls and deliver omens as the spirits of the dead. The new initiates however would prepare to enter the underworld for the first time: the realm of Dionysos Meilichios. This may well have been the start of a period of challenges for the new initiates, before their final initiation into the underworld and admission to the Secret Torchlight Feasts during Dadophorios - the three winter months which would begin with the modern-day November New Moon.

Incidentally, this month also marked the Roman festival of wine, the *Vinalia*, a harvest celebration of Jupiter (the Roman equivalent of the Hellenic Zeus) and Venus (the Roman equivalent of the Hellenic Aphrodite). Aphrodite herself was sometimes conflated with Ariadne[353] (the lover of Dionysos) and the Zeus of Cretan mythology is generally considered by many to be a conflation of Dionysos. The

---

[353] Dictionary of Greek & Roman Antiquities, William George Smith, 1870: P.92

following month of Boedromion would mark the festival of *Ariadneia*, in honour of Ariadne.

Boedromion

The period of Boedromion began with the present-day **September New Moon**. Boedromion marked the end of the Season of Opora (grape harvesting and mead making) which had begun in Hekatombion. As the climate started to become cooler this time was marked by torchbearing ceremonies in Athens, as Dionysos Bakcheus prepared to descend into the underworld and become Dionysos Meilichios, the nocturnal *'shade-face'* Dionysos.

This month marked the festival of *Ariadneia* which was held in remembrance of Ariadne; accounts of this particular festival practice are found on the islands of Naxos and Cyprus, where she was honoured as *Aphrodite-Ariadne*. According to Plutarch this festival was instituted by Theseus, who by some accounts did not abandon Ariadne to her doom but only left her temporarily on the island; he simply did not make it back to the island in time to save her, and she died during childbirth. Rites during this time included the ritual re-enactment of Ariadne's birth pains which would eventually kill her; an intriguing complex of life and death. To further emphasize the importance of paradoxical opposites, male initiates would re-enact the birth pains and not women. Plutarch also suggests that Ariadne may have been worshipped in two different forms during this festival of opposites, to symbolise her happiness with Theseus and then her desperation of his disappearance:

'the festival of the first Ariadne is celebrated with mirth and revels, but the sacrifices performed in honour of the second are attended with sorrow and mourning. [354]

Pyanepsion

The period of Pyanepsion began with the present-day **October New Moon**. After several months of grape harvesting, Athens now celebrated the yield and gave thanks to Dionysos for the harvest. The

---

[354] Plutarch Lives 'Theseus' Pt.20, c. 75 CE, trans. B Perrin

freshly harvested grapes would now be pressed, and the Epilinios *'grape-treading dance'*, was performed at this time as the grape-treaders crushed the fruit to the ritual cry of *euoi!*[355] It is possible that the treading (or at least part of it) was a ritualistic act: depictions found on pottery indicate that the grape treaders may have worn satyr-style animal masks to evoke the wild and shifting nature of Dionysos during the treading.

To mark the conclusion of the grape harvest, the festival of *Oschophoria*, the *'Feast of Boughs'* was held, on approximately the 7th day of the month: a procession of celebrants carried grapevine branches from the temple of Dionysos in Athens towards the ocean, and races between the two sites were sometimes held with the winners receiving prizes such as oil, honey, wine and cheese. Antiquity records that this festival was first instituted by Theseus: the hero of Hellenic mythology who slew the Minotaur, *'the bull of Minos'*. However Plutarch states quite clearly that the deity actually being petitioned during the festival was Dionysos: *'the vine branches ... they carry these in honour of Dionysos and Ariadne ... because they came back home at the time of the vintage.'* [356] We can speculate that the rites held at this time were originally a commemoration of the imminent arrival of the nocturnal Dionysos, later becoming a festival of Theseus and marked by the myth of his return from Crete. According to mythology, the Minotaur was fathered by the Cretan Bull, who we know was conflated with Dionysos Zagreus. It is likely that the Minotaur was yet another embodiment of the Dionysian current - a god of the Cretan Bull Cult, who was associated with both light and dark, or nocturnal flames. The actual slaying of the Minotaur is probably an Athenian perspective, and may have been symbolic of political relations between Athens and Crete; however it may also have been a reminder of the sacrifice of Dionysos that was necessary in order for his next incarnation to be born.

The procession concluded at the shine of Athena Skiras in the seaport square of Phaleron Bay which was about 4 miles away, and to mark the end of the celebrations a great feast was held. The fact that the boughs were carried to a seaport was probably an observance of

---

[355] Greek: *io euoi* Latin: *io evohe*

[356] Plutarch Lives 'Theseus' Pt.23, c. 75 CE, trans. B Perrin

the export of wine, as well as in memory Dionysos' adventures at sea. The procession party was largely made up of women – but also men dressed as women. The significance of cross-dressing during this festival was probably in honour of the androgynous dual nature of Dionysos, and it is known that '*womanish youths*'[357] represented *Dionysos Dimorphos*, the two-natured and effeminate Dionysos, during this festival. Cross-dressing may also have reflected the legend in which Dionysos disguised himself as a woman in order to escape from Hera; or the legend in which Theseus disguised two young soldiers as women to protect the maidens whom had been sent to Crete to be sacrificed to the Minotaur.

'*... he took not with him the full number of virgins ... but selected two youths of his acquaintance, of fair and womanish faces .. and having, by frequent baths ... with a constant use of all the ointments and washes and dresses that serve to the adorning of the head or smoothing of the skin or improving of the complexion ... changed them from what they were before...*'[358]

Another bough-custom associated with Theseus during the festival of *Oschophoria* was a children's competition called the *eiresione*, in which children were invited to decorate olive branches with swinging decorations to mark the return of Theseus from Crete. A similar bough was created during the month of *Thargelion*, which marked the departure of Theseus. Other fruits associated with Dionysos were harvested and celebrated at this time – such as figs and pomegranates. Both fruits were associated with the underworld, and as they ripened they may also have been seen as marking the shift in power between Bakcheus and Meilichios. Just as the fig was associated with underworldly kingship and fertility, so the pomegranate had assured that Persephone remained in the underworld with Hades – a god who is often equated with the chthonic Dionysos and who abducted Persephone at Erineos (a village whose name means *fig*). Both fruits were considered as symbolic of transition and initiation, and came to be used in the rite of Eleusis.

---

[357] The Great Dionysiac Myth Vol.1, Robert Brown, (1877) 2000: P.242
[358] Plutarch Lives 'Theseus' Pt.22, c.75 CE, trans. B Perrin

In other parts of Hellas and beyond, Pyanepsion marked the beginning of waterside rites in which the nocturnal Dionysos was called out from beneath the waves in a prelude to his awakening. The veil between the worlds was considered to be thin at this time which made contact with the underworld easier - especially by using liminal mediums such as water, swamps, fog and smoke. Choruses were held and creatures representing Dionysos, such as goats, lambs or bull calves were flung into the water to placate the underworld beings and to petition for Dionysos' ascent. Other forms of sacrifice were also made to Dionysos in anticipation of his return. Sometimes referred to as the *'son of a cow'* or *'the one who has been born of a cow'* a bull calf was dressed up as the horned infant Dionysos Zagreus in symbols such as hunting boots[359] and then sacrificed to the god. By some reports, the flesh of the animal was then divided up by hand and eaten raw as if eating the flesh of the god; this is just one of the many accounts of *omophagia* (eating of raw flesh) in the worship of Dionysos. A similar account is made in Crete, which is the likely place of origin of this particular rite. Like the celebrations of Oschophoria at Athens, we can suppose that this rite commemorated the withdrawal of the bright and ecstatic Bakcheus and foresaw the arrival of the nocturnal Dionysos Meilichios.

Maimakterion

The period of Maimakterion began with the present-day **November New Moon**. Maimakterion was sometimes described as *'the torchbearing month'* due to the fact that it marked the beginning of *Dadophorios*: three dark winter months, when torchlight processions would be held as part of the Dionysian rites. It is interesting to note that European *'Winter Time'* officially begins on the 30th October - and so November is still considered as the first true month of winter.

The festivities may have begun with the Feast of Torches, or *Lampteria*, which marked the start of a period of awakening in which the nocturnal Dionysos would be invited back to reign over the world of men. Blazing torches would be brought into the sanctuaries and bowls of wine set up throughout the city. A figwood phallus was also used during the Maimakterion rites to symbolise the indestructibility

---

[359] Dionysos: Archetypal Image of Indestructible Life, Karl Kerényi, 1996: P.55

of the nocturnal Dionysos, and in the vineyards this month marked the time to prune back the grapevines to leafless canes. After their pruning the canes appeared as if dead; but like Dionysos, they had only withdrawn their life to the underworld of their roots.

The theme of rebirth continued with the *Festival of Awakening*, which was held approximately on the 8th day of the month (although the date would have varied from year to year, as the festival had to coincide with wine being cleared sufficiently and being ready to drink). By some accounts, a symbol of Dionysos was laid in state in a tomb[360] for a period of time before the thyiades —Dionysian devotees whose ceremonial role was sometimes that of *'nursemaid'* to the baby Dionysos and whom were sometimes referred to as *'storm winds'* due to their movement and nature — began to ritually search for him, in order to awaken him from his slumber. It is recorded in Delphi[361] and also in Thrace, that the ecstatic revelries of the thyiads involved dancing up the mountain paths of Mount Parnassos, singing dithyrambs and undergoing periods of trance and physical exertion as they searched for the underworldly infant; some suggest this practice also acted as an initiation for the young women.[362]

"It is customary for these thyiades, along the road from Athens and elsewhere ... to perform dancing circles ... the chthonic dance of the thyiades."[363]

Their journey ended at the Korykion Antron (*'cave of the leather sack'*) where they enacted the sacred rites of the korykos, the leather sack in which fresh mead was fermented. As the mead was opened, so Dionysos - identified with the mead itself - was seen to be born. As they made their way back down the mountainside, it was said that Dionysos *'danced back down with them'*. It is likely that this particular festival was originally celebrated trieterically (every other year/every third year) but like many other trieteric festivals it eventually became part of the Attic annual festival cycle.

---

[360] Dionysos: Archetypal Image of Indestructible Life, Karl Kerényi, 1996: P.223

[361] Dionysos: Archetypal Image of Indestructible Life, Karl Kerényi, 1996: P.212

[362] The God Who Comes, Rosemarie Taylor-Perry, 2003: P.63

[363] Description of Greece x.4, Pausanias (c. 200 CE) Source: The Great Dionysiac Myth Vol.1, Robert Brown (1877) P.271

Their search and discovery of Dionysos may have been reminiscent of the tale of the goddess Rhea (or Kybele) and her nymphai (nature spirits) who according to mythology found and reared the child Dionysos. Later, these festivals would be reflected in the Liknon ceremonies of the Eleusinian Mysteries, in which the baby Dionysos was said to have been born from the *liknon* (winnowing basket) as *liknites, 'the being in the winnow'*. Rosemarie Taylor-Perry[364] points out the interesting fact that the word *liknon 'winnowing basket'* remains in usage in the modern Greek word *liknizo*, meaning *'to rock a baby'*. According to some accounts, a mask of Dionysos could be found either covering, or inside, the liknon - perhaps symbolizing that the infant Dionysos was the *'revealer'* of the mysteries - or indeed the mysteries themselves. Votive tablets of Persephone, a central character in the Eleusinian Mysteries (and the mother of Dionysos Zagreus, according to several sources) show her opening the Liknon Mystikon; the contents of which are debated, but may well have held objects that were symbolic of the new born infant. Prayers and sacrifices may also have been offered to Persephone at this time, as the mother of the bull-formed child of the underworld.

Certainly the period of Maimakterion was considered a special time for children, in particular those who were considered associated with the underworld. Babies born at this time were considered to be reincarnated souls, who had been conceived during the Anthesteria or the City Dionysia Nine months earlier when the ghosts or *'shades'* of the ancestors were invited back to the upperworld of the living.

Poseidon

The period of Poseidon began with the present-day **December New Moon**. Poseidon marked the beginning of the festival of *Haloa 'festival of the threshing floor'*[365] which was primarily a festival of fruit stores; although in the Eleusinian Mysteries it was also considered a celebration of wine stores (the fruit of Dionysos, viticulture) and grain stores (the seed of his mother Demeter, agriculture).

---

[364] The God Who Comes, Rosemarie Taylor-Perry, 2003: P.64
[365] The Great Dionysiac Myth Vol.1, Robert Brown, (1877) 2000: P.271

Whilst this festival celebrated the abundance of fruit and grain that had been brought into store, it also marked the state of the leafless canes after the grape harvest. The nocturnal Dionysos, who had returned during the festival of awakening in the previous month of Maimakterion, continued to be acknowledged at this time and his association with the underworld and death was emphasized through the Dionysian rites. This month was believed to be a most powerful time to consult with the nocturnal Dionysos Meilichios through divination and oracle, and sacred lots and other types of augury were undertaken by the initiates of Dionysos. The legends of Dionysos and Ikarios were also recalled, and rites held in his memory.

Gamelion

The period of Gamelion began with the present-day **January New Moon**. In the vineyards the grapevines remained as leafless canes, but life was beginning to stir in their roots as the days gradually became warmer. During this time it was considered that the veil between the upperworld and the underworld was thin; and taking advantage of this state of liminality, initiates continued to practice divination and prophecy. Primarily this was done in order to consult with the nocturnal Dionysos, but also to contact the souls of the dead.

Indeed, Dionysos was celebrated for his ability to inspire trance, prophecy and divination of all kinds. In this case, a method of sortilege was used: a young bull was sacrificed as the embodiment of Dionysos, and its bones placed inside a ceremonial kettle. The bones were then cast upon the floor, and read as an oracle. It is likely that the kettle symbolised the underworld, and that the bones symbolised the physical presence of Dionysos. A similar kettle was kept at Delphi – but this time with goat bones inside the kettle. Here too, the bones were believed to be the remainders of Dionysos himself (what was left of his body after dismemberment). Dionysos was associated with the goat in several ways and the infant Dionysos was often described as '*the kid*' who was boiled up in a cooking pot at the hands of the Titans. However the significance of goat bones in this case may also suggest that the prophetic domains of Apollonian Delphi were in fact at one time the realms of Dionysos. According to myth, a goat was said to have discovered the oracular powers of Delphi after accidentally breathing in trance-inducing fumes which were once believed to have arisen from fissures in the rocks beneath the site. The suggestion of intoxication and prophecy – and in particular, discovered by a horned infant - already hints at a Dionysian theme.

Whilst many of the rites undertaken during the period of Gamelion were of an underworldly persuasion, this month also marked the third and last month of the *Dadophorios* (the three winter months) and therefore indicated an end to the reign of the nocturnal Dionysos Meilichios. And so this month was also a time to prepare for the return of Dionysos Bakcheus, or Bromios – the bright and ecstatic god of the returning sun. Devotees of Dionysos reenacted the birth pains of his mother Semele during this time, in anticipation of the rebirth of Dionysos Bakcheus due to occur during the Anthesteria.

And so the month of Gamelion also marked the beginning of the *Festival of Lenaia* - better known as the *Rural Dionysia,* which began on the first full moon after the shortest day of winter but continued until the end of Anthesterion (and was therefore also involved in the rites and folklore of the life-giving Anthesteria). By some accounts the Rural Dionysia was first celebrated in Ikarion, reportedly the first place to have welcomed Dionysos and his gift of wine. Ikarion was also the first place to perform fictional theatre during the intervals between the dithyrambs to Dionysos. During the Lenaia, wine miraculously flowed instead of water in the temples of Dionysos for 7 days – yet if the wine was taken out of the temple, it would immediately transform back into water. This miraculous emergence of wine may have been symbolic of the imminent return of the Ecstatic One, whose presence was described as *'bursting forth'* into the world, as well as the opening of the first new wine which had been fermenting during the colder months and would soon be ready to drink. In Elis in southern Hellas, a similar miracle occurred: three sealed and empty pitchers were placed within a sealed temple, and when the temple was opened up again the pitchers were miraculously full of wine. Another account of water turning into wine at this time of year was also recorded on the island of Andros: here too, it was said that Dionysos was reborn when the sunlight was beginning to renew itself[366] a process which would have begun at the winter

---

[366] Dionysus Myth & Cult, Walter F Otto (1960) 1995: P.194

solstice but would have become more evident during the following months running up to the month of Anthesterion; a period of honouring Dionysos as lord of vitality and new life. By some accounts, the Lenaia also marked the beginning of the rites of the *Gerairai* (priestesses of Dionysos) who aided with the sacred marriage rites at the *Sanctuary of Limnae* (see Anthesterion) and the Lenaia was considered a festival period which was sacred to both the son and the mother.

Another tradition was carried out during this time called the *Askoliasmos*, or *'leaping on the wine skin'*. During this sport a he-goat would be sacrificed and its skin would be filled with wine or oil until it was round. It was then greased; after which contestants would try to balance on the skin and whoever balanced (or *'danced'*) upon it for the longest was the winner.[367] The winner could then take home the skin, which was full of expensive oil or wine. This tradition also finds its origins in Ikarion, where according to legend King Ikarios slaughtered a goat for eating his grapevines and then made a bag from its skin. He made a bag from the skin which he filled with wine, and danced upon it in honour of Dionysos.

Anthesterion

The period of Anthesterion began with the present-day **February New Moon**. This month marked the first of the new wine, which had been fermenting during the winter and was now opened and poured upon the earth in libation. This month symbolized the return of Dionysos Bakcheus, the ecstatic god of the warmer months, and as such it was also in honour of *Dionysos Lampter*, *'light bringer'*. Unlike the nocturnal Meilichios – who had ruled during the winter months but was usually considered as remaining *'apart'* from the physical world – the presence of Dionysos Bakcheus was believed to be absolutely literal. As the embodiment of new life, he was identified with blossom and growth, and was referred to as *Dionysos Antheus*, *'the blooming'*.

During the *Festival of Anthesteria*, an icon of Dionysos was brought into Athens which symbolised his return, and was thought of

---

[367] Dionysos: Archetypal Image of Indestructible Life, Karl Kerényi, 1996: P.312

and treated as the god himself. Actual statues of Dionysos were rare and so it was more common for an object, or a combination of objects, to represent the god. Sometimes two wooden masks similar to the masks of Bakcheus and Meilichios were used as the icon: these were placed back to back or mounted upon a post, creating a duality which marked the exchange of reign from one guise of the god to the other. Indeed, the chthonic guise of Dionysos continued to be honoured during this time: offerings were made to *Dionysos Nyktelios 'nocturnal'* during the Anthesteria. A similar ritual occurred at this time in the city of Sikyon, where an icon of Dionysos entered the city by night accompanied by torchbearers who left bowls of wine around the city. The leader of the torch procession was called the *Bakcheios*, an epithet of Dionysos which means *'exciter to frenzy'*. Several accounts recall that the icon of Dionysos used during the Anthesteria entered the city upon a wooden ship, and this may have been significant for several reasons. The first was that it was often considered that during his absence Dionysos had been travelling to foreign territories across the sea, and this festival marked his triumphant return. This travel was probably symbolic of the export of wine to other countries, although this fact was probably not something that the average worshipper would have been aware of. Secondly, water was considered a liminal substance: a portal between the worlds. As Dionysos returned from the chthonic depths it was believed that the gates of the underworld were swung wide open - and as he ascended up into the world of the living he brought with him a host of wandering spirits.

This occurred on the first day of the festival - the **11th day** of the month named the ***Pithoigia*** or *'tap-barrel day'* when the first of the wine fermentation jars (pithoi) were opened and in doing so the souls of the dead emerged from the underworld. It is possible that the pithoi were considered akin to cremation urns, hence the links with the dead and necromantic rites at this time.[368] Shrines and temples were closed off; statues of the gods were covered or wrapped with cloth; and people chewed hawthorn to protect themselves from malignant spirits on this ghostly day. Dionysos himself was also considered to emerge from the pithoi, a rite which paralleled the more obvious entrance that the god made by ship on the same day.

---

[368] The God Who Comes, Rosemarie Taylor-Perry, 2003: P.70

This wine would then be taken to the ceremonial space where the icon or statue from the ship had been placed, and the wine was mixed there with sacred spring water by a band of Satyrs and shared out with the initiates, who would then toast the return of the bright god to the sound of trumpet blasts. Rites were also held outside of the temples in general festival street celebrations, and libations were offered to the Agathos Daemon, the household spirit of good fortune.

Erigone, the daughter of King Ikarios who learnt the skill of viticulture from Dionysos, was also commemorated during the Pithoigia. She hung herself from her father's corpse after he was murdered for serving wine to the men of his court – not understanding the effects of the wine, they believed that he had poisoned them. During the festival, swings were set up in the courtyards where the *pithoi* were stored and young Athenian girls would swing upon them to recreate the swinging of Erigone during the opening of the wine fermentation jars. It is possible that the swinging was seen as an activity which aided the transition of the spirits from the underworld into the upperworld, much like ritual swinging and whirring was seen to aid trance states and visions. The swinging followed a period of *'roaming'*, which re-enacted Erigone *'seeking'* her father – but also reinforced the idea of *'seeking'* the god – an activity which had been a major part of the rites during the winter months. In some places, the myth of Ikarios was combined with the rites of calling the god up from lakes – by some accounts, the body of Ikarios (who could be considered as a mythological embodiment of Dionysos) was tossed into a deep well of water.[369] The celebrants would take the opportunity to honour the spirits of their ancestors who had returned during the Pithoigia, and would eat with them, much like the *Dumb Supper* of neo-pagan Samhain.

But the Anthesteria was not just a time for the ancestors to be remembered and honoured; more importantly, it was also a time when the dead had the opportunity to be reborn. On the second day of the Anthesteria, the **12th day** of the month, named ***Khoes Day***, the souls who had emerged from the underworld had the chance to

---

[369] A Different God? Dionysos & Ancient Polytheism 'Dionysos, the Wine, and Ikarios' Philippe Borgeaud (2009) 2011: P.166

be reconceived during hieros gamos: ritual lovemaking. Indeed the festival of Anthesteria is recorded to have possessed a particularly erotic atmosphere as the spirits attended the nuptial rites; and Dionysos was perceived as both *'lord of souls'* and *'bridegroom'*.[370] These ceremonies were often held by the common revelers on the marshes adjacent to the sealed temple of *Dionysos Limnaios 'Dionysos of the Marsh'* – or, *Sanctuary of Limnae* – which lay just outside of Athens. They were held at dusk and accompanied by sacrifices.

Dionysos himself was believed to participate in Sacred Marriage during this time, and the *Sanctuary of Limnae* played an important part in these mysteries. The 12th day of the Anthesterion marked the only time when the temple opened its doors, and it was here that the Basilinna (*'Queen' of Athens*) would be united with Dionysos. By other accounts, a procession began here which led to the *Boukoleon* or *'bull stable'* sanctuary at the central marketplace where the rite took place; indeed, the Boukoleon was often referred to as the Archon's *'bedchamber'*. During the sacred marriage they would ritually conceive Dionysos Meilichios, born nine months later at the *Festival of Awakening*.

The *Gerairai* (fourteen4 elder priestesses of Dionysos) are said to have held an important role during the sacred marriage rites, both in terms of purification and sympathetic magic. The Greek orator Demosthenes recalled that the Gerairai swore oaths during the rites of heiros gamos and attended fourteen special altars *'with baskets'*. This particular element of the Anthesteria was known as the *Theoinia* - a name which also referred to these fourteen shrines at which the Gerairai attended. Offerings - and specifically purificatory rites - were made at these special shrines and may have been considered crucial to the success of the sacred marriage rites. The ancient Greeks always gave special attention to their altars and shrines: the decoration and offerings upon the altar acted as a form of permanent dedication to the deity and reinforced the ritual and magic undertaken there. Grain and salt were sprinkled to consecrate the sacred area, and lustration (a form of purification by washing or anointing with water or blood) was carried out before entering the space.[371] Blood was also

---

[370] The God Who Comes, Rosemarie Taylor-Perry, 2003: P.70

[371] Prolegomena to the Study of Greek Religions, Jane Ellen Harrison 1908: P.60

sometimes sprinkled around the outskirts of the shine to keep evil spirits from entering the sacred space (as it was believed they remained preoccupied with the blood around the perimeter). The significance of specifically fourteen women possibly reflects the fourteen youths who were sent to the Minotaur in the ancient legends; this rite may therefore have some connection with Theseus – the Dionysian-style hero who slew the Bull of Minos, and who is often considered as akin to Dionysos himself.

Another rite is often mentioned in conjunction with the Theoinia, although even less is known about its purpose: the *Iobakcheia 'hail bacchus rites*[372] in which priestesses declared themselves as pure. The two rites may have expressed two different forms of Dionysos being worshipped at this time, i.e. the mild/composed and the ecstatic, especially when we consider that this month also signified a shift from Mellichios to Bakcheus. These rites are said to have been performed at very specific times during the sacred marriage ceremonies, although by some accounts the rituals of the Gerairai began several weeks before, at the Rural Dionysia.

Libations of wine continued to be offered during this time, and from Khoes Day until the end of the Anthesteria Dionysos held the name of *Choöpotes 'deep drinker'*. Drinking competitions were held and he who could drink the most was declared the winner and crowned with a wreath of leaves; an accessory that Dionysos himself was said to have invented. More extravagant leaf wreaths were crafted out of pure gold, and are known to have been worn for religious and political occasions alike.

Whilst the wandering spirits of the Anthesteria were rightfully honoured, by their nature they were also feared. Any spirits who had not been reconceived during Khoes Day were now driven back down to the underworld on **Khytroi Day** - the third day of the festival and the **13th day** of the month - with cries of *'Out of the doors, ye Keres! It is no longer Anthesteria!'*[373] Rites were held on the banks of marshes and lakes and food and oil was offered within clay food pots (khytroi) encouraging the spirits to descend into the chthonic depths of the

---

[372] Suidas s.v. Theoinion c. 10 CE

[373] Prolegomena to the Study of Greek Religions, Jane Ellen Harrison 1908: P.35

underworld. During this day, Dionysos was recognised in his role as psychopomp as he directed the ghosts and spirits back to the underworld. It is interesting to note that the Greek name for this day, χύτροι, is actually a masculine word meaning natural pots, i.e. holes in the ground[374] chasms, caves and natural pools – liminal places regarded as entrances to the underworld - those used as offering pits to the chthonic gods: bothroi. A baked offering of grain, mixed seeds, figs and honey was also offered at this time to Hermes Chthonios, underworldly psychopomp identified with Dionysos. The cake was not intended to be eaten by mortals – even the Priests, who would often partake of food offered to the gods, were forbidden to eat this particular sacred offering. Hesychius mentions that a purificatory censor was made out of a khytroi pot, inside which incense and sometimes the baked honey-seed cakes were burnt. The smoke was used to fumigate the home or shrine and the ashes scattered to Hekate at the meeting of three ways, after which the homeowner or temple keeper would walk away without looking back. A cacophony of noise and revelry, quite fitting to the Dionysian atmosphere, accompanied these offerings and fumigations with cymbals and drums being played[375] to drive the spirits back into the realm of the dead.

Theatre and choral dances were also popular during this time, as well as games, sacrifice and masked dance to mark the birthday of the ecstatic god. Aside from the religious meanings of the festival, the Anthesteria was also a time to celebrate communal production: something which was extremely important to Dionysos, who embodied the ecstasy of the group. Richard Seaford[376] wrote that the Dionysos cult encouraged *'seasonally determined communality'*, emphasizing the importance of the average working person; indeed the opening of the wine signified the success of the previous winemaking period, and gave people hope for the next season. As with many of the Dionysian festivals, equality also featured during the Anthesteria. Slaves and poor workers were invited to join in during the festivities and allowed access to food, wine and other pleasures of the city. In fact some researchers believe that the rituals used during

---

374 Prolegomena to the Study of Greek Religions, Jane Ellen Harrison 1908: P.37

375 The God Who Comes, Rosemarie Taylor-Perry, 2003: P.37

376 Dionysos, Richard Seaford, 2006: P.17

Khytroi Day to drive out the wandering ghosts also acted to drive out these people, as the festival ended and the city returned to normal.

Another related festival was held during this period, called the *Diasia*: a feast held in honour of Zeus Meilichios[377] which involved sacrifices and oracular messages. As we have already examined, it is likely that Zeus Meilichios was an adaption of the older underworld snake-god or daemon Meilichios, who was much more closely connected to the chthonic cults of Dionysos than the Olympian Zeus. There are also accounts in Crete of a private trieteric rite which occurred at this time of the year which involved taking bulls out into the wild and ripping the creatures to pieces alive, and then madly devouring the raw flesh in the name of *Dionysos Omestes, 'devourer'*. We must keep in mind that this particular account was made by a Christian writer who actively worked to discredit pagan religion.

Elaphebolion

The period of Elaphebolion began with the present-day **March New Moon**. This month marked the festival known as the *City Dionysia* (or *Greater Dionysia*) which is generally considered as one of the most important and widely celebrated of the Athenian festivals, drawing people to Athens from all over Hellas and beyond. Earlier during the festival year, icons, statues and symbols of Dionysos had been moved to a secret shrine where they had been kept hidden, only to be brought back into the city at this time to mark the arrival of Dionysos. The icon would enter the city temple or sacred space to the accompaniment of dance and song, led by a youth carrying a blazing torch; perhaps symbolizing the return of the bright god and his association with the sun as well as his role as torchbearing psychopomp.

You may have noticed that this *'arrival'* of an icon or statue seems to be of a similar nature to the entrance of Dionysos upon a wooden boat during the Anthesteria in the previous month, suggesting it may be a continuation of the theme. But this is not where the similarities end. Once the icon had entered the temple, a

---

[377] Dictionary of Greek & Roman Antiquities, William George Smith, 1870

bull was singled out as the embodiment of Dionysos. It was named *axios taurus 'worthy bull'* - that is, considered worthy of carrying the spirit or soul of Dionysos. The bull was then slaughtered, and thereafter the literal presence of Dionysos Bakcheus was celebrated. At first it might seem confusing as to why a bull (which embodies Dionysos) should be sacrificed at a time when the god has only just arrived, or been *'born'*. This may in fact have been a continuation of the sexual theme of spirit reincarnation from Anthesteria, when spirits were invited back and had the opportunity to be reborn through hieros gamos (ritual lovemaking). Although the City Dionysia is accounted to have been a time of sexual union, it is generally believed that it had nowhere near the sexual atmosphere that was associated with the earlier festival of Anthesteria – instead, it heavily focused on honouring the ancestors (in particular celebrating family and military civic honour). If hieros gamos was still being practiced during the Greater Dionysia (which by many accounts it was) then the sacrifice of Dionysos at a time when his rebirth was being celebrated is in fact quite appropriate: one soul was reborn simultaneously at the death of another.

A cheerful atmosphere remained however, and theatrical competitions were held throughout the festival with the winners of the competition having the chance to perform at the next Rural Dionysia. Satirical street processions were also popular during this time, and participants called the *Phallophoroi* carried large phalloi decorated with ivy and vine leaves through the streets, accompanied by *Ithyphalloi* who were dressed in women's clothing and wore the phalloi. *Kanephori*, or basket-bearers, followed them carrying baskets full of fruit – and by some accounts carrying snakes, a symbol reminiscent of the *kista mystica* – a basket which held sacred objects. The *Liknophoroi* also took part in the processions carrying the *Liknon*, the sacred winnowing fan of Dionysos Iakchos.

A festival may also have been held to Semele at this time: in honour of her position as the mother of Dionysos Bromios, but also in commemoration of her death. It is also possible that a rite of resurrection was part of this festival, in remembrance of Dionysos' descent into the underworld to revive his mother from the dead. This Semelian festival may have been of trieteric origin, although it eventually became part of the Attic annual festival cycle.

Munychion

The period of Munychion began with the present-day **April New Moon**. During this month, the festival of *Agrionia* was celebrated which honoured Dionysos Agrionios, *'the wild'*. Primarily, this festival recalled the disappearance of Dionysos. The attending Maenads searched for him only to return unsuccessfully, declaring that Dionysos was gone; he was with the Muses, or with the goddess Thetis (i.e., he was in the underworld). The theme of the absent god at this time of the year (when Dionysos Bakcheus is considered as being very literally present) seems a rather strange practice, although according to some accounts this particular festival was originally part of the biennial or trieteric festival cycles, and therefore the time of year would not have been significant. The myths of King Lykourgos of Edonia in Thrace, who had also denied the cult of Dionysos, were also recalled at this time.

According to the Hellenic traveler Pausanias[378] this month marked a ceremony called the Skiereia, or *'the festival of the shade'*, in the Hellenic village of Alea: *'there is a temple of Dionysos with an image. In honour of Dionysos they celebrate every other year a festival called Skiereia, and at this festival, in obedience to a response from Delphi, women are flogged.'* Pausanias compared this ceremony to the flogging of Spartan youths at the festival of Artemis; the goddess who demanded blood as part of the coming of age initiation of young boys. This could be a fairly accurate comparison, as Walter Otto speculates that the flogging of the women at the Skiereia was to recall the fate of the daughters of King Minyas of Orchomenos, who had refused the cult of Dionysos and having been driven mad by the god, bloodily disemboweled one of their sons, Hippasos. It is possible that the flogging was performed as a ritualized punishment for those who had refused to worship Dionysos, with the women of Alea *'standing in'* for the offenders. According to some sources, the blood which had flowed during the flogging was then offered to the statues or icons of Dionysos, a substitute for the human sacrifice that the gods would otherwise demand.

---

[378] Description of Greece, 8. 46.5, Pausanias (c. 200 CE) 1979 trans. WHS Jones

Munychion also marked a Feast of the Dead in the Hellenic city of Argos. Sometimes seen as a parallel to the Anthesteria of Athens, spirits were encouraged to return to the upperworld of the living where they were honoured, and asked for favours. When the feast was over, a tradition followed which was not dissimilar to the final rites of the Anthesteria, in which a cacophony of noise was created to send the spirits back and then food offered in appeasement.

Thargelion

The period of Thargelion began with the present-day **May New Moon**. In terms of later Athenian celebrations, the month of Thargelion - and the festival of *Thargelia* - were sacred to the orderly inversion of Dionysos, the Olympian god Apollo (as well as the goddess Artemis). However, many aspects of the Thargelia appear to be Dionysian in nature and quite possibly originated in earlier rites to Dionysos, who predated Apollo by some time. It is clear that Dionysos was at one time involved in this festival, either as the principle deity or evoked as a guise of Apollo. At the very least, his presence continued in this festival through the atmosphere and practices undertaken during the celebrations. Plutarch wrote that Dionysos was no less important than Apollo in the sacred mysteries, and suggested that the two gods were hardly distinguishable at one time. This is further supported by Homer who wrote of Apollo as an older, dual being who brought both pestilence and healing.

For in the first instance, the Thargelia was a festival of purification. A practice existed during the Thargelia in which a poor worker or slave - referred to as the Scapegoat or *Pharmakos* [379] - would be invited to the celebrations to eat well, drink wine and enjoy the pleasures of the city. However once the feast was over, offerings of barley cakes, cheese and figs were put in the hands of the scapegoat and they were then driven out of the city - the unfortunate ones were stoned to death as they left. It was believed that as they left the city, and crossed the boundaries between inside and outside, any concerns and impurities of the city such as poverty or sickness would leave with them. These themes of driving out and crossing boundaries was

---

[379] Encyclopedia of Religion & Ethics Part 21, James Hastings (1921) 2003: P.221

of course a common motif of Dionysian rites; and certainly, the offerings given to the scapegoat are reminiscent of those given to Chthonios: those offerings that must not be eaten by mortals.

But the fig is perhaps even more significant: the wild fig tree is named after the Ram - *Caprificus* in Latin – and the name of *Fig-Bakkhoi* was given to the scapegoat as they were expelled.[380] Philostratus the Elder likened the goat to a Bakkhoi of Dionysos, describing that it *'leaps lightly like a Bacchae'*. Perhaps this name was reminiscent of the human scapegoats' more ancient association with Dionysos, but in any case the symbolism of the goat is a clear indication of the involvement of Dionysos in these rites. The goat or ram had always been a popular sacrifice to Dionysos, especially in relation to his dual nature and was considered as the embodiment of him as well as being one of his favourite shapeshifting forms.

Cooked vegetables and seeds were also considered as sacred offerings during this time, and were carried in a pot named the Thargelos[381] in a procession between Athens and the Python Sanctuary at Delphi where Dionysos had once protected the earth goddess in his serpent form. Certainly, underlying themes of Delphi were present during the Thargelia: music and dance competitions were held during the festival for both for Apollo and for Dionysos with the winners receiving a sacred tripod which was dedicated to Python. Offerings of *Eiresione* are also reported to have been made during the Thargelia, together with figs, wine and oil. These decorated boughs were created by children and used to decorate the temples to Apollo. However they were also associated with the legends of Theseus who was said to have departed for Crete at this time.

Skirophorion

The period of Skirophorion began with the present-day **June New Moon**. As the climate drew near to the hottest point of the year, this month marked the beginning of *Bouphonia*, meaning *'sound of the bull'* - a period of time in which oracles were taken from the sound

[380] Athenian Institution of the Khoregia, Peter Wilson, 2000: P. 33
[381] Athenian Institution of the Khoregia, Peter Wilson, 2000: P. 33

that a sacrificial bull made, as it was being sacrificed. The bull that was chosen was believed to be the embodiment of *Dionysos Erechtheus*, '*earth born one*', and given the temperature at this time of year this sacrifice may have been a petition for the return of the cooler months and the beginning of grape harvesting. The blade that was used to perform the sacrifice was then cast into the sea.[382] This practice was well known in ancient Hellas; casting an item which embodied '*an unclean act*' into deep water was seen as sparing the soul of the offender – just like the unfortunate *Pharmakos*, the '*scapegoat*' was sent to the underworld for judgment instead of the offender themselves.

---

[382] The God Who Comes, Rosemarie Taylor-Perry, 2003: P.36

Conclusion

Dionysos is a unique and diverse deity who is both underrated and misunderstood, yet he stands as one of the most archaic and primordial deities known to mankind. As one of the most widely spread of the ancient mysteries, his cult had a profound effect on the human condition, both socially and culturally; and his intimate connection with mysticism both influenced and strengthened his effect on the developing world as a whole. As an emblem of social equality, the myths of Dionysos were performed on grain-threshing floors and grand marble stages alike; and far from being simple tales to amuse, his myths held many clues to the practices of his mystery cults, reflecting his many guises and giving us some indication of how he was worshipped in the past.

Dionysos could not be controlled or contained; he was the essence of freedom and liberation. He ruled over all the realms and travelled between them with ease: from the starry heavens to the depths of the underworld, and to the far reaches of the great outer spaces. Indeed to many of his followers he was known as an animating and cosmogenic god, an intermediary force between the material world and the source of all things. To him, all things were equal – and as such, he was an inclusive character and a defender of the marginalised. Even his physical appearance was not fixed; he had the ability to change into any form or gender he liked, and was also known to be reborn into different incarnations.

Certainly, Dionysos is a god of cycles; although perhaps different cycles than many of us are familiar with in neo-paganism. In many ways, this challenges us to re-think how we see the world and how we interact with it, and encourages us to think outside the box. It also helps us connect to our ancestors in a rather unique way, as we start to work with the patterns honoured by our forefathers which otherwise would be lost. Yet, we can also recognise similarities between ancient Dionysian practices and more contemporary mystery/occult traditions; even in modern rites today, we instinctively use the same ancient themes and practices which have crossed time and space on the Dionysian current. The use of the oracular arts is just one of these instinctive and atavistic practices; his prophetic legacy is second to none, and intrinsically linked to his role as an underworld psychopomp and lord of initiatory processes. Yet, as a god of paradoxes he is also a solar god of energy and motion, life and sensuality.

Unlike so many other ancient deities, the name of Dionysos has never faded away. Remaining a relevant and prominent figure throughout history, his name is recognised by people from all walks of life. And far from being a remnant of a bygone era, Dionysos is perhaps more relevant than ever today as we leave behind the somewhat distorted values of the Piscean Age and strive towards the principles of freedom, equality and self-expression. I have no doubt that the rise of interest in Dionysos and other deities like him is a result of this shift. These deities who have lain in slumber are now being reawakened, and making themselves known. Incidentally, it was never my original intention to work with Dionysos in a practical sense, and especially not to write a book about him! Sometimes we just have to go with the flow, and allow the Dionysian current to take us where it will.

"Earth breaker, Ground Shaker! Hidden Lord of the Mound. Reveal to us thy sweet honey, O' whisperer of bees. Serpent-adorned and Serpent-born, you bring to flourish thy blooms! O' Provider! Between thy jaws the secret flows: they pure and vibrant wine. O Tumbler of prophetic lots, Inspirer of Sacred Trance; O'Earth Dragon: Euoi! Cooling tendrils are thine. O'Mild One, O'Tamer of Heat: Meilichios! Escort to underworld shades: Initiator, Divider! We sing for you, and carry thy flame aloft."[383]

---

[383] The Book of Ways, PJ Ralls & V Bramshaw, Private Unpublished Text, 1999

Bibliography

Aeneid, Virgil, c. 29-19 BCE, trans. J Dryden

Aeschylus: Fragments (from Strabo, *Geography*, Aristophanes, *Birds* 1247, trans. W Smith)

Alkmeonis, Author Unknown

Ancient Mystery Cults, Walter Burkert (1931) 1987

Antigone, Sophocles, c. 440 BCE, trans. Sir RC Jebb

Antiquities of Greece Vol.1, John Potter, 1740

Aristotle: Poetics, Richard Janko, 1987

Ashmolean Catalogue: Heracles to Alexander the Great, 2011

Astronomica, Pseudo-Hyginus, c. 100 CE, trans. M Grant

Athenian Institution of the Khoregia, Peter Wilson, 2000

Byzantine Magic (edited by Henry Maguire) *'The Theory & Practice of Magic'* John Duffy, 1995

Classical Antiquity 17, 'Dionysos and Katharsis in Antigone', Scott Scullion, 1998

Classical Journal XVI-XVII: Collection of the Chaldean Oracles, Thomas Taylor, 1817-1818

Cockfights, Contradictions & the Mythopoetics of Ancient Greek Culture, Eric Csapo, (lecture) 2006

Craft of the Wise, Vikki Bramshaw, 2009

Cretan Cults and Festivals, RF Willetts, 1962

Cynegetica, Oppian, c.300 CE trans. Mair

Description of Greece, Pausanias (c.200 CE) 1979 trans. WHS Jones

Dictionary of Greek & Roman Antiquities, William George Smith, 1870

Die Musik nach dem Chaos, Michael Janda, 2010

Dionysiaca, Nonnus c. 500 CE trans. Rouse

Dionysos & Ancient Polytheism 'Dionysos, the Wine, and Ikarios' Philippe Borgeaud (2009) 2011

Dionysos in Archaic Greece, Cornelia Isler- Kerényi, 2007

Dionysos in the Underworld - An interpretation of the Toledo Krater, Stian Sundell Torjussen, University ofTromsø Nordlit 20, 2006

Dionysos, Richard Seaford, 2006

Dionysos: Archetypal Image of Indestructible Life, Karl Kerényi, 1996

Dionysus Myth & Cult, Walter F Otto (1960) 1995

Dogme et Rituel de La Haute Magie Vol.1, Eliphas Levi, 1854

Ecstatic Religion, HJ Lewis (1971) 2003

Eleusis: Archetypal Image of Mother & Daughter, Karl Kerényi (1960) 1991

Encyclopedia of Religion & Ethics Part 21, James Hastings (1921) 2003

Epicorum Graecorum Fragmenta, G. Kinkel, 1878

Euripides & Alcestis, Kiki Gounaridou, 1998

Fasti, Ovid, C1st BCE - C1st CE trans. Boyle

Five Stages of Greek Religion, (studies based on a course of lectures, 1912) Gilbert Murray, 1955

Frogs, Aristophanes, c. 400 BCE, trans. Frere

Frogs, Aristophanes, c. 400 BCE, trans. M. Dillon

Geography, Strabo, c. 7 BCE

Georgics, Virgil c. 29 BCE

Gnosticism & the New Testament, Pheme Perkins, 1993

Greek Mysteries, Michael Cosmopoulos, 2003

Greek Religion, Walter Burkert (1931) 1985

Greek to English Lexicon, 1940, Liddel & Scott (on Perseus)

Harvests of Joy, Robert Mondavi, 1999

Hecuba, Euripides, c. 424 BCE, trans. ED Coleridge

Hekate Her Sacred Fires, edited by Sorita d'Este, 2010

Herakleitos of Ephesos, fragments, c. 500 BCE

Hercules Furens 16, Seneca, c. 100 CE, trans. Miller

Histories, Herodotus, c. 450 CE

Homo Necans: Greek Sacrificial Ritual & Myth, Walter Burkert, 1986

Horos Dios: An Athenian Shrine & Cult of Zeus, Gerald Lalonde, 2006

Imagines, Philostratus the Elder, c. 300 CE, trans. Fairbanks

In Search of God the Mother - The Cult of Anatolian Cybele, Lynn Roller, 1999

Isis Unveiled Vol. 2, H.P. Blavatsky (1877) 2008

Isthmian Odes, Pindar, c. 458 BCE

Jewish & Christian Self Definition, 1982

Kratylos Vol 12, Plato, c. 500 BCE trans. HN Fowler

Kretes, Porphyry (Source: *The Great Dionysiac Myth Vol.1*, Robert Brown ,1877, 2000)

Liber LXV, Aleister Crowley, 1919: Part II

Liber XV The Gnostic Mass, Aleister Crowley, 1913

Library of History, Diodorus Siculus, c. 60 – 30 BCE

Life of Apollonius of Tyana 2.2, Philostratus, c. 200 CE, trans. Conybeare

Lykymnios, Euripides, c. 400 BCE

Metamorphoses, Ovid, C1st BCE - C1st CE trans. AS Kline

Metamorphoses, Ovid, C1st BCE - C1st CE trans. Melville

Moralia, Plutarch, c. 100 CE

Myths of Greece and Rome, Jane Harrison (1927) 2007

Natural History XIV, Pliny the Elder, 77-79 CE (Perseus Project)

Odes, Horace, 13 BCE (from *Thespis*, TH Gaster, 1975)

Oedipus Tyrannus, Sophocles, c. 429 BCE

Oedipus, Lucias Seneca, c. 100 CE

On the Characteristics of Animals, Aelian, circa C2nd CE

On the Crown, Demosthenes, c. 300 BCE trans. CA Vince & JH Vince

Orphic Hymn 53 to Amphietus

Othello, Scene II, William Shakespeare, 1603

Parallel Lives, Plutarch c.75 CE

Peace, Aristophanes, c. 420 BCE, trans. Eugene O' Neill, Jr., Ed.

Phaedo, Plato, c. 360 BCE, trans. B Jowett

Phaedra, Seneca, c. 50 CE

Phaedrus, Plato c. C3rd.BCE

Plutarch's Lives 'Theseus' c.75 CE, trans. B Perrin

Plutarch's Morals, G Bell, 1889

Prolegomena to the Study of Greek Religions, Jane Ellen Harrison 1908

Psyche (Vol 6) Erwin Rohde (1925) 2006

Python A Study of Delphic Myth and its Origins, Joseph Eddy Fontenrose (1959) 1980

Savage Energies, Walter Burkert, (1931) 2001

Seidr: The Gate is Open, Katie Gerrard, 2011

Seidways: Shaking, Swaying and the Serpent Mysteries, Jan Fries, 2009

Semele or Dionysos, Eubulus c. 300 BCE

Shiva and Dionysus: Gods of Love and Ecstasy, Alain Daniélou, (1979) 1992

Symboles fondamentaux de la science scarée, Réne Guenon, 1962

Tantra Raja (VIII)

Tatian, Adv.Gr8.68

Tearing Apart the Zagreus Myth, Radcliffe Edmonds, 1999

The Alex Sanders Lectures, Alex Sanders, 1984

The Archanians, Aristophanes, c. 425 BCE, trans. anon

The Attic Theatre, AE Haigh (1898) 1969

The Bacchae, Euripides, c. 400 BCE, trans. Ian Johnston

The Bacchae, Euripides, c. 400 BCE, trans. Kirk

The Bacchae, Euripides, c. 400 BCE, trans. R Lattimore

The Bacchae, Euripides, c. 400 BCE, trans. TA Buckley

The Concise Dictionary of European Proverbs, 1998: P.989 (proverb 986 Phaedrus)

The Craft of Zeus: Myths of Weaving and Fabric, John Scheid, 2001

The Divine Thunderbolt, JT Sibley, 2009

The God Who Comes, Rosemarie Taylor-Perry, 2003

The Great Dionysiac Myth Vol.1, Robert Brown, (1877) 2000

The Greek Colonisation of the Black Sea, GR Tsetskhladze, 1998

The Harvard Theological Review Vol.72, 'Ecstasy and Possession', Ross S Kraemer, 1979

The Homeric Hymns, Hymn to Dionysos Frag.1, Apostolos Athanasskis, 1976

The Iliad, Homer, c. 800 BCE, trans. AT Murray

The Mythology of the Aryan Nations Vol.1, George Cox, 1870

The Mythology of the Aryan Nations Vol.2, George Cox (1870) 2004

The Religions of the Roman Empire, John Ferguson, 1985

The Roebuck in the Thicket, Evan John Jones, 2001

The Secret Teachings of All Ages, Manly P. Hall (1928) 2008

The Star Crossed Stone, Kenneth J McNamara, 2010

The Triumph of the Moon, Professor Ronald Hutton, 1999

The Vishnu Purana, c. 320 CE, trans. HH Wilson

The Works, Ralph Cudworth, 1829

Theatre of the Greeks, JW Donaldson, 1860

Themis - A Study of the Social Origins of Greek Religion, Jane Ellen Harrison, 2010

Timaios, Plato, c. 360 BCE

Trachiniae, Sophocles, c. 450 BCE, trans. Sir RC Jebb

Vision of Poets, Elizabeth Barrett Browning, 1844

VS: Duality & Conflict in Magick, Mythology & Paganism, edited by Kim Huggens, 2011

Index

A

Abraxas, 37, 94, 132
Acteon, 139
Aegae, 129, 130, 186
Aeschylus, 93, 96, 97, 98, 175
Africa, 12, 18, 39, 157, 159, 161
Agathae Tyche, 35
Agathos Daimon, 35, 36, 37, 79, 100, 116
Agaue, 71
Agrionia, 196, 200, 219
Aigobolos, 34
Aiskhylos, 154
Alea, 219
Alexander the Great, 23, 34, 36, 92, 96, 114, 119, 120, 121, 128, 129, 130, 131, 135, 137, 142, 151, 155, 168, 186
Alexandria, 36, 76, 144
Alkyonian Lake, 75, 121, 135, 176
Amathus, 83
Amphiktyon, 31
Anatolia, 114, 121, 122, 123
Anax Agreus, 92, 137
Anthesteria, 31, 36, 51, 54, 104, 169, 172, 177, 180, 184, 199, 208, 210, 211, 213, 214, 215, 216, 217, 218, 220
Anthesterion, 61, 134, 166, 198, 199, 210, 211, 214
Antigone, 24, 78, 148
Antimachus, 19
Apaturia, 113
Aphrodite, 83, 162, 202, 203
Apis, 121
Apollo, 7, 36, 41, 47, 63, 91, 97, 112, 116, 119, 134, 141, 162, 163, 164, 165, 166, 200, 201, 220, 221
Apollonius Rhodius, 19
Ares, 140

Argos, 74, 75, 114, 130, 139, 176, 220
Ariadne, 27, 74, 75, 76, 77, 82, 121, 124, 125, 135, 176, 178, 185, 197, 202, 203, 204
Ariadneia, 203
Aristaios, 68
Aristophanes, 27, 44, 77, 78, 81, 83, 97, 108, 132, 136, 141, 176, 182
Aristotle, 56, 57, 151, 184
Artemis, 24, 75, 82, 83, 84, 122, 124, 139, 219, 220
Astronomica, 69, 75, 173
Athamas, 67, 68
Athena, 140, 204
Athens, 12, 18, 24, 25, 31, 47, 48, 52, 79, 80, 86, 113, 125, 132, 134, 150, 152, 162, 169, 177, 183, 187, 190, 193, 194, 202, 203, 204, 206, 207, 211, 214, 217, 220, 221
Attica, 25
Attis, 20, 122, 165
Aura, 77, 80, 82, 83
Auroch, 21, 39, 89, 110
Axio Tauros, 122

B

Bacchanalia, 33, 183
Bacchantes, 59, 120
Bacchants, 59, 144
Bacchus, 25, 33, 45, 82, 94, 101, 120, 155, 157, 174, 182, 183, 190
Bakcheus, 23, 43, 46, 48, 51, 52, 57, 63, 64, 65, 76, 93, 189, 193, 194, 196, 198, 199, 200, 203, 205, 206, 212, 215
Bakkhoi, 48, 55, 59, 87, 89, 90, 98, 106, 108, 109, 111, 112, 118, 138, 144, 147, 151, 158, 161, 168, 170, 183, 221
Baphomet, 113
Basilinna, 183, 184, 214

231

N

O

P

R

S

Sabazios, 13, 21, 22, 23, 24, 25, 41, 62, 66, 92, 94, 105, 116, 130, 131, 139
Salamis, 78
Samothrace, 43, 63, 122, 130
Satyrs, 50, 57, 66, 67, 69, 70, 74, 107, 108, 112, 130, 132, 136, 151, 161, 182, 183, 213
Semele, 26, 32, 40, 43, 59, 63, 64, 65, 67, 71, 75, 76, 77, 80, 81, 82, 84, 95, 99, 102, 176, 186, 192, 193, 198, 201, 210, 218
Semele or Dionysos, 32
Serpent, 13, 21, 35, 36, 62, 63, 65, 91, 105, 116, 117, 118, 140, 144, 156, 164, 166, 221
Shiva, 20, 118, 128, 149, 153, 161
Sicily, 93, 113
Silenus, 108, 136, 179
Sirius, 26, 27, 28, 67, 79, 125, 192, 197, 199, 200
Skiereia, 219
Skirophorion, 198, 200, 201, 221
Snake, 13, 21, 35, 43, 54, 62, 66, 67, 86, 102, 103, 109, 116, 117, 118, 133, 161, 183, 217
Socrates, 59, 93, 178, 188, 189
Sophocles, 21, 24, 78, 107
Sparta, 55, 67, 90, 131, 187
St Athanasius, 23
St Denys, 13, 34
Staphylus, 74
Strabo, 23, 24, 92, 96
Strategems of War, 185
Syracuse, 113

T

Tauropolus, 74
Tenedos, 97
Thargelia, 200, 220, 221
Thargelion, 125, 173, 198, 200, 205, 220
The Bacchae, 11, 17, 27, 39, 57, 62, 65, 71, 72, 82, 95, 98, 104, 105, 115, 140, 146, 147, 150, 154, 157, 159,
163, 166, 167, 180, 183, 185, 188, 189
The Golden Bough, 48
The Iliad, 39, 201
Thebes, 26, 41, 57, 71, 72, 101, 119, 139, 147, 163
Themis, 57, 98, 140, 158, 165
Theoinos, 32
Theseus, 74, 113, 124, 127, 173, 195, 203, 204, 205, 215, 221
Thespis, 56, 97
Thessaly, 111, 122, 170, 187
Thetis, 70, 170, 176, 185, 219
Thorikos, 31
Thrace, 20, 21, 22, 25, 31, 70, 81, 92, 110, 111, 116, 121, 129, 130, 139, 207, 219
Thrassos, 91
Thyia, 129, 189
Thyiad, 189
Thyone, 76, 82
Thyrsus, 11, 35, 52, 68, 75, 89, 94, 101, 105, 176, 188
Tiger, 63, 115
Titans, 29, 42, 43, 59, 62, 63, 86, 92, 94, 95, 110, 138, 166, 201, 209
Trophonios, 37

V

Venus, 202
Virgil, 26, 29, 92, 111, 121, 174

W

Wine, 23, 28, 30, 31, 32, 33, 34, 35, 36, 37, 40, 51, 53, 54, 55, 56, 60, 61, 64, 66, 67, 69, 73, 74, 79, 83, 86, 100, 101, 104, 105, 111, 112, 114, 127, 133, 134, 136, 141, 142, 144, 148, 161, 165, 167, 171, 172, 173, 180, 181, 188, 189, 194, 195, 197, 198, 201, 202, 204, 205, 206, 207, 208, 210, 211, 212, 213, 215, 216, 220, 221, 225
World Soul, 87, 88, 89, 94

X

Y

Z

Avalonia *is an independent publisher producing outstanding and innovative books which push the boundaries of their subjects and illuminate the spirit of the sacred in its many manifestations.*

Other titles in our catalogue include:

Anahita: Ancient Persian Goddess and Zoroastrian Yazata, edited by Payam Nabarz

Dragon Bones, by Jan Fries

Momento Mori, edited by Kim Huggens

Seidr: The Gate is Open, by Katie Gerrard

The Complete Grimoire of Pope Honorius, by David Rankine and Paul Harry Barron

The Faerie Queens, edited by Sorita d'Este and David Rankine

The Gods of the Vikings, by Marion Pearce

Hekate Liminal Rites, by Sorita d'Este and David Rankine

THOTH, by Lesley Jackson

Thracian Magic, by Georgi Mishev

To explore these and other titles by **Avalonia**, visit:
www.avaloniabooks.co.uk

Lightning Source UK Ltd.
Milton Keynes UK
UKOW03f2204110214

226312UK00003B/441/P